To

Wi

Lesley.

Zen and the Art of Hip-joint Maintenance

Zen and the Art of Hip-joint Maintenance

John Caunt

Chineway Press

First Published in 2003 by Chineway Press.

Chineway Press
18 Ethelburt Avenue
Southampton
SO16 3DD

www.chineway.co.uk

ISBN: 0-9546493-0-3

Cover design by: Ian Tyrrell - RPM Print and Design.

Printed and bound by: Antony Rowe Ltd.

Cover photography by: John Caunt

Chapter 1

The birthday cards were what started it. One Victor Meldrew card would have been bad enough. Two would have set alarm bells ringing. But three!

'That's not really how people see me, is it?'

The pause before my wife responds says it all. 'Well…'

'Well, what?'

'I sometimes worry that you're turning into a …'

'A what?'

'Well, um… an obsessive old git, if you really want to know.'

She laughs, one of those laughs that implies she's only joking, but it's less than convincing. I pretend not to notice and press her for evidence to support her allegation.

'The egg incident.'

'No really! You're not serious. I couldn't just ignore it, could I? And as for that cheeky bastard with the Audi putting his spoke in. All very well for him. It wasn't his front door they threw it at.'

'What about the dog-mess campaign?'

'It's a menace, you've said so yourself. And I still reckon the warning flags were a good idea. OK, I'll admit a bit more research might have been wise before posting it back through their letterboxes, but you can't deny that those two women did look very similar.'

We continue in this vein, one purported example after another. It's as if she's been saving them up. I'm beginning to wish I hadn't asked the question. She latches on to my mounting irritation and proffers a solution.

'You know what I think the problem is? You're stuck around the house too much. Working from home is all very well but, when you're not crouching over that bloody computer or monopolising the phone, you're glowering at the neighbours and turning trivial irritations into major incidents. You really ought to try and get out more.'

She's right. I have to own up to it. My horizons have shrunk since I stopped going out to work every day. Not enough variety and inter- action I suppose. And I'm responding by becoming more boring, grouchy and obsessive by the week. That bloke with the Audi could have been more polite about it, but he hit the nail on the head. I *do* need to get a life. But I'm only fifty-five for God's sake! I'm becoming an old git before my time.

The answer to my problem surely doesn't lie in shackling myself to some dreary employer once again. It's more a case of getting some balance back into my life – new people, new activities, that sort of thing. I consider the possibilities. What could I choose as a way of kick-starting a more varied existence? Perhaps I should join the over- fifties group at the leisure centre – bobbing grey heads up and down the swimming pool every Tuesday and Thursday. No, I'm not quite that far gone. If I'm to be true to my baby-boomer pedigree and recover the spirit of my youth, I need to think about something a bit more challenging.

I fish around in my limited think tank, pulling out and throwing back one pitiful idea after another – too small, too silly, too boring, too tough. Then, one sprat refuses to be thrown back. What about an expedition? I've always fancied tackling a long distance walk, just never got around to it previously. Now could be the time. What could I go for – the Pennine Way perhaps, or Offa's Dike, or maybe the South West Coastal Path? But why stop there? Why not do the whole country – Land's End to John O'Groats? I'm a stranger to much of it – about time I discovered a little more about the place that's nurtured me for the last fifty-five years. I'm moderately fit – shouldn't be too much of a struggle. And doing it on my own would certainly be the way to meet people. Give me plenty of time to sort my thoughts out too – get the world back into proportion.

Over the next few days the idea takes shape. I'm told it's just short of nine-hundred miles from end to end by the shortest route. And I sure as hell wouldn't want to take the shortest route – pounding along busy main roads, lungs full of hydrocarbons and blood spurting from my heels. If I'm going to enjoy it, I'll have to go by footpaths and minor lanes. That's likely to bump the distance well above a thousand miles – maybe eleven hundred. Still, I shan't be trying to smash any speed or endurance records, so no point in turning it into a slog. I could even divide the journey into three or four stages, take a break between each and do some of the less spectacular bits by bike. Yeah! This is beginning to look like a piece of cake – Land's End to John O'Groats for softies – all I need now is to get myself organised.

I take myself off to the public library and spend two and a half hours poring over travel books and walking guides until one of the Geography Section's permanent fixtures, a man with seventy percent proof breath and the look of Rasputin about him, decides I'm a kindred spirit and worth cultivating. As my feigned deafness is clearly unconvincing, I cut short the visit and get out into the fresh air. So much for the planning phase.

In my new-found *Easy Rider* mode, I tell myself that too much in the way of detailed planning would spoil the enjoyment. At least I've got a rough idea of where I'm going. As far as I can judge, it's just a case of following the cliff in a northerly direction out of the Land's End car park and bearing left when you get to Bristol, making sure you don't stray far into Wales. I'm sure I can play the thing by ear. Precise target mileages and pre-booked accommodation would be too much hassle. I'll take my chance with youth hostels and cheap B&Bs and see how I get on from day to day. That's it then – John O'Groats here we come. Now what about some kit?

The last time I undertook any significant exploration of this country on my own was at the age of seventeen when I sought to demonstrate my self-sufficiency by embarking on a hitchhiking tour of the West Country. In those days you could do that sort of thing without your parents automatically assuming they would next see you on a mortuary slab after your trussed-up naked body had floated onto some empty Cornish beach.

The trip required a rucksack, and the only place I knew that sold such things was an army surplus shop next to the fruit and veg market. There was quite a range to choose from: cavernous grey ones on metal frames at prices higher than I was planning to spend on the whole trip, little khaki ones that could fit comfortably between the shoulder-blades – ideal provided you wished to carry no more than a Bronco toilet roll and a packet of Spangles. Underneath some Swedish Army greatcoats I discovered a shapeless, olive green monstrosity made of that rubber-backed, imitation canvas fabric which, in the 1960s, was the material of choice for inferior raincoats and those ubiquitous duffel bags. Just the ticket, big and cheap. I bought it.

Come the departure day and my new rucksack was stuffed to the point that I couldn't pull the drawstring tight enough to close the top flap.

'Ah what the hell! It'll probably stretch with use.'

My mum and sister steadied the load on the corner of the kitchen table as I slipped my arms into the straps and drew myself up to a semi-crouch, slightly alarmed at the sensation that my innards were about to drop out onto the floor.

'Isn't it a bit too full?'

'No, it'll be fine,' I croaked. 'Just need to get used to it.'

Twenty miles into the journey, the straps parted company with the rucksack and I was reduced to waddling along with it in my arms like a grossly oversized infant. I stopped at a sewing shop to buy carpet twine and a darning needle and spent half an hour at the side of the road sewing the straps back on. This did the trick for all of three hours before I was back to the monstrous baby routine. Clearly, this state of affairs could not continue. Duffel bag fabric was never intended to take such punishment and neither, it was increasingly apparent, were my shoulders. Next morning found me in a post office cringing at the cost of sending a large parcel to my home address, but then walking out almost upright with a heavily stitched olive green object on my back that was still just about recognisable as a rucksack.

Thirty-eight years on I'm wiser to the value of good equipment and, it has to be said, considerably better off than I was in the sixties but, alas, I'm no less of a cheapskate, and the prospect of shelling out hundreds of pounds to equip myself with state-of-the-art gear for this trip horrifies me. But I've got to bite the bullet. I'm the owner of a waterproof that has long since ceased to be worthy of the name, a pair of boots that seem slightly narrower than the feet for which they are intended, and some shiny polyester walking trousers that would go down a storm at a zip fetishists' convention but leave a lot to be desired as far as normal human movement is concerned. I poke around the darker recesses of outdoor shops looking for items that will be light, waterproof, durable and cheap.

My salvation comes in the form of a factory outlet selling branded gear at knock-down prices. In one wild afternoon I equip myself with tough and not unstylish trousers, Goretex lined boots, new water-proofs, rucksack and 1000 mile socks. Now there's a piece of marketing brilliance – walking socks guaranteed to last for at least a thousand miles. It sounds such a bloody long way, and who but a complete nerd is actually going to count. 'Dear Sirs, I am returning the enclosed socks which have sprung a hole after only 972 miles. I should be obliged etc.'

How about a technical vest to complete my purchases? A what? Well, it's just a fancy name for a tee-shirt fashioned from artificial fibres that are supposed to wick the sweat away and dry you in next to no time. I'm undecided. I've been wary of putting artificial fibres next to the skin of my upper body ever since I was a teenager, and had to abandon fashionable nylon polo necks because they induced within minutes the sort of underarm odour that would not have been out of place on a sex-starved ferret.

Textile technology must have sorted that one out by now.

I head for the pay point clutching my technical vest.

It is a source of astonishment to me how a few light items combined can suddenly produce one very heavy item. Spread them out on the ground and they would blow away in a moderate breeze. Put them together in a rucksack and you're dealing with something that has all the attributes of a sack of coal. In the spare room I gather up those things essential for an extended walking trip and carefully pack them into my nice new rucksack. On the bathroom scales with the resulting package on my back, I discover that my weight has gone up by almost two and a half stone. Unacceptable. This is meant to be a lean and fast moving unit. The image I catch of myself in the bathroom mirror has more in common with the top-weight entry in a snail race. Time for some serious trimming of requirements. Out go the binoculars. Out goes the sweatshirt – replaced by a lightweight fleece. Out goes the spare pair of shorts.

My survey of the weightiest items in my pack shows towels to be a major issue. Anything bigger than a hand towel adds considerably to the bulk. The outdoor shop appears to offer a solution in the form of a 'camping towel' – lightweight and highly absorbent. I buy one, undeterred by the fact that it has the size, texture and appearance of a yellow duster. I give it a trial run. Absorbent? This thing is the fabric equivalent of those electric hand dryers you find in public lavatories. It doesn't remove moisture, just moves it around. Running on the spot would be a far more effective way of getting dry. And another thing – how am I going to manage on the beach? I'm not a man of particularly large proportions but maintaining my modesty behind this small rectangle of yellow fluff could be a challenge too far. I don't think I could cope with the ridicule. No, hang the extra weight! A proper towel is the only thing.

To compensate, I redouble my efforts on other equipment. The standard water bottle is discarded in favour of a dinky soft plastic one which packs flat and rolls up when empty. It looks not much stronger than a shampoo sachet, but the manufacturers claim that John Prescott could sit upon it with Ann Widdecombe on his knee without it bursting. I have neither the confidence nor the contacts to put it to the test; I'll take their word for it. And while I'm at it, I'll buy the optional extra 'drinking system' – a two foot length of plastic tubing that clips to your shoulder straps and allows you to take a drink any time without troubling to get the bottle out of your rucksack. A bit pretentious, I know, but unhitching and re-hitching yourself every time you want something from your bag can, they say, significantly slow your progress and add to the hassle. I could get an extra half mile a day out of this piece of tube.

I'm overly preoccupied with how to record my journey as I go. A notebook and pencil is the obvious answer, but I'm an inveterate techno-freak and I crave something sophisticated. The prospect of weeks spent attempting to transcribe my impenetrable scribble after the event doesn't appeal at all. Wouldn't it be nice to have my material in a form that could be transferred straight to my word processor for a bit of gentle tidying? My attention turns to the new generation of hand held computers – light, portable and packing the amount of power that twenty years ago would have been regarded as adequate for a NASA moon shot. But there's a difficulty – getting the information into them in the first place. Anything that meets my weight requirements sports a Lilliputian keyboard or relies on recognition of handwriting entered with a stylus on a pressure sensitive screen. Given my inadequacy with pen and paper, this doesn't sound like a recipe for success. The answer to my needs emerges in the form of a product hailed as a design miracle with a small but genuine touch type keyboard. What's more, it weighs in at no more than two pairs of underpants, and works off standard batteries with a promised life of thirty hours – important on a journey where the opportunity to top up the rechargeable variety can't be relied upon. Yes, this is the one for me.

Just one small problem – I'm unwilling to go out and buy one. I write to the manufacturers with an offer they can't refuse. If they are prepared to provide me with one of these technological wonders, I will happily give it a one thousand mile road test, and compile a full length book on it as I go. More, I will make sure that my readers know this masterpiece has been produced on their pocket sized PA. Excellent cheap promotion, eh?

They don't trouble to reply.

Swallowing my pride I buy one anyway, determined that as revenge I will expose its weaknesses and bring the company's share price crashing down. Unfortunately, I discover that the bursting of the dotcom bubble has already done that for me, and anyway weaknesses are hard to find. After a bit of practice I can type at up to twenty-odd words a minute and can manage about half an hour before I go completely bog-eyed staring at the tiny screen. In final triumph I discover that the space bar doesn't work unless it is struck precisely on the middle, and this frequently results in text where six or seven words are run together. But even this source of complaint is denied me when the assistant at John Lewis cheerfully exchanges my defective machine for one that operates properly. Bugger!

All the walking books warn about pitching in to solid long distance stuff without adequate preparation. I reason that it would be a good idea to get in some day walks before embarking on the real thing, but the weather and my body conspire to deny me much needed practice. It rains throughout the early spring and, worse, I acquire a pain in my hip that keeps me awake at night and makes walking to the front gate a misery. Psychosomatic? Surely not. Must be something desperately serious. I'm convinced that hip replacement is an inevitability, but the osteopath diagnoses referred pain from a trapped nerve and charges outrageous sums to pinion me and subject my spine to the sort of treatment that, in any other circumstances, would find him answering a charge in the Magistrate's Court.

After three weeks of this indignity the pain starts to ease a little. The weather has improved too. I'm suddenly convinced that I must seize the moment before some further impediment crops up. I cancel the remaining osteopath appointments and buy a single ticket to Penzance. But my decisiveness is accompanied by anxiety. How will my hip respond to twenty miles a day of cliff walking? And what about the boots? I've had no opportunity to break in the new ones. Should I take a chance on them or stick with the old ones?

I plod round and round the bedroom, one from each pair on my feet, trying to work out which will be the better bet. As a road test it leaves something to be desired but, after fifteen minutes of dithering, I plump for the old ones. Five minutes later I change my mind in favour of the new.

Salisbury to Penzance is surely not one of the great railway journeys of the world. We lurch from one minor west-country station to another, taking on and disgorging successive waves of shoppers, school kids and frazzled commuters. The only other long distance travellers in the compartment are three new-agers – funny, I thought they always went by VW camper van – and a man who bears an uncanny resemblance to the office prankster from *The Fast Show*. He sits opposite me, busily shuffling through a folder entitled '50 Activities for Self Improvement'. He endlessly orders and reorders them, tearing some up – presumably the ones that didn't work – and making little marks in red felt tip on others. I can't help but think that number one on his list of activities might be to pop down to the charity shop with his tartan trousers and gingham shirt.

But who am I to criticise? Here I am in my new walking trousers, my technical vest, my old boots (Hmm – I think I should have brought the new ones after all) gobbling Kendal Mintcake that was meant for emergencies and feeling like a fraud. I may look the part, but I'm distinctly uncertain that this enterprise will end up on my list of fifty activities for self improvement. Far from embarking on a great end-to-end adventure, I'm not at all sure I will make it past the first couple of days.

Penzance certainly has an end of Britain feel to it. There's nowhere further to go – just a big set of buffers and a very large PENZANCE sign to put the boot in on those who were travelling to Exeter but fell asleep at Yeovil. Outside is a grey sky, grey buildings, grey sea flecked with white horses. Welcome to Penzance! As I leave the station yard, it starts to rain heavily and I have to shelter in a shop doorway while I struggle to put on my brand new waterproofs.

The route to the youth hostel seemed simplicity itself when I studied the book on the train. Walk though the town and turn right just past the YMCA building. What YMCA building? No sign of it. As shops and houses give way to open countryside, I figure I must have missed the turning and begin to retrace my steps. My God! Lost already, and I haven't even started.

Of course, I could ask somebody, but I've got this terrible thing about wanting to appear as if I know what I'm doing, even when I patently don't. It's a failing that has caused me to spend huge chunks of my time on this earth in fruitless activity and seething frustration as instruction books remain unread and advice stays unsought. Here I am, looking like a walker, dressed up in my walker's clothes. How can I fail to find my way around this piddling place?

I steal a furtive glance at the book and conclude that the sketch map must relate to a different Penzance from the one I'm in. But after a circular tour of the town and an embarrassed nod or two to locals who have watched me pass by three times, I stumble by chance on a sign directing me to the slightly worn but still impressive mansion that is the youth hostel.

My pleasure at successfully negotiating this first challenge is tempered by the presence of a school minibus and a coach in the car park. The warden reassures me: 'You won't hear them where you are,' but I'm less than convinced as I make my way to my room and a stream of animated little girls scamper past me down the stairs like lemmings on speed. The warden was right though. I neither hear nor see anything more of them. Whether what I witnessed was their migration to the nearest cliff, I'm not really sure.

There are four middle-aged Germans in my room and they already have their towels on the best beds. Honestly, I'm not making it up. We're talking major stereotype fulfilment here. Only the bunk by the door is free. I choose the lower bed, judging the upper one too squeaky. Bad move. Half an hour later the upper berth is occupied by a cyclist who will squeak the night away above my head. But to tell the truth, this is the least of the nocturnal disturbances. One of my roommates has a quite unbelievable snore. It starts up almost as soon as the light goes off, deep and gurgling, like an elephant blowing through its trunk into a bucket of blancmange. A few minutes later and we have a duet. The second participant produces a short, sharp hurrumph perfectly timed at the end of each of the first performer's rumbles. And, yes, there's more – I become acutely aware that somebody is farting in his sleep. Just when I think things can't get any worse, a third snorer takes the stage. He utters a small sexual groan which works very nicely with the other two. I'm put in mind of the Singing Dogs – barked versions of 'Jingle Bells' and 'How Much Is That Doggy In The Window?' that topped the Christmas charts in the late fifties and early sixties. As a child I used to wonder what cruelty they inflicted on the creatures to get them to perform in that way. I didn't know much about the magic of sound editing in those days. In a vain attempt to silence tonight's singing dogs, I stuff my ears with damp toilet paper. Can't do anything about my nose, unfortunately.

I open my eyes at seven in the morning with one of those leaden headaches that point to a wholly inadequate night's sleep. Outside the rain is coming down in stair rods. I lie still, foetus-like. Am I seriously considering waddling off across the cliffs in this lot? What's the alternative? Sitting around in some steamy Penzance café? Certainly can't stick around here – they kick you out at ten. I join the gloomy parade into the washrooms and, with just a smidgen of vitality showered into my system, trail miserably down to breakfast.

I never, ever, eat a cooked breakfast at home, but this is an occasion where a bit of serious fuelling is called for. It's all the wrong stuff of course, but I wade into bacon sausage, eggs, beans, even fried bread, as if my very survival depends on it. My table-mate is a walker going in the opposite direction. My God! He looks so fit and young. I notice that he has eschewed the fatty garbage I'm consuming in favour of cereal and toast. He tells me it has taken him a week and a half to come from Clovelly and he thinks he has pushed it too hard. Hmmm – makes my hoped-for twenty miles a day look a shade optimistic. And he's using the trip as an opportunity to sort his life out. I listen politely as he enumerates the problems he has grappled with along the coastal path – failed relationships, unsatisfactory job, the pressures of urban life. Well I guess a cliff path is as good a place as any to deal with these issues. There is, after all, an on-hand solution if you reach the conclusion that life is no longer worth the effort. And what has he decided? A pretty literal dose of downshifting actually. Ten days on his own around this corner of Britain and he has resolved to give up his job, move down to Cornwall and join the ranks of the tele-commuters. I'm slightly alarmed. If this is what ten days of lone walking does for you, what am I going to be like by the time I reach John O'Groats? Could be all set for a Trappist monastery.

I spin out breakfast on the pretext of gathering intelligence for my trip, but eventually there's nothing else for it. I have to make a move. Fortunately the rain has diminished to a light drizzle. I ask at reception about buses to Land's End, and am informed that there's a bus stop a quarter of a mile down the road, but the hostel's own bus departs from the front door in fifteen minutes. That will do for me – I scurry off to pack my rucksack.

What the hostel receptionist neglected to tell me was that this is most certainly not the express service to Land's End. In fact the journey starts in quite the wrong direction. The bus heads back into Penzance and stops for five minutes outside the railway station. Being back where I started the previous afternoon does nothing for my sense of progress. After that it's a meandering route around the peninsular, taking in such essential sights as Newlyn Harbour, the Merry Maidens Bronze Age Standing Stones, and The Minack Open Air Theatre at Porthcurno. All very interesting, but I'm anxious to get walking and I'm starting to feel a little travel sick on these winding lanes. My fellow passengers are up for the ride rather than the destination. There are three of them – a Swedish woman with her teenage daughter, and an elderly man from Shrewsbury who has spent the last thirty years tracing his Cornish ancestry and wants the rest of us to appreciate his knowledge of the county's history and legend. The Swedes provide a willing audience, although I'm not sure that, between his gabbled delivery and the noise of the engine, there's a great deal they are able to comprehend. But they display the correct body language and make all the right noises, so he is greatly encouraged. The driver, not to be outdone, joins in with gusto. So entranced are they all by the hotch-potch of fact, myth and complete nonsense they are able to weave together that, when we finally arrive at Land's End, I'm the only one who wants to get off. The rest remain on board, to complete the circular route back to Penzance.

Everyone I have spoken to says Land's End is horrible – utterly spoilt by the modern tourist complex. But it's not nearly as ghastly as I had expected. Sure, there's an air of theme park to it, but the buildings are compact and low rise and most of the attractions are contained within them. There isn't the tackiness one finds in many of the country's tourist traps. I'm almost tempted to enter the 'Miles of Memories' exhibition which offers to let me experience the sights, the smells, the stories and some of the amazing modes of transport used by intrepid travellers between Land's End and John O'Groats. I'm fascinated by what the smells might be, but I reluctantly conclude it will delay my departure. Perhaps next time.

I wander into one of the shops. In my rush to get started I haven't yet picked up a map. My hand hovers over Sheet 102 in the Ordnance Survey Explorer Series. Nah! What's the point of a large scale map? I'll have walked off it by tomorrow. For the next hundred and eighty miles before I hit Exmoor all I need to do is keep the sea on my left. Can't go too wrong with that. I buy a general touring map of Cornwall and a guide to the Coastal Path. These, together with a large bar of nougat, should see me all right.

There's a notice at the main entrance to the complex inviting would-be end-to-enders to register at the post office. I'm again seized by doubt at the prospect. Will I make it to John O'Groats? Will my hip start to play up again? Have I made the right decision on boots? Does it count if you are planning to do the trip in stages. 'Don't be silly' I tell myself 'Making the commitment will be good for you.' I wander inside and, with as much casualness as I can muster, announce my intention to a counter clerk who looks a lot like Postman Pat's younger brother. He puts my name in a book and gives me a form which I must have authenticated at least six times along the way if I want the privilege of joining the End to End Club. As I'm already feeling acutely self conscious about admitting what I'm up to, the prospect of queuing in half a dozen post offices across the country to have my form stamped doesn't sound immediately appealing. And the benefits that membership confers – a certificate, a newsletter, an end-to-ender's tie – don't strike me as prizes beyond measure.

Out on the cliff there's one final task before I depart – a photo, framed against an angry sky with the offshore rocks and the Longships lighthouse lurking in the lower background. There's a man who will do the job for you next to a signpost showing the distance to John O'Groats and various world cities. Into it, he will slot one for your home town. He can manage pretty well anywhere you want. I toy with the idea of asking him to do Nome, Alaska for me, but conclude that this sort of thing isn't really my scene and opt instead for the self-timer device on my own camera.

I wonder if there is anybody in the world who manages to use these things successfully. I have never yet found a surface of suitable height and stability to frame the shot I wanted, and this occasion is no exception. Yes, I know you can buy mini tripods, but it's simpler to get someone to take the photo for you than carry one of those on the off-chance you might want to take a snap of yourself. After a lot of experimentation I finally find a spot on a low stone wall that is just about level and will get me in shot if I stand well back by the cliff edge. I set it up, walk carefully backwards and try to look suitably disinterested as the countdown timer flashes. A gust of wind causes the camera to wobble wildly and I rush to rescue it. I try again. This time it flashes for an age and I conclude I must have failed to set it properly. I walk forward and put my face two inches from the lens as the shutter goes. On the third attempt a couple of economy-sized inflatable tourists drift between me and the camera at the crucial moment. I give up and ask a passer-by to take my photo.

That's it. I'm ready to go. It's 11:30, I've wasted half the day and it looks like rain again, but I'm off on the longest walk of my life.

Chapter 2

I'm so glad to be away that I almost bounce along the first couple of miles. The going is pleasant and easy, but my new telescopic hiking stick is no more than an inconvenience. After tripping over it several times, I strap it to the back of my rucksack. And there's an immediate problem with the coastal path guide. I realise that it's written for somebody walking in the opposite direction. In order to follow it, I'm required to read from the bottom of the page to the top and then turn back to the previous page. This shouldn't be too hard for an averagely intelligent being, but I appear pathetically incapable of mastering it. Try as I might, I can't stop myself re-reading the directions for stretches of ground I've already covered. I idly wonder whether walking backwards would make the task easier.

At Sennan Cove I meet the Swedish pair from the bus. They have a slightly shell-shocked air about them, and tell me that they have given up on Cornish history and legend in favour of a gentle walk back to Land's End. Two miles further on I make a quite unnecessary detour inland by failing to spot a junction in the path. At the same time I confidently misdirect a couple who have stopped to consult their map. After half a mile, my mistake is only too clear. I can see the misdirected couple trudging along behind me, and decide to put a spurt on to prevent them catching up.

My guide book tells me that Cape Cornwall is the only cape in England. This surprises me as the French coast is littered with the things – Cap this or Cap that everywhere you go. I gamely attempt to interrogate the last vestiges of my O-level Geography in the hope of unearthing some recollection of the difference between a cape and other sorts of headland, but nothing comes out. Still, Cape Cornwall is an impressive sight with its conical outline and old mine buildings. Apparently it was bought by Heinz, the food company, before being handed over to the National Trust. I muse on this piece of useless information for at least a mile. What could Heinz possibly have wanted from this scrap of the Cornish coast? I'm gaily kicking around images of offshore baked bean factories when it occurs to me that I may be on the edge of hallucination. Perhaps this foolishness is down to low blood sugar. It's five hours since my fatty breakfast. Time to get some carbohydrate into my system. I gnaw dementedly at the slab of Land's End nougat, risking several fillings in the process.

I'm feeling quite pleased with my progress but, when I stop and look back over my route, I realise I've been walking briskly for two hours and I can still see Land's End.

For all the attractiveness of the surroundings, this is grim industrial country with a hard past. Relics of tin mining are everywhere – derelict engine houses, robust chimneys, roofless buildings, home to unruly shrubs that jostle in the empty doors and windows. It's odd how the years lend romance and austere beauty to these ruined workings. I'm sure there was precious little of it when they were active. I wonder whether future generations will thrill at the sight of some of our contemporary eyesores. In a post-motorway age will spaghetti junction reveal its true aesthetic splendour? Hard to imagine.

The mining of tin and copper has been a feature of Cornwall since before Roman times. Early extraction was from surface streaming or shallow workings and it was not until the eighteenth century that developments in mining technology permitted exploitation of the deeper deposits. The abandoned mines that are so much a feature of this area were largely the result of huge expansion generated by nineteenth century industrialisation. At the peak of Cornish mining prosperity in the 1850s, a majority of the world's tin and copper was being mined in the county. But within ten years a savage downturn occurred. Huge deposits of more accessible ore were discovered in the USA, South America and Australia, and the Cornish mines couldn't compete. A few hung on after the 1930s, but the 1985 slump in the price of tin put paid to all bar two. The final mine closed in 1998.

The Levant mine typifies the nineteenth century boom. Opened in 1820, it employed more than 600 miners at its peak and had 60 miles of tunnels. In 1919 it was the scene of the worst mining disaster in Cornish history when thirty-one miners were killed. By 1930 it was closed. And what is there to show for it now? Well, apart from some old workings, just the engine house with its restored winding-engine, owned by The National Trust and maintained by volunteers.

I join the short queue at the engine house door, entrance money in hand, thinking I'm going to be in for a fascinating bit of history. I've reckoned without that heady combination of volunteers and steam-engines. You come across it on steam railways up and down the country. The volunteers are always men of huge enthusiasm but arrested development. Some mental shutter came down when they got their first piece of Hornby Dublo rolling-stock, and they have never quite been able to move on. On the surface they will deal competently with other human beings, but if you wave an oily rag in front of their faces, their eyes will glaze and it will be instantly clear where their true interests and affections lie. And so it is at Levant. The engine has broken down and everyone, from the guy who collects the entrance fee to the one making the coffee, has that distracted look of a mother whose infant has gone down with something yet to be diagnosed. Visitors, in such circumstances, are an intrusion on family suffering even if they have paid good money to be there.

Several of us shoe-horn ourselves into the tiny boiler-house waiting for the promised tour to begin. Each time I move, my rucksack jams some poor soul into an even tighter corner. Embarrassed at this, and having screwed as much interest as I can muster from the meagre photographic display, I take a stroll outside and return several minutes later as four of my fellow customers emerge from the building. One speaks.

'He says the tour will start in ten minutes, but he said that ten minutes ago.'

We exchange a look of mutual resolve and turn as one for the short walk back to the car park and the coastal path. 'That's a pound up my cassock. Bloody volunteers!'

A few hundred yards on from Levant is the unsightly legacy of the Geevor Pit. Geevor was a late arrival at the party, having been set up by expatriate miners who returned to Cornwall from South Africa at the time of the Boer War. The company took over a previously worked site and managed to continue in production until 1990. Now it is open again, but this time as a museum with mining artefacts and displays showing how miners lived and worked. Visitors can tour the surface processing plant and venture a little way underground.

The site looks hideous – recent spoil heaps and grey concrete buildings. Somehow I doubt that tourists of the twenty second century will be pointing their experience-processors at this lot. Prefabricated concrete falls short of the sturdy stone engine houses and brick-topped stacks of the nineteenth century.

A little way after Pendeen I take an inland path to the quiet coast road in order to make up some quick miles. It's late afternoon and my coastal path guide indicates that there is no accommodation to be had before Zennor some five miles away. What's more, the path ahead is ominously described as 'severe' and I'm concerned about overdoing it on day one.

Well, it seems I may have left it too late. The first human being I encounter on hitting the road is a weaselly figure in a knitted bobble hat without a bobble who emerges from a dilapidated lean-to. I'm just thinking what a pleasant rural caricature he presents and am about to greet him cheerily when he points at me, laughs loudly and says, 'Yer knackered you.' I glower my affront and stride out with an angry bounce. Sure, my feet hurt – this choice of boots may have been a mistake – but I'm buggered if I'm going to be laughed at by yokels in bobbleless bobble hats appearing out of sheds.

In fact I do make some quicker progress along the road and it isn't unpleasant. There are plenty of wild flowers along the verge and very little traffic. The sea is still there just off to the left beyond tiny stone bordered fields. The bus driver this morning said that these fields had to be small to protect crops and animals from the prevailing winds, but there are neither crops nor animals to be seen – only rabbits, plenty of rabbits.

Halfway between Morvah and Zennor my attention is caught by a pair of men's boots on a flat stone near a bend in the road. I step up for a closer look and see that there is also a bunch of dead flowers and a note testifying to the loss of a beloved son. It's both poignant and slightly macabre. The empty boots, what strange objects to leave. I can't quite shake out the image of Albert and the Lion – Albert's parents offering his cap as evidence that the lion had eaten him. I walk on disturbed, wondering about the nature of the tragedy that should have moved a parent to place their dead son's boots at the side of the road.

This practice of leaving roadside tributes seems to have taken off in the last six or seven years. You never used to see bouquets at the sites of fatal accidents or scenes of crime in the way you do today. I wonder why we have got into it. Have we become more accustomed to public displays of grief and emotion since the great Diana watershed? Has our famous British reserve been more exposed to the touchy-feely practices of other countries? Or are we reacting to the disappearance of other more permanent tributes? Now that very few of us have a permanent resting place marked with a headstone, do we have to confer some sanctity on the place where a person breathed their last, regardless of whether it's a busy road junction, a railway embankment or even, as in an example I saw recently, a gents public lavatory?

On the approaches to Zennor, I notice a house displaying a bed and breakfast sign. I had been aiming for a hostel in the village, but figure this could be a more comfortable option. I don't particularly want to spend a second sleepless night in a communal dorm. As I walk through the garden I'm just slightly put off by the sight of broken beds and a profusion of assorted household junk piled in an open outhouse. By the porch there hangs a bell – no clapper, just a stick on a piece of string and a rough sign which says 'Please ring the bell hard.' The last word is underlined three times in magic marker. I lift the stick and at the same time glance up at the windows. Now I'm all for saving on window cleaning bills, but these look as if they haven't seen a chamois since Queen Elizabeth came to the throne. And I'm not talking about the present Queen. From what I can see of the curtains, they don't look too good either. I lower the stick, sneak back out of the gate and continue on my way.

Zennor comes upon me suddenly. It's a delightful little village nestling in a hollow – characterful unspoilt pub, attractive church, all the right ingredients. DH Lawrence lived here with his wife and two friends while he was writing *Women In Love*, staying initially at the Tinner's Arms and later renting a house. It seems that the villagers disapproved of Lawrence's free and easy attitudes towards relationships, and were deeply suspicious of his German wife Frieda who was a member of the von Richtofen family. We're talking the latter part of the First World War here, not the best of times to be stomping around Cornwall with a German accent. A number of ships had been sunk by German submarine action within nearby waters, and a local rumour began to grow that the Lawrences might be spies. There was absolutely

18

no basis to it but, in October 1917, they were interrogated by the police and given three days to leave the village. A clear case of Zennorphobia you might say. Sorry about that, I just couldn't help myself.

The hostel is a converted Wesleyan chapel close by the pub. Nineteenth century Zennor boasted an astonishing total of six chapels as assorted brands of non-conformity fought for the souls of dissolute miners. This one has adapted remarkably to its new role. It's clean, bright and comfortably appointed. What's more, it's almost empty. Just me and four Germans. The cheery New Zealander in charge shows me to my room. 'Six beds, take your pick. You've got the room to yourself.' Hmm, this is more like it.

A good meal with several cold beers sees to it that I sleep like the proverbial infant and I wake much more positive than yesterday, despite some worrying redness and pain in my little toes. I knew I should have brought the new boots. These are obviously going to cause me problems.

Additional hostellers have been beamed in from the planet Nerd during the night. A middle-aged couple in matching outfits sit in total silence throughout breakfast. Or at least, one of them does. The male member – I use the term in both senses – has chosen to introduce an element of technology into that age-old conversation stopper of burying one's nose in the newspaper. Just in case his hapless wife should be tempted to speak to him, he has adopted the personal stereo as essential breakfast accessory.

Before I hit the trail, I feel I must visit the Zennor Folklore Museum, which is right next door. The thatched exterior and waterwheel signal a degree of tweeness, but it's a treasure-trove of life enhancing artefacts such as the Reverend Hitchens' collection of cutthroat razors. And there are quaint hand-written accounts of ancient local customs and personalities of the past. One recounts the habits of a nineteenth century neighbour from hell who used to take to his bed and hibernate throughout the winter months, but would make up for it in summer by rising at three in the morning and ranting around the village – hammering on doors and windows and berating residents for their laziness.

The Ordnance Survey map in the hostel shows two paths to St Ives, the coastal path and a slightly more direct one 'The Tinner's Way' which cuts across fields about half a mile inland. Even though I've told myself that speed doesn't matter on this trip, I'm still keen to put some distance between myself and Land's End. Turning the corner at St Ives is an important psychological shift towards the Northeast – the direction of John O' Groats. A mile saved by taking the more direct route is attractive, but it requires a bit more navigation than the coastal path. Following the latter is largely a matter of keeping the sea to your left and walking as close as possible to it without actually falling in. With no Ordnance Survey map of my own, I squint long and hard at the hostel map, attempting to commit to memory the course of the inland path. Unsuccessful. All recollection of it has disappeared by the time I am ten yards from the hostel gate, but initially the footpath is easy to find and to follow. It runs flat, straight and level through empty fields, between each of which is a stone cattle grid, every slab solidly cut and laid in position as if for a thousand years. The people who made these, clearly didn't expect to be moving on for a while.

But then I run across junctions in the path that leave me confused and undecided. I choose the likeliest looking one, but soon find myself heading down into a deep valley and, without the benefit of a decent map, I don't know whether it will re-emerge or whether I have taken a wrong turning. I retrace my steps, surely a mistake, and have to put up with several minutes of road walking before I'm able to join another footpath. This one runs purposefully for a few hundred yards before dawdling off into a welter of similarly weighted cattle tracks. I climb a fence and struggle up a steep lane, only to find myself back on the road. OK, I give up – I follow the road down into St Ives.

My first impression of St Ives isn't helped by the fact that my feet are now hurting quite a lot. They have become the main focus of my thoughts. I curse my decision to leave the new boots behind. Little more than a day of walking and I'm crippled. But even allowing for an element of distraction, I'm hard pressed to find something good to say about this town. Whatever it was that attracted Barbara Hepworth, Bernard Leach et al has been diminished by roaming packs of visitors with vests and tattoos. And too many of the shops are parading ubiquitous holiday tat. Sure, there's classy stuff too and the place still has clear attractions – you don't get a branch of the Tate Gallery in a small seaside town for nothing – but there are just too many fat trailing wallies and less than wholesome cooking smells for my comfort. I buy an, admittedly excellent, pasty and change into my shorts on the beach. The sun has come out and it seems like the sensible thing to do. A seagull the size of a golden eagle skis my head as I'm standing on one leg with my trousers round my ankles, almost causing me to drop my towel. I complete the task sitting down and scoop half the beach into my shorts.

As I prepare to leave the town my attention is caught by a boot shop displaying a large red 'Sale' sign in its window. The two things dearest to my heart at this moment are comfortable footwear and the chance to save money. The combination proves irresistible and five minutes later I'm walking out of the shop, the proud owner of a pair of lightweight, waterproof jobbies – twenty-five percent off, this week only. It's a purchase I quickly regret. The other boots go into the pack where they immediately make their presence felt on my shoulders. What's more, even though the new boots felt sublime as I slipped my feet into them in the shop, I quickly realise that the sensation was one of contrast with a pair in which I'd already been walking hard for two hours. A couple of wellingtons stuffed with cabbage stalks would probably have felt equally comfortable. After half an hour my belief that the new boots represent the ultimate in footwear has been revealed as premature to say the least. Once up to normal running temperature they are scarcely any more comfortable than the ones they have usurped, and – Shit! – they are quite a bit hotter. The sun is beaming down and I decide to relinquish the new boots in favour of my sandals. This is madness! There are now two pairs of boots in my bag and, with each foot weighing in around 850 grams, that's a pretty significant extra half a stone on the weight of my pack. I resolve that I will post one pair back home some time in the next couple of days. But which pair?

Boots notwithstanding, the path out of St Ives is pleasant and easy, past hotels and large comfortable houses and then alongside the railway line till I'm standing above the broad sweep of Porthkidney sands. Looking back, St Ives is attractive again – picturesque harbour, once the fourth busiest in England, toy houses stacked up behind. Ahead is the Hayle estuary and a necessary inland detour, initially through bungalow land, but before too long there is no alternative but to schlep along the busy main road, across the bridge and into Hayle. The guide book has warned me about this and I'm expecting it to be worse than it actually is.

Hayle is not a particularly nice place. Its great claim to fame is as a one-time centre for the manufacture of mining machinery. In the nineteenth century the town supplied pumps and drills to the world. Now it has the air of somewhere with not a lot to do, but making quite a meal about not doing it. Bored teenagers drape themselves, scowling, over dreary benches by the busy junction that seems to constitute the town's centre.

I move on quickly and, stopping only to buy five out-of-date energy bars for a pound, head out once again towards the coast. I note with irritation that places I walked an hour and a half previously are only a couple of hundred yards away across the estuary. To put them out of sight and mind I attempt a short cut through the sand dunes, but find myself repeatedly coming up against barbed wire and signs threatening to deprive me of my basic human rights if I dare to venture into the private caravan sites and chalet parks they protect. Being a law abiding chap, I veer away each time along the numerous rabbit tracks that criss-cross the sandy humps. Finally, I stumble over a rise and come face to face with a man shovelling rubbish from a pick-up truck into a skip. He makes no attempt to shoot me, but jumps so violently with surprise that I'm moved to run through a mental checklist of the procedures for dealing with cardiac arrest. Once he has recovered his composure, he tells me to ignore the signs and go straight through the holiday park to the beach. I do so, and emerge onto a vast open shore. High point of my day is a two mile stroll along flat, wet, soft-centred sand.

It's five thirty and I need to start thinking about accommodation. There's the village of Gwithian and then nothing else for several miles. So Gwithian it is – a quiet little place – pub, church, a few houses, caravan site and just a couple of bed and breakfasts. The Calize Country House looks like an attractive bet and turns out to be exactly that. The friendly proprietor offers me a comfortable room with a lovely sea view and makes me a cup of tea while I run a wonderful hot bath. And it all comes at a price little more than a youth hostel.

My preoccupation with sore feet has shifted to an even more urgent area – the most incredibly painful bum. That sand I scooped off St Ives beach while I was changing into my shorts has insinuated itself into the parts other minerals do not reach. It has been scouring away all afternoon and has rubbed me absolutely raw. I shuffle the contents of my meagre first-aid kit for something that will help. Blister dressings, insect repellent, triangular bandage, safety pins. Why in God's name did I neglect antiseptic cream? At the very bottom of the pack I locate one of those spirit wet wipes. It'll have to do. I brace myself and just about manage to summon the courage to apply it to my delicate rear, then listen in surprise to the trapped animal squeal that seems to come from a point about three feet above my head.

There's a pub just down the road that does evening meals. I hobble in at a quarter past seven, get myself a pint and ask if I can order some food.

'What, for tonight?' says the landlord.

I nod.

'Well, I can't say when you'll get it.' He gestures towards the dozen or so people eating in the dining room. 'And these people' – he points to a smiley couple seated by the bar – 'are waiting for a table.'

I'm a touch nonplussed. Wholesome this place may be, but I can tell from a five-second glance at the menu that it's not Rick Stein's. What do you have to do to get plaice and chips in these parts? But it's the only eatery in the village and, in my physical condition, a couple of miles walk to the next one is a less attractive option than starvation. I decide on a policy of negotiation and offer to eat at one of the little circular tables in the bar rather than wait for a larger one in the main dining area. As there is only one of me, I figure that I'll be taking up less room and freeing a dining table for people who might otherwise have to wait until a week next Tuesday. The landlord, however, treats the suggestion like a proposition from Wittgenstein. I've made the mistake of putting this revolutionary idea to somebody who isn't ready for it. Here is a man who likes things in their place. The bar is where drinks are served, the dining area for food. Confusing the two could lead to disorder and chaos. In no time at all there would be people drinking from the urinals and pissing into pint pots. Fortunately, the landlady proves more flexible and happily agrees to serve me in the bar. Fifteen minutes and I have my plaice and chips. The other poor sods are still waiting for a table.

I am entertained during my meal by a medley of what are clearly the landlord's favourite pop songs. Some of them I've not heard since the seventies and had rather hoped to keep it that way. Each time there is one he particularly likes, he turns up the volume. The Lowry song is the hands-down winner. Matchstick men and matchstick cats and dogs not only get more decibels than the others, but the regulars even join in with the chorus.

I'm still very sore in the morning, and not really looking forward to the day. To put off the moment of departure I pootle around the pretty little Gwithian church – its graveyard well stocked with shipwreck victims pre-dating the Godrevy Lighthouse. But I'm unable to make this last more than ten minutes and reluctantly head for the path once more. The first mile is agony, but with muscles warmed up it becomes easier. I recall reading somewhere that, in long distance walking, the first three days are the worst. This encourages me. Here I am on day three. Should get better from tomorrow.

The three day watershed focus starts me thinking early about my bed for the night. Perranporth seems like a reasonable target. It has a youth hostel but, before I enquire about vacant beds, I'll try another tactic. There's an old friend I haven't seen for a good twenty-five years, but I'm pretty sure he included the words 'give us a call if you're in the area' on at least one of the last twenty-five Christmas cards. He lives in Falmouth on the south coast, but it's only a dozen miles from my intended destination. I'll try phoning him.

Sure enough my call results in the offer of a bed for the night and, even better, a pick up and return service from Perranporth. That has to be better than a youth hostel full of surfers.

It's pretty easy terrain across Godrevy Point and on past Hell's Mouth a rather grandiose name for a fairly run-of-the-mill cleft in the cliffs – and by lunch time I'm at Portreath. I've kept my motivation high throughout the morning by the thought of a delicious pub lunch washed down by a fine pint or two. As I trundle through Portreath, I spot a hostelry down by the harbour that looks ideal.

I've always been too influenced by outward appearances. In my younger days, it took me a long time to cotton on to the fact that pretty girls aren't always nice people. Unfortunately, I've yet to learn the same lesson when it comes to pubs. Once inside, my mistake is clear. The place has a gloomy and claustrophobic air; customers huddle in silence over flat beer and grim rations. I order a swift half, and move on.

The path between Portreath and Porthtowan would be very enjoyable were it not for a bloody great fence that encloses a large Ministry of Defence site and runs right next to the path for about three miles. Nancekuke the place is called, and apparently the fence is one of the lesser problems associated with it. In the years after the Second World War it housed a chemical weapons factory manufacturing the deadly nerve gas sarin. Recently there have been questions raised in parliament and the press about high levels of serious illness and premature death among former workers at the plant and it has emerged that, when it was closed in 1970, equipment was dumped down disused mine-shafts and that some environmental contamination may have resulted. The Ministry of Defensiveness is adamant that all stocks of sarin were taken elsewhere, but has admitted that it doesn't know exactly what is in the shafts. I quicken my pace and aim muttered curses at this monolithic organisation that has managed to muck up so many beautiful areas of our countryside, but has simultaneously preserved them from the modern excesses of commercial development and agriculture. I recently read about a species of butterfly that only exists on MoD land. Ironic, isn't it?

I'm becoming a little concerned that on day three of the trip I haven't yet started to ponder any of the great questions of life. That guy I met back in Penzance had successfully plotted his position in the grand scheme of things by this point. Being alone with my thoughts is all very well but, try as I might, the spirit of enquiry doesn't seem to stretch much further than reflecting upon how far I've walked, how far still to go, and how soon I can stop for something to eat. Could it be that I'm not cut out for a contemplative existence, or is it that I'm just out of practice? As far as I can recall, my only serious attempt at probing my own existence was at the age of six when I spent a good deal of time and energy considering the question: 'How do I know I'm not a squirrel, dreaming that I'm a human during my long winter hibernation?' It's a question I never successfully answered, except that the older I became, the less likely it was that the range of reminiscences I thought I possessed could be contained within even a six-month-long squirrel dream. Unless, of course, the reminiscences themselves were simply invented to order as background for my ongoing dream. Hmmm. Perhaps I should stick to consideration of how far I've still to go and when I can have the next Mars bar.

After Porthtowan I'm well and truly back in mining country. Disused workings are everywhere. Up ahead is the hefty lump of St

Agnes Beacon – one of the chain of hills used to relay warning of the arrival of the Spanish Armada. There are fine views in all directions. I'm told you can see thirty parish churches and, at night, twelve lighthouses, but I'm not sticking around to count. At my current rate of progress, I'm getting twitchy about making my evening rendezvous.

The village of St Agnes, nestling beyond the beacon, was founded on mining. Now, it's a place for holidays and retirement with property prices rising faster than anywhere else in Cornwall, It's altogether an attractive little place and, if I hadn't already made other arrangements, I think I would be knocking on one or two B&B doors. There are echoes of old St Agnes in the Miners' and Mechanics' Institute in the main street and in some of the cottages stacked, almost one on top of another, down precipitous slopes. The harbour which served as the gateway for incoming coal and outgoing ore is long gone, washed away nearly a century ago as others had been before it. The only evidence of its existence, some large granite blocks strewn around the base of the cliff. It was a vital conduit for local industry, but container port it certainly wasn't. Everything that entered or left from it had to be conveyed by winch or chute from the top of the cliff.

The Canine Precision Defecation Team has been demonstrating its skills along the path out of St Agnes, and I'm forced to engage in a dangerous game of hop-scotch. It must take considerable dedication and training to get your animal to perform in the middle of a one-foot-wide path when the creature's natural instincts are surely to retreat to the undergrowth. But they clearly take the art seriously around here and delight in showing their contempt for the notices threatening paltry fines. I observe too that, presumably as a result of the damp climate, the less recent deposits have grown a highly artistic bacterial fur that makes them look like small dead creatures dotted along the path.

The day becomes a little wearisome from this point in. Not least the spell when I'm repeatedly buzzed by a small aircraft practising its landing approaches at Trevallas airfield. As it ruffles my immaculate coiffeur for the umpteenth time I begin to imagine that I'm Cary Grant in that sequence from *North by North West*. I look around for a handy cornfield to dive into, but unfortunately there isn't one to hand.

It's gone seven when I finally lumber over Cligga Head and see the wide sands of Perranporth laid out before me. Despite the hour, there are still dozens of surfers bobbing about in very small waves. I suspect that as long as there's daylight there'll be surfers, any day of the year. I can understand the attraction when there's something to surf on, but today few waves are more than a foot high. That doesn't seem to put them off. They sit around like mounted tadpoles waiting for some piddling wave, marginally bigger than the rest, that will carry them all of five yards before they flop back, straddling their boards, scanning the horizon for the next bit of paltry excitement.

It's an addictive business surfing, and as bad for your health as smoking. At least that's the impression I get from talking to a rather elderly enthusiast who's half out of his wetsuit, rubber arms flapping around his knees, and taking a drink of some meaty-smelling liquid next to his camper van which sports a sticker announcing that 'Surfers do it standing up'. I had always thought that there were just two risks – drowning or running across myopic sharks that can't tell the difference between humans and seals. Seems I was wrong. My informant reels off a veritable inventory of complaints that can afflict the surfing fanatic: back pain, lacerations, bunions, hypothermia, skin problems, cataracts, pollution related infections and surfer's ear. This last is caused by long term exposure to cold sea water and can result in hearing loss. I wonder whether the brine might have a pickling effect on other faculties too, but feel it wouldn't be diplomatic to give voice to my thoughts.

I'm hobbling along the main drag in Perranporth when a car draws alongside me. The middle-aged driver winds down the window, sticks out a scaly, hairless head, like a tortoise peeping out of its shell, and proceeds to insult me loudly. I jump back in surprise. What's with this geezer? He laughs and gestures towards the passenger seat.

'Oh, hello Tony.'

Odd, isn't it? You forget that other people change and get older too while they're out of your sight.

Meeting someone after twenty-five years isn't so different from meeting them for the first time. There appears to be no concurrence in the recollections we have of three years spent sharing seedy student bedsits. So little history do we have in common, I even begin to fear that the creature I am speaking to might be an interloper substituted by some alien intelligence in place of my erstwhile flatmate. And as for the family and career baggage that has rolled around the carousel since we were students, where to start is the question. Our conversation rapidly shifts from 1970s catch-up to third-millennium chit-chat. At least that way his wife, whom I have never met before, can join in. After a very pleasant meal, I'm persuaded to coax my legs into a jaunt around the best of Falmouth's pubs. They protest, but we go anyway. It's an attractive town with some characterful drinking places, but even three pints of excellent beer fails to drown the din of my screaming muscles.

Next morning I'm delivered back to Perranporth, refreshed and invigorated. Adele has put most of my garments through the washing machine, and my load is eased by the absence of a pair of boots – the old ones – that remain in Falmouth to be picked up at some unspecified time in the future. I start off at a cracking pace, keen to discover whether it really does get easier after three days.

At Holywell beach I take a swim. The first of the trip. As I towel off my shivering body I'm suddenly aware how many fat people there are around me. It's like finding yourself in the middle of a colony of sea lions. They bask and trumpet to each other. And so many of them are startlingly young. I'm not talking podgy here, I'm talking seriously gross – children of six or seven. It's a graphic illustration of how far we've moved as a country into the premier league of world heavyweights. I can't help but draw comparisons with the family beach scene of my own childhood. You came across the occasional fat kid, but in the main they were like me – stick thin, ribs you could play a tune on. In an instant it all floods back to me: permanently chattering teeth on windswept beaches; the orange, hand-knitted, woollen swimming trunks that, weighed down with sand and sea water, hung halfway to my knees; the moth hole in the front that periodically pitched me into acute peep-through embarrassment; the painfully chafed inner thighs from running around all day in wet, sandy wool; the ritual smearing of calamine lotion on evening crimson skin; the itch and the agony that accompanied wholesale peeling. Perhaps modern obesity isn't so bad after all.

I've often wondered why it is we feel so comfortable and relaxed on beaches. Stick me in a conventional bed and I'll lie awake for half the night, but stretch me out on a beach and I'm asleep in moments. I recall reading one semi-plausible explanation that suggested it could be traced back to early human evolution along the coastal fringes of southern Africa. We're comforted by the proximity of sea, so the theory went, because it represented safety. When confronted by vicious predators with a taste for early humanoids, our ancestors were able to scamper into the water, safe from the creatures that wanted to eat them. Ignoring the fact that lots of nasty predators can swim a deal better than we can, the theorists went on to suggest that the amount of time our ancestors spent standing up to their necks in the sea while lions patrolled the shoreline had a further effect on our bodily evolution – the disappearance of hair from all but the tops of our heads. Well now, that's not quite accurate, is it? There are other hirsute underwater areas that would tend to put the mockers on the theory. Unless, of course, our ancestors felt so protected by the sea that they were able to lie on their backs in the water and wave their genitalia at the furious predators on the shore.

Arriving in Newquay I'm a little surprised that I'm permitted to walk down the main street, even though I'm clearly devoid of tattoos. Perhaps I'll be required to get some before I'm allowed to leave. I last came to this town at the age of eleven on a day trip from a Boys' Brigade summer camp near St Austell. It was, I thought, the most magical place I had ever visited and I marked the occasion by purchasing a souvenir tea towel and a pot of clotted cream to take home for my mum. I was sick on the tea towel during the winding coach journey back to St Austell but, after a thorough boiling, it still did service for many years. The cream, though, had to be given to the cat; several days inside a hot tent had taken it past its best.

And so it is with Newquay today – sell-by date well past. The town centre has a run down and slightly threatening air with tatty shops and black splodges on the pavement that speak of dropped ice creams and ground-in chips. Youths with cans of lager and backward facing caps dangle around aimlessly – three of them crowd my personal space as I top up my dwindling supplies of cash from a hole in the wall.

Have you noticed how a backward facing cap instantly lowers the wearer's IQ by a minimum of twenty points? I'm surprised that education experts haven't yet cottoned on to this. It's so obvious. The problem of under-performance among teenage boys could be solved at a stroke, simply by getting them to wear their caps the right way round.

Back on the cliff-top path, a little old lady tootles up from the road with two large carrier bags. A group of fractious seagulls has already gathered in preparation for her arrival and, as she empties her bags on the ground, their numbers are massively augmented as if by magic. There are scores of them, wheeling, diving, scrapping and squawking over the giant heap of crusts she has delivered. The old lady stands back, flushed with parental pride, smiling and encouraging them. This is clearly a daily ritual. I can picture her trekking around the shops and guesthouses, collecting up the stale bread and uneaten toast that will sustain her unruly charges and give her an interest in life. And as I walk on, I fancy I can hear a groan from the nearby bungalow residents who will have to contend yet again with bird-shit on the washing and crusts down the chimney.

At the Merrymoor Inn by the beach in Mawgen Porth I'm offered an excellent room at a very reasonable price – sea view and immaculate en-suite bathroom. I enjoy some nice grilled lamb and a couple of pints of Bass on the terrace before moving back inside as the sun dips. There's just one small drawback – the live music. It comes in the form of a singer-guitarist equipped with a rhythm box who churns his way through Dire Straits and Simon and Garfunkel standards. I'm in danger of being unkind, because he is perfectly competent, but I can't help but feel that this sort of act is past its zenith. It's too hackneyed to make you want to listen, but too intrusive to be treated as background. I retire to bed, where I can still hear 'Money for Nothing' thumping up through my pillow.

It's the usual English breakfast they dish up in the morning, but at least there's grapefruit and muesli on offer. The friendly waitress offers me extra bacon in place of the sausage I can't face. I detect an Essex accent and we get to talking about Southend where she lives for most of the year. But she tells me with pride that she is actually Scottish, having moved down from Edinburgh some seven years ago and worked hard to lose her Scottish accent so that she would fit in at school. I'm both impressed and appalled. To my mind, Edinburgh could lay claim to the most attractive accent in the UK. Exchanging it for Estuary English seems nothing short of sacrilegious. She agrees, but says that's not the way you think when you're fourteen.

I'm prompted to reflect on the accents I've heard so far on the trip. Plenty of Midlands, and North, both sides of the Pennines, but precious few Cornish. It's as if they're hiding in caves, preserving their threatened heritage, leaving the shops, inns and guesthouses to be run by outsiders.

The stretch between Mawgan Porth and Padstow is quite delightful walking. Gone are the spoil heaps and ruined buildings of the mining areas. Gone too the military establishments that border much of the path between Portreath and Newquay. The rocky outcrops have given way to more rounded contours with springy turf, and there are far fewer of the stiff ups and downs that characterised earlier sections.

One of the noticeable features of this path is that the well known beauty spots I come upon every so often are actually no more attractive than some of the places I have never heard of. In fact they are rendered less so by the cars and people that are inevitably present. Bedruthan Steps is a case in point. The subject of thousands of postcards, it's an interesting and impressive collection of rocks. But is it the highlight of my morning? I don't think so. I've been delighted by so many views and glimpses along the way. This is just one more, and so familiar that it doesn't quite count as a proper view.

At Porthcothan an old man in a navy style peaked cap and thick black and yellow fleece – I'm sweating in just my shorts – greets me:

'Isn't it a lovely day. First day of summer.'

I agree. He might think me rude if I were to point out that, as yesterday was just as sunny, it has to be at least the second day of summer. He goes on,

'Up in England I hear they've had summer for a little while now.'

This is heady stuff. I've obviously run across one of the revered elders of the Popular Front for the Liberation of Cornwall, just emerged from his cave. But I'm unsure how to respond. Is the question a trap? Will I be seized by his accomplices and interrogated if I make any remark that suggests his country and mine are one and the same, and that the weather has been uniformly awful across the whole of it.

I know there's a long tradition in Cornwall of not wanting to be associated with the rest of the country. But these days, do any of us want to own up to being English? British we may not mind. But English! It's one of those characteristics you feel you should apologise for – as if all the crassness and jingoistic exploitation ever committed by your countrymen and forbears can be attributed to you personally.

'Where do you come from?'

'I'm from England, actually. Sorry about that.'

And if being English is a reason for apology, what about being English, male, white, heterosexual and middle-class? That's a burden of guilt almost too great to carry. We must be one of the few minority groups it's still acceptable to make fun of. I almost feel that I should book myself into the Edinburgh Fringe, get up on stage and invite the audience to laugh at me directly. Cut out the middle man, so to speak.

As I move inland along the Camel estuary I start to meet more people along the path and there's a strange similarity about them. They are all traditionally English and in their late fifties: good solid boots, baggy shorts and white legs with just a hint of varicose veins. They carry knobbly sticks – some of which have those little metal badges that tell of ancient trips to the English Lakes and the Austrian Tyrol. And they protect their thinning scalps with those off-white floppy brimmed pudding hats that have been an essential element of sensible middle-class holiday luggage since 1959. I meet or pass so many in almost identical gear that I begin to think the same ones are coming round again, like extras in an old budget movie. Eventually I study the map and realise that the coastal path at this point has joined up with a thirty mile footpath called the Saint's Way which links the River Camel in the north with the River Fowey in the south of Cornwall, along an ancient route that has associations with a number of Celtic saints and holy men. Realisation dawns. Of course! Pilgrims, that's what they are – old-style vicars and scoutmasters, stalwart members of rural church congregations.

Now Padstow is a nice place. Definitely one of the best I've passed through so far. Quite busy with holidaymakers, but retaining its character and integrity. The picturesque harbour still has something of a working port about it, and there is less undiluted tourist trash than Newquay or St Ives. But on the pasty front Padstow has to be in a league of its own. Pasty shops are everywhere. In a street just behind the quay there are even two next door to each other. Given that they are also on sale in every grocery shop, pub and café throughout the county, I have to ask myself whether the market might be reaching saturation point. I reckon that even if everyone in Padstow on this day ate five of the things, the pasty shelves of the town would still not be cleared. Are there alternative uses that I'm overlooking? Do people use them as door stops perhaps, or fancy edging for ornamental borders?

I take the little ferry across the estuary to Rock, or 'Knightsbridge-On-Sea' as it has become known in acknowledgement of its holiday-making clientele. The sons and daughters of the seriously loaded flock here to party away the summer months. And it's noticeable that the car park contains not a single resprayed Ford Capri or rusty Montego with go-faster stripes. Nearby is the tiny fifteenth century church of St Enodoc where Sir John Betjeman is buried. This building, on the site of a sixth century oratory, is a sweet little place nestling in the dunes. For many years it nestled so successfully that it completely disappeared from view beneath the sand.

At the mouth of the estuary is Polzeath – a place I feel I should already know. I've never been there, but an old friend, who died a couple of years back, described it as her favourite place in all the world. I'm keen to discover some of the magic it had for her. It's nearly five o'clock and I settle on it as my destination for the day. I pluck a guest house from my guide book accommodation list and phone ahead to arrange a room.

I can't stop myself being delighted by this new-found use for my mobile phone. I've had the thing for quite a while now. It's the size of a house brick, and I've carted it from place to place like so much ballast. The week after I bought it, every electronics shop was full of models a quarter the size and half the price. But I've stuck with my ugly giant. Not out of any love for it, but because I've hitherto been unable to find any sensible use for my first ten quid's worth of free call credit, and I'm sure as hell not going to donate the thing to the Science Museum with as much as a penny left in the pot. Suddenly, however, there's a chance that I might have to top it up before the end of the trip.

But I mustn't get carried away. I remain stubbornly incapable of making that conceptual leap from mobile phone as emergency equip-ment to mobile phone as recreational accessory. I can sort myself a room for the night or let my wife know that I haven't yet fallen over a cliff, but even here I'm severely troubled by a slightly out-of-date mental cash register that keeps urging me to keep it brief.

It's such a shame, and I really must try harder. I'm guilty of wasting that enormous investment in infrastructure, those masts sprouting from the top of every tall building and hillside. I resolve not to rest until I've exchanged text messages with somebody six feet away from me in the same room, and managed an entire supermarket shopping trip without breaking off a conversation with my cousin's best friend's dog.

A pity that video-phone technology has not yet taken off in a big way. The Polzeath B&B turns out to be less than well appointed – decrepit furniture, threadbare blankets, towels you can spit through, dust, cobwebs and curtains that won't close properly. If stained and chipped plywood utility furniture ever becomes collectable, I know where there is an excellent example of a wardrobe and chest of drawers. But I do have a brilliant sea view, and I'm too knackered for the hassle of turning the room down and seeking somewhere else.

I wash my feet in the sink, get an attack of cramp and nearly pull the rickety object off the wall. Judging by the bodged tile-work and sealant at the back of it, I wouldn't be the first to have done so.

My late friend told me about this wonderful café down by the beach that served excellent fresh fish, and I am looking forward to eating there. I'm somewhat taken aback to find that it's the garishly painted building that had so offended my senses as I approached the village. But never judge a book by its cover, and all that. I wander in. The menu looks interesting, then …

'Sorry, we're not serving food tonight.'

I take a beer at one of the tables outside, and look around for an alternative. As far as I can see there's only a fish and chip shop.

I've eaten some pretty dreadful fish and chips in my time, but these surely have to rank among the five worst examples. Even the idyllic setting of a beautiful empty beach with the sun dipping gently towards the horizon cannot diminish their utter vileness. Later I find a restaurant and pub situated on either flank of the bay, but by then I'm not hungry any more.

I've walked some distance today, but I still feel as if there are a few miles left in my legs. Perhaps I really am getting into my stride. I put myself to the test by trekking up the steep path to the top of Pentire Head. It's absolutely worth the effort. I'm entirely alone in the late evening sunshine at the small flat summit – sea, cliff and bay on three sides – and it's so peaceful, so glorious that I literally stretch out my arms and shout for the delight of it. I guess I came here hoping to discover something to remember my old friend by, and in this scene I think I have.

I bounce back down the precipitous path as the sun slips away, and reach the beach in time to watch it slide perfectly into a burnished sea. Not a hint of haze to mar its descent right down to the last tiny golden sliver. It's an awful cliché but I do feel glad to be alive.

Back in the guest house, I become aware that there are other poor sods staying here. Somebody in the next room is having a wash, and when they let out the water it bubbles up into my bowl. Outside, the quiet road is suddenly alive with herds of teenagers in fancy dress. Nuns, fairies, pirates and gorillas make their noisy way up the hill and the place falls silent again, apart from the second-hand water which continues to gurgle grumpily in my wash basin.

Chapter 3

At breakfast, they don't even ask what I want. Just wheel out the usual suspects – wizened bacon, brazen sausage, furtive eggs. Cooked breakfast novelty is definitely wearing thin. I'm not sure how many more of these I can take. In a corner of the dining room are stacked some bar stools and spirit optics – relics from a previous failed venture perhaps.

The section from Polzeath to Port Isaac is very pretty but gets increasingly tougher as it goes, and my progress slows accordingly. The rock formation at Lundy Hole and the beach at Lundy Bay are particularly striking, the more so for being deserted. Hardly any trace of habitation all morning apart from Port Quin – just a clutch of holiday cottages, now owned by the National Trust, at the head of a peaceful inlet. A one time fishing village, Port Quin has the distinction of having been abandoned twice – the first occasion was early in the nineteenth century when all the men of the village drowned at sea, while the second, and decisive, exodus came when the pilchard shoals failed in the 1840s. Everything about the location shouts 'this would be a nice place for a little fishing village.' Alas, you can have the best location in the world, but it's not much use if there are no fish. So there it sits, quietly harbouring its lost life.

The terrain towards Port Isaac becomes tougher still. I meet a struggling couple who are hoping to have a nice lunch at Port Quin and catch the bus back. They think it is just around the next headland, and seek my confirmation. I don't know which piece of bad news to deliver first. Should I tell them it's another half hour of hard walking or that there's no bus stop, let alone a café or pub? It seems unkind to reveal any of these truths – it will certainly ruin a beautiful walk – and for a moment I consider letting them soldier on in joyful ignorance. But I tell them everything, sure that they will curse me for it. Glancing back, several minutes after leaving them, I see they are still rooted to the spot where we met, doubtless debating whether to turn back along the route they have already struggled over for the best part of an hour or carry on in the knowledge that, when they do get to Port Quin, they'll have to trek back by road with empty bellies.

Port Isaac is picturesque enough to be regularly in demand for film locations. It's easy to see why: unspoiled harbour, whitewashed stone cottages, narrow lanes. The narrowest, Squeezebelly Alley, is only eighteen inches wide. The village offers a choice of lunchtime pubs – always a nuisance for worriers like me. Such occasions allow ample opportunity to dither over which one appears to have the pleasantest outlook, the tastiest pint or the best ploughman's. Even when the food comes and it's OK, I'm haunted by the thought that a few yards down the road they might be serving something exquisite. I settle on the Red Lion because it has a nice terrace overlooking the harbour, but I'm still a little concerned that the food board looked better on the one fifty yards down the road. A man from Cromer with a voice like Larry Grayson is sounding off to a couple from Lancashire about how Cornwall has been ruined by excessive coastal development and money grubbing tourist fleecers. The Lancashire man agrees.

'Yes, for what we pay to stay a fortnight at our caravan site, we could take a decent holiday abroad. Mind you, it is nice. Right next to the sea, and all mod cons.'

After a strenuous morning I'm in no great hurry to get started again along a stretch that the guide book describes as some of the toughest walking on the whole 600 mile South West Coast Path. Given that there are more ups and downs per mile on this long distance trail than there are on the Pennine Way, it's obviously not going to be a Sunday afternoon stroll. But I can't sit around listening to other people's conversations. I press on.

I have been walking in my four-wheel-drive sandals for the last couple of days but, not only are there some very steep climbs and descents on this section, the going is very rough and overgrown in places. I figure that I might make faster progress with my boots on. After a couple of miles they have to come off again. It feels as if my feet are on fire. I remove the boots and my dripping socks and struggle on in my sandals. I'm starting to become very irritable. A light aircraft circles interminably overhead, and further sours my mood. Fortunately, there is nobody else around to witness the spectacle of a sweating middle-aged man waving a pointy stick at an aeroplane and shouting 'Fuck off' at the top of his voice. The aeroplane ignores me.

After Trebarwith Strand the walking is more level. Long abandoned slate quarries are carved out of the cliff. In a couple of places Jenga-like stacks jut up from the quarry floor - inferior slate that was not worth the trouble of mining. Under the cliffs at Penhallic point the wharf is still visible where slates were loaded onto sailing ships, and along the path are the anchor blocks for donkey winches. I notice something new about the walls surrounding nearby fields. They're made of slate too, arranged in a neat herringbone pattern. Very stylish.

A procession of around thirty school kids, teachers front and back like mountain railway engines, jangles towards me. Every single one of the kids is wired up to a personal stereo. They exchange staccato bursts of conversation in unnaturally loud voices and sing tuneless snatches of whatever is blasting their eardrums.

Tintagel Youth Hostel is housed in former slate quarry offices about a mile from the village. Like most hostels it doesn't respond to phone calls until 5 pm. I'm hoping they'll have some room left, but when I arrive there just before five, there's already a 'hostel full' sign on the door. 'Bet it's that bloody school party.' I consider walking to the next hostel at Boscastle, but that's another five miles and the phone number is continuously engaged. So it's into Tintagel to look for a B&B.

Just by the attractive Norman church of St Materiana on the outskirts of the village, a film crew is in action. Lights, cameras, support vehicles and several emaciated actors in long black hooded cloaks and deathly green-grey make-up. Clearly not *Songs of Praise*. A group of sunburned holidaymakers in shorts and beer bellies, contrasting comically with the actors, looks on in eager anticipation. They could be in for a long wait. The director and his assistant are closeted in deep conversation and every other member of the outfit has that expression of bored resignation so familiar to those who frequent hospital waiting rooms and railway station buffets.

Tintagel is a village that owes most of its business to Arthurian legend. They've got Geoffrey of Monmouth to thank for that. Back in the twelfth century he earmarked the castle here as the place where King Arthur had been conceived some seven centuries previously. Quite where Geoff got his information from I'm not sure, but he tells how Uther Pendragon seduced and impregnated a certain Princess Ygerna by turning himself into a likeness of her husband with the assistance of a potion provided by Merlin the wizard. Then, as if he hadn't already done enough damage, Pendragon killed the poor husband to boot. For seaside sex, drugs and violence it sounds as if fifth century Tintagel was a match for twenty-first century Faliraki.

The story has been embroidered and argued over ever since Geoffrey committed it to vellum. Much of the Arthurian legend, including the elements of medieval chivalry, is the result of invention by later writers. And while there is widespread acceptance that a Celtic military leader by the name of Arthur may well have existed, there is little in the way of unanimity that he came from around these parts.

Nevertheless, the people of Tintagel have milked the connection for all it is worth. You have the King Arthur's Arms, Merlin's Gift Shop, the Guinevere Lounge and the Camelot Castle Hotel to name but four. There might even be a Sir Lancelot Fish and Chip Shop, or perhaps I imagined that. But there's not a lot in the village to stir the imagination. Apart from the castle and the church, both on the outskirts, the only building of any consequence is the post office, housed in a fourteenth century manor house. Otherwise it's a sprawling and rather undistinguished jumble.

At Merlin's Gifts, they sell toffee cow pats and white chocolate seagull droppings. I note that the seagull droppings also come in a packet labelled 'Seagull Poo' for those who might find the word 'droppings' a little too subtle.

I try several B&Bs. They all have plenty of rooms but they're doubles and the proprietors want to make an additional charge for single occupancy. It's six thirty, the place is almost deserted and they are more likely to experience a meteor shower than a sudden influx of tourists. Common sense should dictate that having one person in a room is preferable to having none, but they happily let me go on my way even when I give them every cue to reconsider their price. 'Oh really, I haven't been paying an extra charge in other places.' I can't even put their stupidity down to centuries of Cornish in-breeding because for the most part they seem to be Londoners.

At one particularly grotty pub the landlord offers me a single room for £24. When I demur at the price he adds that I will be able to use the heated pool free of charge and even takes me to see it. It is down at the end of a yard which has all the attractiveness of a builder's depot and it is both deserted and covered with a grubby plastic sheet. Concerned that I am still not biting, he reduces the price by £2 and throws in free snooker. Little does he know that the last time I played snooker, some twenty years ago, my only score of any note was the one I made on the baize. And even if I were to be tempted back to the table, where would I find someone to play with? 'Please come in here and play snooker with me. I've only ever played twice and I was crap.' Not a selling point. His final ploy is to point out that the room includes a proper breakfast.

'You've got yer cooked.'

I look at the dirty windows and the drab paintwork, gag at the thought of yet another bacon and egg breakfast and tell him politely that I think I'll look elsewhere. At the Bosayne Guest House I'm offered an en suite double for the price of a single. Very pleasant and well appointed, if furnished throughout in cardinal red. Could make for some interesting nightmares.

In the pub where I eat my evening meal – great, no chips for once – I encounter the first significant grouping of genuine born and bred Cornish since leaving Land's End. Fifteen of them around one table, celebrating a sixtieth birthday. And what are they talking about? Illnesses and house prices. There you go! Proof if ever it was needed that the Cornish are no different from the rest of the population.

I have to admit that the ruins of Tintagel Castle are impressive. The rocky island location, close against wave-lashed cliffs – bridge crossing to steep stepped access. Even a cynic like me feels the pull of Arthurian legend. But then I read that the existing fortress ruin was built in the twelfth century by Reginald, Earl of Cornwall, illegitimate son of Henry I. And sadly, knowledge that the guy responsible for this edifice was a bastard called Reg takes away some of the mystique. He is transformed in an instant from chivalrous knight to beer-bellied builder. I can picture him standing on the battlements, scratching his backside and flicking his fag ends into the sea as he seeks to convince his tenants that water dripping from the ceiling of the Great Hall isn't the result of inadequate roofing but simply a bit of condensation.

There was much earlier habitation though. The likelihood is that the site was the stronghold of a Celtic king as early as the fifth century. Recent excavations have uncovered fifth century pottery and sixth century glassware from southern Spain. Also unearthed was a piece of slate with a Latin inscription which, translated, says: 'Artognou, father of a descendent of Coll has had this made.' All pretty meaningless you may think, but the first three letters have got the Camelot brigade pretty excited. 'Nonsense' say the experts, 'This has nothing to do with King Arthur.' I'm inclined to think they're right. The person who wrote this was quite clearly a sad case. What's the guy saying? That there's nothing in his own family history he can boast about, so he'll attempt to appropriate the kudos attached to his wife's more distinguished forebears. Pathetic!

And what was this piece of slate? Well, the archaeologists say it was a drain cover, and the words were scribbled rather than inscribed. That does it. What we have here is a piece of graffiti from Artognou, the educated plumber, who was quite good at drains, but had a chip on the shoulder about his family history.

My coastal path book describes the path from Tintagel to Boscastle as moderate, but it feels pretty strenuous to me. I look for the promised seals and puffins but see neither. Hardly any people either until I get within spitting distance of Boscastle and then there are dozens. They're all taking a comfy stroll from the harbour up to the Daymark and back. I feel both superior and annoyed with myself for feeling superior.

Boscastle is lovely, with a delightful harbour built in the sixteenth century by Sir Richard Grenville, while he was taking a break from harassing the Spanish. There are whitewashed cottages, decent tea rooms and not a kiss-me-quick hat in sight. In the Visitors' Centre a man with a plummy face and accent to match earnestly surveys the display of drawings, photographs and artefacts that trace the history of the village. He is one of those people who have to ask a question whenever they are presented with any form of exhibition, no matter how informative the commentary. I can see him preparing himself to strike. He furrows his brow, purses his lips and then... Yep, he's got one. He approaches the attendant – a benign but capable looking elderly lady.

'When did the first road come to Boscastle?'

She looks surprised. 'I've really no idea. I wasn't here. There must have been a road of sorts back in Norman times.'

This isn't good enough. What he wants is a precise date, together with drawings, scale models and nails from the original construction workers' boots. He shakes his head gently in disappointment and wanders back to the exhibition grumbling.

'It says here somewhere that Boscastle's inhabitants arrived by sea.'

Does the chap really think that people came and went by water and had no relationship with the surrounding area until someone decided to bring them a nice new road?

The attendant is instantly accommodating to my more mundane question about the location of a tap to fill my water bottle. She offers to fill it from her own little kitchen, leaving me with an unattended counter arrayed with all manner of nickable goods. I'm pleased at this demonstration of trust. It seems to call up images of a more innocent time. I hope that others will respond in similar way to her helpfulness.

The stretch from Boscastle to Crackington Haven is just as tough as yesterday's and more remote. The only people I see are serious walkers. They fall into two groups: those out to stretch their legs, and those more interested in exercising their egos. I meet a man from the second category at the top of a very stiff and quite hairy climb that has left me breathless and sweating. My 'That was a tough one' is greeted by a dismissive 'You ain't seen nothing yet.' As if I've just stepped out of my front door while he is returning from a walk to the North Pole with Ranulph Fiennes. He is keen to tell me that he has walked almost the whole South West Way, and looks at me pityingly when I ask if he did it in a single stint. 'No, of course not.' He has been doing it one day at a time for the last ten years.

I don't know why I find it necessary to be so polite to strangers. I smile and nod while he plods through a tedious and long-winded description of his exploits, without a single question aimed in my direction, when by rights I should be rendering a service to the community by kicking him over the cliff.

Later I meet a complete contrast. Seriously scruffy, beard from eyebrows to navel, the type who believes that walking gear is not to be discarded until it falls apart of its own accord, he ambles into view like an amiable hedgehog. He has started from Minehead and is on his way to Land's End. Here we are passing about half way. He gives not a toss about distances, guide books, maps even. He's just enjoying being out there and he'll stop when he's ready.

It's interesting that those I encounter experiencing difficulty with the path are exclusively youngsters. Near Boscastle a badly sunburned couple stumble down the path with fixed expressions of terminal desperation that suggest they might have just crossed the Negev desert without camels or water. And at the café in Crackington a girl who only started at Bude is buying sticking plasters and stuffing her boots with chewed dock leaves in an attempt to deal with blisters that have the appearance of large overripe grapes. Both the couples I meet between Crackington and Millook stop to ask urgently how much further they have to go. All have one thing in common, they are seriously overloaded – tents, sleeping bags, mugs dangling on strings – and appear to have started a tough coastal path on one of its most difficult sections. They have the effect of making me feel, without justification, venerable, wise and immensely hardy.

For the first time since I started the trip, the wind has shifted and is now coming from a southerly direction. This means that, instead of the salt and wet rock smell of the sea, it is the sugar and warm-sick odour of cow shit that is constantly in my nose. It's a timely reminder that clotted cream teas and dairy ice cream come at a price.

Miserable git of the day award goes to the owner of the Bosun's Locker at Millook who has a notice on his gate saying, 'This is a private dwelling, not an information bureau.' Millook is a six house hamlet and, considering I have only met five people in the last two hours, one might think he would be grateful for a bit of outside contact. Surely the enquiries he is objecting to can't be anything more than the occasional tired walker seeking confirmation of distance to the next habitation. If you ask me, it should be a feature of our countryside access legislation that people who own houses on beautiful sections of long distance paths be obliged to provide bona-fide walkers with information, water and toilet facilities – a sort of community service in lieu of scenery tax.

It's half past seven when I finally schlep up to the door of the Bay View Inn at Widemouth Bay. A long hard day and I've had enough. I put away another pub meal, almost too tired to register what I'm eating, drag myself to my room, and crash out straight away.

There's easy walking next morning from Widemouth to Bude, but I take it steadily, conserving energy, because the book says that after Bude it gets really tough again. I can't say much about Bude. It has a fine beach but, beyond that, its main attraction seems to be a canal that

was built in the early nineteenth century to carry sea sand to improve the poor agricultural soils inland (Interesting Facts No. 361). It's not a pretty town by any standard, but neither is it gone to pot like Newquay. Just a bland resort with Saga coaches in the car park and reserved parking for the vicar and the organist outside the church. Verily I say unto you. It is easier for a camel to pass through the eye of a needle than for a casual motorist to park outside the parish church at Bude.

In the absence of anything else of interest, that Limerick about the young lady from Bude who stood on a stage in the nude keeps running around in my head.

I notice that here, as in all the more populated places, there are memory benches. I've passed loads of them. More benches than walkers, that's for sure. Councils all around the West Country must be getting desperate about where to put the next one. Perhaps it's time to think of some other form of cliff-top memorial to the departed. What are the things that I have most missed as I walk along the path – a pair of binoculars, a drinking fountain, a boot scraper? And while we're about it, maybe it's time to rethink the memorial plaques. I passed one that was dedicated to Joe Bloggs 'beloved father and optician'. I had never realised that the professionals down at Specsavers inspired such strong emotions. Another was dedicated to a woman who died aged 76 and is described as 'a good provider.' After three quarters of a century on this earth, is that really the best that her nearest and dearest could say about her? Makes the poor lady sound like a branch of the Co-op. The plaque I found most touching was one simply labelled 'Geoff's Seat' – no surname, no date, no message.

The steep ups and downs start again about a mile and a half from Bude, but it's attractive walking apart from the bit past the satellite tracking station close to Sharpnose Point. This has a double perimeter fence with barbed wire and CCTV cameras pointing in all directions. Notices warn that it is a prohibited place under the terms of the Official Secrets Act and that you are liable to be sent to the Tower for hanging, drawing and quartering if you happen to find yourself on the wrong side of the fence. It strikes me as faintly ludicrous that an organisation whose whole raison d'être is spying on others should be quite so twitchy about others spying on it. The station is part of a set-up called Echelon which operates through a partnership with the USA,

44

Canada, Australia and New Zealand to intercept and monitor the billions of ordinary telephone conversations, faxes, and emails that travel across the world's communication networks every day. There have been complaints from other EU member countries that the brief goes beyond national security, and that access to commercially sensitive information obtained through this clandestine process has been used to give Britain an unfair trading advantage. However, the puff has rather been taken out of the protests by the revelation that these same European governments have tracking stations of their own which are up to identical tricks. At least I can be sure that nobody has ever gained economic or security advantage from phone calls I have made. In fact, I feel sorry for any poor sod who has had to listen in on me. I give the CCTV cameras a sympathetic wave and press on.

Morwenstow is the last village in Cornwall and deserving of a slight detour for its impressive church. The Reverend R S Hawker was vicar here for more than forty years, from 1834 until his death in 1875. He was, by all accounts, a slightly wacko individual who kept a large pet pig, smoked opium and wrote poetry in a cliff top hut he had constructed out of driftwood. The hut is still there, just off the path. Hawker's best known work was a piece that floats back to me from the mists of my schooldays with the memorable lines, 'And should Trelawny die; There's twenty thousand Cornishmen will know the reason why.' Try as I might, I can't remember what Trelawny's problem was, or why so many people knew about it. Could it be that the guy had a formidable reputation around the county for guzzling clotted cream teas and Cornish pasties – a famous heart attack waiting to happen?

The Morwenstow churchyard contains the graves of many shipwrecked sailors. Prior to Reverend Hawker's tenure it had been customary to bury washed-up bodies on the beach without any ceremony, the argument being that there was no way of determining that the victims were indeed Christians. But Hawker insisted on conducting a dignified burial for all the seamen who fell foul of this stretch of coast, and there was no shortage of customers. He seems to have been particularly busy in 1842. A stone inscribed 'Unknown yet well known' marks the mass grave of thirty who perished in the wreck of the Alonzo. Nine more died that same year when the Caledonia broke up on the rocks – their grave marked by a wooden figurehead. It seems that Hawker was fond of using upturned boats to mark shipwreck graves. A rather bizarre practice you might think, but there were plenty washed up along with the bodies, and he thought it a shame not to use them. For Hawker they symbolised the security of the Ark. Sadly for modern churchyard photo-opportunities, they have long since rotted away.

At Marsland Mouth there's a little wooden bridge over a small stream and, on the far side a sign 'Welcome to Devon.' I prop my camera up on the Cornish side and run across to the Devon side in time to smile smugly and point my stick at the sign as the shutter clicks. As ever, it takes three goes before I'm reasonably confident that I have a shot with me stationary and properly framed within it.

A little further on, high on the northern side of the stunning Welcombe Valley, is another writer's hut. This one belonged to Ronald Duncan, the author, poet and playwright who came to live in West Mill at Welcombe in 1937. Perhaps he took his inspiration from Reverend Hawker, but like a wise little pig he chose to build his cliff hut of stone rather than driftwood. It's a sturdy structure in which Duncan used to spend most of his summers working. His daughter, Briony, who now lives at the Mill in the valley below, restored it in his memory after his death. The door is unlocked and there is an invitation to any passing walker to rest or take shelter there. Inside I find seats, fresh drinking water on the table and an amazing view from the window. It's a quite delightful memorial. The visitor's book shows no entries for today, but I notice that ten days ago someone else passed through on their way from Land's End to John O'Groats. The entry that really grabs me, though, is from a couple who have decided to enter into the literary spirit of the place and record their presence in verse. It goes:

Today when we were here;
There was a lot of rain, Oh dear!
But we thought the weather;
Could only get better;
And so we say goodbye to all;
We are going on the paths wide or small.

Must have had poor old Ronald Duncan squirming in his grave.

On a high, exposed headland near a place called South Hole, I meet a couple who are pitching a small tent about three feet from the cliff edge. I express the hope that neither of them is troubled by sleep

46

walking, to which they earnestly respond that they always like to pick a site with a view. But they're not sure they have chosen the best location. They point to the previous headland I've just crossed.

'What's the view like from there?'

I look back to an almost identical piece of cliff about a quarter of a mile away.

'Well, um, pretty much the same as here.'

They eye me suspiciously, unsure whether I'm telling them the full truth. Maybe there's an extra-special view just over there that I'm keeping for myself.

Here we are confronting as good a view as you'll find anywhere in Europe and yet they're not satisfied. It's one of the worst features of modern life in my opinion – this inability to enjoy what we currently possess out of concern that we may be missing something even better. We're all at it: constantly and obsessively assessing our situation against every point of reference like hyperactive GSP systems. And always we find ourselves wanting, selectively homing in on those we consider to have a better job, house, lifestyle, appearance or even cliff-top view. We agonise over our failure and labour miserably to remedy our perceived deficiencies, only to find that when we do so, a whole new level of negative comparisons has opened up, and we start all over again.

The pair agree they won't move the tent – they've already got it up anyway – but they're immediately off into other comparisons. Quite unprompted, the bloke launches into a passionate appraisal of the different brands of bivvy bag currently on the market. I am unable to contribute, being only vaguely aware what a bivvy bag is, so I simply nod and grunt at appropriate points in his discourse. Oblivious to my limited participation, he moves on to consider the merits of one-man Goretex tents. The guy is in his late forties, and I'm thinking perhaps he should have grown out of such boy scout ardour by now, but I guess he's someone who needs a passion. If he wasn't extolling the virtues of lightweight tents, he'd probably be salivating over a motor magazine or computer catalogue.

The encounter leaves me feeling I've had enough for the day, and I decide that a nearby youth hostel will be my accommodation target. It's a short detour off the path through the pretty village of Elmscott to the former Victorian schoolhouse. Looks quiet enough – just two vehicles in the car park and a couple of girls tucking into mounds of pasta at one of the bench tables in the garden. I wander inside to the reception area and ring the bell. A small, quite elderly, lady bobs up instantly from somewhere underneath the counter and views me with astonishment. My own confusion deepens when, in response to my enquiry about a bed for the night, she laughs.

'We're closed.' She can't believe I wouldn't know this. 'It's in the book – closed Thursdays.'

Now, one of those aspects of bus and train timetables I've never quite mastered is the wretched X:Mon tucked away in the small print at the bottom. Invariably it means that the service I'm expecting to use doesn't run on the precise day and time I wish to travel. It's the same with the YHA Handbook. Squirreled away among the symbols and directions that make up each hostel's entry are the departures from normal opening. And sure enough, when I check, Elmscott has an X:Thu 12/4 – 30/6 cunningly placed to catch me out when I ramble by, late on a Thursday afternoon.

What makes this incident worthy of note, is not my failure to spot the closure, but the warden's incomprehension that anyone should make such a mistake. She's very nice about it, but there's no mistaking that she and I inhabit different planets. She can't understand how anyone who had even a smidgen of common sense would set out without carefully planning their accommodation along the way and booking ahead.

But then, just as I'm mentally adjusting to the idea of another hour's walk to a likely B&B village, she says that I can stay at the hostel after all. Two German girls have begged to be allowed to stay on for an extra night and there's a man who has to drive back north tomorrow and doesn't want the hassle of moving to another hostel. I show the appropriate gratitude for her generosity while secretly wondering why we had to enact the closure charade before getting to this point. She books me in, sells me a frozen ready-meal and points me in the direction of the male dormitory.

I'm devouring my ocean pie, more pie than ocean, in the garden, when the other male resident for the night appears on the scene. He's in his late fifties with a real boozer's face – red cheeks, spongy nose, half closed lids – and a serious beer gut. My attention moves from his physical attributes to his holiday garb: sandals with black socks, baggy khaki shorts, Hawaiian shirt and a home-knitted light blue cardigan that appears to have been made for someone quite a bit smaller. His arms and legs are a mass of scratches, the result, I discover later, of a one-sided quarrel with a bramble patch while searching for wild flowers. He turns his radar scanner in my direction, rolls himself a very slim ciggy and locks on for the duration.

I've met plenty of people who can talk endlessly about themselves, never experiencing a gram of curiosity about the people they are addressing, but this guy is world class. He would make the ancient mariner appear positively tongue tied. In the course of an hour and a half, I am treated to a blow by blow account of the thirty years he spent single-handedly steering the UK textile industry – trips he made to outlying factories, put-downs he delivered to managing directors who dared to disagree with him, intricate details of technology and processes that were hitherto a mystery to me, and might reasonably have been expected to remain that way. I'm beginning to wonder whether suicide might offer an attractive alternative to more of these revelations when he suddenly asks if I fancy a pint.

I'm in a terrible dilemma. On the one hand it means yet more time in his company; but on the other, the nearest pub is three miles away, he has a car and I could certainly use a drink.

It's apparent from his driving that he's had one or two already. We lurch along at eighteen miles an hour, gears crashing horribly. He is quickly lost in the narrow lanes and we conduct an extensive exploration of this corner of North Devon before finally arriving at the pub in Hartland. As we enter the public bar, the expressions on the patrons' faces clearly indicate that he has been in there previously, boring the arses off them.

My companion's conversation switches from textiles to holidays. He had intended this holiday to be a tour of Cornwall but muddled up Plymouth with Portsmouth and consequently spent most of his time in Salisbury which, he tells me, is populated by the most terrible drivers. North Devon is as far west as he has gone. Tomorrow he is due to drive home to Lancashire, and his wife is going on holiday by herself as soon as he gets back. This is a woman I understand.

Trapped now until closing time, there is ample opportunity for me to learn about every place my new friend has visited in his life and quite a few that he hasn't. His most enthusiastic comments of the whole evening are reserved for Iceland. He gives me an in-depth description of the geology, history, culture and natural environment of this wonderful country. I venture to ask how long he spent there, and discover that he went on a day trip from Manchester Airport.

Remembering the outward journey, I'm a little concerned about getting back into the car, particularly now the driver has consumed an additional three pints. But I'm unwilling to contemplate a three mile walk, reasoning that on these empty lanes the worst he can do is run us into a ditch and, at the speed he likes to travel, that's unlikely to be fatal.

To say that he is a little the worse for wear is to understate the case. It's clear he can barely see beyond the windscreen and without me to tell him when to brake or turn the wheel, God knows where he would have ended up. We proceed at milk float pace along, thankfully, deserted lanes, fan belt slipping and shrieking, never out of second gear. By the time we get back to the hostel I'm beyond words. I make an immediate bolt for my bed and pretend to fall asleep.

He said he was going to make an early start in the morning, but five thirty is ridiculous. It feels as if I've only been asleep for half an hour. Any normal person sharing a dormitory would try to leave quietly to avoid disturbing others. Not this guy. He eschews the adjacent washrooms and carries out his lengthy ablutions at the wash basin in the dorm, gargling merrily and hacking into the sink. There's a lull in his activities, presumably while he eats his breakfast somewhere, then he's back and forth between room and car a dozen times, letting the dormitory door slam shut on every occasion, and all the while whistling tunelessly under his breath. What the hell's going on here? He has no more luggage than I have. I'm convinced he is doing everything he can to wake me. I lie still, desperately willing myself not to get angry – never get back to sleep again if I do. And I'm damned if I'm going to enter into any more conversations with the bugger. Finally, after an elaborate ritual of dusting imaginary sand off his bed, and three or four minutes of car door slamming practice, I hear the engine start followed by the progress of his screaming fan belt away down the valley. I glance at my watch – a quarter to eight.

I decide to walk down the lanes through Hartland and Brownsham, rejoining the coastal path where it cuts back in an easterly direction towards Clovelly. This, I reckon, will save me two or three miles walking around Hartland Point and I need to make some rapid progress because there's a long stretch with no accommodation at all between Clovelly and Westward Ho!. I don't want to get stranded at the end of the day. Unfortunately, not all the lanes are marked on my map and I take a wrong turning, emerging onto the A39 with no alternative but to retrace my steps or walk along the main road for a mile and a half. There follows the least pleasant half hour of the trip so far. The road bends every couple of hundred yards; it has no verge and is heavy with traffic. I press myself as close to the edge as possible and skip from one side of the road to the other to maximise my visibility on the bends, but I remain in genuine fear of being mown down. Most uncomfortable of all is the sense that my status has changed. Out on the cliff or even the empty lanes I can hold my head up. I'm a hardy walker – a prince of the outdoors – I've chosen to be there, in control of what I'm doing. But no-one other than a fool or a vagrant skips along a busy trunk road like this. Suddenly I'm a seedy, middle-aged fugitive, and I don't like it.

The experience calls to mind the time in my youth when I first started hitchhiking. I had this naïve notion that motorists would show more sympathy for the plucky individual who demonstrated that he was ready to tackle some of the miles himself, rather than loafing by the side of the road with his arm out. So I trudged along, head down, sticking out my thumb when I heard a vehicle coming up behind me. It was the worst possible strategy, of course. Nobody picks up a hitch-hiker if they can only see him from the back. For all the motorist knows, he might have an axe in his hand, or even worse, a copy of Watchtower. Pretty quickly I learned to stand in the places where drivers could stop easily, to make eye contact and to will them to acknowledge me. Much easier and more productive.

But I don't want lifts today. It would destroy the whole purpose of the trip, and at fifty-five I'm a bit long in the tooth for that game. What I want is to get away from this road as soon as possible. It's an immense relief when, at last, I'm able to turn off down a minor lane and back to sanity. I shudder at the thought that the end-to-end speed merchants – those who complete the Land's End to John O'Groats walk by the shortest possible route – do a large part of the trip on roads like the one I have just escaped.

Clovelly has for so long been acclaimed the most attractive village in the whole Southwest, that I'm quite ready to find fault with it. But I can't really. Sure, there are too many tourists but, as one of them, I'm part of that problem. The precipitous main street, down which goods are still carted by sledge and donkey, and the flower bedecked cottages live up to their picture postcard image. I decide against lunch at the pleasant looking pub by the harbour – it's somewhat crowded – but I linger a while on the quay, watching a man hose down the Clovelly lifeboat. The setting – steep wooded slopes, beached fishing boats – is delightful. The morning's tribulations gently subside.

The village has not been so well preserved by accident. Much has been due to the paternalistic influence of the successive families who have owned the estate of which it forms a part. One of the most notable of these was the Hamlyn family who owned the place in the late nineteenth and early twentieth centuries. A considerable amount of restoration work was carried out at the instigation of Christine Hamlyn, and many of the cottages bear her initials along with the date when they were restored.

The Hamlyns also constructed the Hobby Drive, as a means of providing winter work for fishermen, and the long distance path takes its leave of the village along this broad, level and easy track. It winds through the woods for a couple of miles with occasional glimpses of the sea, before the coastal path breaks away and reassumes its familiar unruly character.

At Buck's Mills, a glorious little place without any of Clovelly's tourist excess, there's a very welcome tea room where I stop for a latish lunch. The next table is occupied by a slightly overweight middle-aged man – checked shirt and beach shorts – for all the world like a Sunday afternoon ambler. Only his hefty rucksack tells a different story. I discover he is a Norwegian, walking the coastal path in the opposite direction to me, and currently enjoying a beer while he waits for his somewhat slower cousin to catch up. I ask him what he thinks of the West Country and the coastal path so far, only for him to tell me modestly that he has walked the whole 630 miles of it previously. And in response to my questions, he admits that he has done most of the UK's other long distance paths as well – last year walking the entire length of England from the top of the Pennine Way to Brighton. It's refreshing to meet someone so unpretentious, and what an antidote to last evening's companion. We take another beer together. The cousin, younger, but also overweight, struggles in after about ten minutes. Her expression suggests that she may not be enjoying the trip quite as much as he is.

For the next three hours I see, quite literally, not a soul. This stretch of path doesn't have the same fearsome climbs and descents of some of the earlier sections, but it is terribly overgrown. I spend the afternoon hacking my way through brambles, bracken and nettles, whacking the ground ahead of me with my stick out of concern not to tread on any sleeping adders, for I'm still in my Ranulph Fiennes sandals. After several days in them, my feet have swelled so much that I can't get the wretched St Ives boots on at all.

Westward Ho! has the distinction of being the only town in Britain with an exclamation in its name, but it isn't one of delight. The town sadly fails to come anywhere close to the image of romance and adventure suggested by its title. It's a dreary, clapped out, third rate resort. I cannot imagine what sort of nineteenth century marketing nonsense led its founders to seize on the idea of naming a town after a Charles Kingsley novel. Did they seriously think that it might take on the character of the book? And if so, did they consider any other popular novels of the time? Did they contemplate the sort of community that might develop if they named the place *Frankenstein* or *Bleak House*?

I approach the town along a concrete promenade that's liberally decorated with dog shit, past a gloomy caravan park and into a central area mainly comprising amusement arcades and candy floss stalls. The flat brown sea off to the left does nothing to enhance my first impression, nor does the rain that now starts to fall steadily. But I'm certainly not going any further today, so I need to find a room, and quickly.

The Eversley Guest House just back from the seafront looks a cut above the rest, and turns out to be so – spotlessly clean, lovingly decorated and furnished. This will do.

I don't think I have ever seen a house with quite as many knick-knacks. They are everywhere – pots, plants, teddy bears, ornaments, pictures, artefacts. The amount of dusting, polishing and watering must be phenomenal. Even the bathroom is crammed with them – curtains around the bath, eight large candlesticks, a huge basket of toiletries, cabbage patch dolls, antique bedpans, large framed pictures. It's both delightfully different and ever so slightly over the top.

At breakfast all the guests are seated around one large table, beautifully set with willow pattern crockery. It beats the standard guest house segregation – the mini cornflake packets and individual one-splodge marmalades – silence broken only by clink of spoon on cup. But with all these identical pots and jugs it's hard to know what you're getting. I guess wrongly and pour orange juice into my tea.

At the far end of the table is a young woman whose husband's job is soon to be relocated from Worthing. She's here with her mother on a house hunting expedition. They appear to have looked at every new development in Devon and found them all wanting – too remote, too central, too exposed, too sheltered. Now she is reluctantly thinking about extending her search to include what she quaintly calls 'second hand houses'. I love this. I feel it calls for a new style of estate agency descriptions – 'One careful lady owner from new. Economical to run. Very clean inside and out.'

Twenty minutes down the road from the guest house, I realise I've left my telescopic hiking stick back in my room. The thing has been little more than a nuisance for the entire trip, but it's twenty-five quid's worth of aluminium and cork, and who knows when I might really need it. If I had been walking for half an hour, I could have said 'sod it', but twenty minutes is not quite long enough for that. I hoof my way back, cursing every step. Then I discover that the tide is now too low for the Appledore to Instow ferry across the Torridge estuary. This means a slog round via Bideford and the busy main road crossing.

As a reward for all this discomfort, I allow myself an early pint at Instow in the knowledge that there won't be another refreshment stop before Barnstaple. At eleven-thirty the bar is pretty full. Guests for an imminent wedding, who have stayed overnight in the pub's accommodation, are fortifying themselves for the ceremony. I take my drink to the seats outside. In twos and threes the wedding guests emerge from the pub and make off for the church. Several minutes after all the others have gone, a youth in a denim shirt worn outside baggy black trousers dives out of the bar, peers anxiously up and down the road and asks me if I know where the church is and whether I have seen a taxi. When I'm unable to help him with either request, he jitters back and forth in frustration, lights a fag, coughs horribly and spits on the ground right next to me.

It infuriates me that spitting has become positively decorous of late. Once upon a time the only people who spat were playground bullies and little ferrety men who wore greasy caps and had thin roll-ups permanently glued to their lower lips. Now this dirty old gits' pursuit is becoming acceptable – anywhere, anytime. Millionaire icons of the sporting world have to take a lot of the blame. The pampered oiks who go by the name of football stars have been at it for ages, but these days even the Centre Court at Wimbledon is awash with saliva – Fred Perry would have been appalled. And it's nothing more than an affectation – very few sportspeople *need* to spit. Just look at track athletes for proof of that – they've probably got the greatest reason to spit but you seldom see them doing it. Everywhere I go there are people aged five to thirty-five spitting on the ground – big spits, small spits, spits for no reason at all. It wouldn't surprise me to hear that people have started spitting at the Queen's Garden Parties. It's vile and I want the habit outlawed, punishable by flogging and lengthy terms in solitary confinement.

In time a taxi arrives, but it is kept waiting for several minutes while the young man's girlfriend gets ready. All the time, our gallant hero keeps up a running commentary on the deficiencies of women in general and his girlfriend in particular. Eventually she appears in a white, sparkly almost transparent number with a bright pink shawl the size, shape and consistency of a racing spinnaker. The youth takes a final drag on his latest cigarette, spits again and tells the driver to step on it.

The coastal path from Instow to Barnstaple joins up with the Tarka Trail Cycleway along a disused railway line. It is very flat, gritty and boring. I am repeatedly stopping to shake bits of gravel out of my sandal. As I trudge wearily along, bikes sweep past at four times my pace. Pausing to relieve myself becomes a new occasion for anxiety with cyclists appearing out of nowhere in mid-flow.

At Barnstaple, the path goes directly past the railway station. There's a train due to depart in ten minutes and it's looking a lot like rain. The prospect of plodding up onto Exmoor, then on towards Minehead tomorrow is suddenly deeply unattractive. Almost without thinking, I buy a ticket to Southampton and unhitch my rucksack. Soddit! Stage One finishes here.

Chapter 4

Stage Two requires an element of re-equipping. My walking clothes are clearly not right for a cycling stage, but neither am I keen to start shelling out on a set of pukka cycling gear. It's not just about penny-pinching; it also has quite a bit to do with not wanting to look a complete arse. I know that visibility and aerodynamics are the reason why cycle clothing comes in bright, figure hugging polyester, but is it really necessary to produce the stuff in such vile colour combinations or cut the garments so that they emphasise the less flattering parts of one's anatomy quite so mercilessly? In my walking gear I'm happy to go into a pub or a supermarket – even to amble around an art gallery or a stately home, but I'd as soon visit one of these places in my underpants as do so wearing cycling gear.

So I search around for garments that will offer comfortable safe cycling without turning me into a multi-coloured figure of fun. Here's a jacket that's bright and windproof, but could be put to a variety of outdoor uses. Now this is an interesting idea, special cyclist's underpants, padded in the appropriate places, that can be worn under ordinary shorts or track suit bottoms. They have the appearance of a grown-up nappy, but they do the job and are unobtrusive, in a manner of speaking. And so I go on, selecting the most serviceable things from my existing wardrobe and supplementing them with the odd new purchase.

What about the bike? I have one that is quite adequate, but it's a mountain bike – not the first choice for touring. I pay a visit to my local cycle shop and am gently ushered through a breathtaking range of models that goes from more than I'm prepared to pay to a lot more than I'm prepared to pay. I hover for a while over a nice light hybrid – touring frame, all-terrain tyres – but come away with just a pair of panniers for my existing machine and a dinky clip-on handlebar bag.

The mountain bike will be fine, I tell myself. It may be a bit heavier than some of these other models, but I'm not planning to do too many miles in a day, and at least I'll have the option of going off-road when suitable opportunities present themselves.

Come departure day, my first mistake is to roll up at the station expecting just to buy a ticket and get on. Things have changed since the last time I travelled by train with a bike. The man in the ticket office shakes his head slowly and directs me to the travel centre – a ticket office with comfy seats – where I must make a bicycle reservation. I queue behind two enormous ladies conducting an interminable enquiry about a trip to Newcastle in three weeks time while the train I had hoped to catch arrives, sits around for a bit, and then departs. For want of arriving a few minutes earlier, my journey is delayed by two hours.

And why did I choose to end the previous stage in Barnstaple? Taunton would have been so much more convenient. I have lengthy waits for connections at Salisbury and Exeter before a final hour in a two carriage diesel with almost opaque windows that deposits me in Barnstaple at four in the afternoon.

I negotiate my way through the surprisingly busy town, but then take a turning too soon and find myself on one of those 1960s circular roads from which it's impossible to escape. It takes me on a tour around a grey prefabricated council estate before plonking me back where I started. Three youths on skateboards look as if they are about to shout something but maybe, just maybe, my expression deters them.

Once free of the town, the lane I've chosen to take me up onto Exmoor is very pretty but a bloody hard slog. The stretch from Brayford up to Fyldon Common is a particularly tough test of my virgin cycling muscles and I begin to wonder whether my choice of transport for this stage was quite such a good idea. But it's much easier going when I finally make it to the high moor and I arrive at Exford around six-thirty satisfied that I've at least put a few miles in the bank.

The youth hostel is my chosen billet for the night. It's a very clean, characterful and welcoming Victorian house right in the centre of the village. After selecting the best bunk in a six-bed room – other roommates yet to arrive – I remedy my travel stained condition then drift across the road to the pub for a monster portion of poacher's pie and chips that induces an attack of food hostility well before the glaze on my plate is fully visible. Not that there's anything wrong with the food, it's very good, but I find the Desperate Dan quantities that are becoming so prevalent in pubs produce in me contradictory responses. My initial delight as the laden plate is set before me soon gives way to resentment as I struggle to devour what I have paid for. I know I won't manage it, but I carry on stuffing yet one more forkful into my reluctant gob. Is this down to my stinginess or does it stem from the exhortations to clear my plate that dogged my 1950s childhood? Almost fifty years on, am I doomed endlessly to replay my response to the harridans of the school dinner hall who regarded my failure to consume their windpipe stew and vomit custard as an affront to God and the civilised world?

The pub walls are covered with hunting pictures and photos. It's clear that some of them have been taken outside this very bar. Come to think of it, that noise of baying hounds I could hear from my room in the hostel wasn't just a household pet complaining about being locked in. There must be a hunt kennels somewhere nearby. Of course! I realise with a jolt that I've seen this place before in news footage – angry protestors milling outside the pub at the start of the Boxing Day meeting. We're into quintessential hunting territory here. It's one of those villages where locals claim they would be reduced to eating grass and begging on the highway if a hunting ban were to be enacted. I look around furtively. Is there anything about my demeanour that marks me out as a Guardian reading, erstwhile member of the League Against Cruel Sports? There are no crimson jackets and riding crops visible among the customers, but that doesn't stop me feeling anxious. I'm sure they have undercover agents disguised as human beings. An awful vision surfaces – I'm being chased out of the village by ruddy-cheeked landowners, horsy-faced women and salivating dogs; then cornered, gasping and defeated, in some steep-sided moorland coombe and battered to death with Countryside Alliance placards. Better scurry back to the bohemian sanctuary of the youth hostel before I'm rumbled.

Over cocoa I get talking to a pleasantly old fashioned couple from Workington who are commencing a tour of the Southwest without any real plan. They've never been this far south before and they are keen to know where to go. I use my self-appointed expert status to advise them on the places to visit and to avoid, and I inject my advice with all the prejudices I have acquired or reinforced along the way – go to Padstow, avoid Newquay, steer clear of boot shops in St Ives, don't get into conversations with men in Hawaiian shirts. They thank me for my observations and doubtless go back to their guidebooks, filing my remarks under L for lunatic.

It's pissing with rain in the morning when I set off, and I'm soon as wet on the inside of my supposedly breathable waterproofs as I am on the exterior. As far as I'm concerned this whole notion of water-proof breathable fabrics is nothing more than a con. The principle behind it is that the waterproof membrane is studded with tiny holes, large enough for the warm vapour of perspiration to escape, but too small for liquid rain to enter. That's fine in theory, but my perspiration doesn't come conveniently in vapour form. With anything more than moderate effort I can turn a tee-shirt into a dishcloth inside five min-utes. Sweat springs from my skin in fully formed rivulets that have as much chance of getting through the holes in my breathable jacket as a hippo of sneaking down a rabbit burrow. I suspect that only a garment that incorporated gutters and downpipes would really be able to cope. Am I alone in this affliction? I don't think so. Whenever I mention it to others they say, 'Ooh I know,' and launch into stories of how they had to be treated for dehydration after hurrying to catch trains during thunderstorms.

The weather switches my brain to worst case scenario mode. I contemplate days of damp gloomy pedalling, struggling up impossible gradients, scythed by horizontal rain and vicious winds straight out of the Arctic. I picture my jacket billowing like a spinnaker, and sudden side gusts threatening to throw me under the wheels of passing jugger-nauts as I struggle with the bucking handlebars. But within an hour I leave the rain behind and swoop down from the moor into a valley filled with bright glancing sunshine. Looking back, the grey mass crouching over the hills seems no more than a bit of low cloud.

Swooping is the big advantage that cycling has over walking. The opportunity to coast down a hill at thirty or forty miles an hour with no effort at all, makes even the most tedious climb worthwhile. For the walker, descents can be just as slow and punishing as any climb. It's just the site of the pain that changes – from muscles and lungs going up, to knees and ankles coming down.

In the exhilaration that comes from my new turn of speed, I take a wrong turning and find myself arriving at the astonishingly traffic clogged A39. Solid lines of cars, all packed to the gunwales, trundling to or from their holiday destinations. I make a detour through Watchet which avoids the worst of it, and when I'm forced to rejoin the main road at West Quantoxhead, I'm relieved to discover a wide pavement for the best part of a mile. Then, more relief, there's another possible detour along unclassified roads almost to Bridgewater.

But this means I will have to miss Coleridge's cottage close to the main road on the edge of the Quantocks at Nether Stowey. Its National Trust symbol glares at me from the map and admonishes me for daring to pass without a visit. But, come on, why should I feel it's essential to go there? This whole business of 'must visit' attractions is just a device we use to inject spurious meaning into the pointless activity of tourism. Would a visit change my life? Unlikely. What's so special about a house that an eighteenth century poet lived in? Not a lot. Have I ever been a fan of Coleridge? Not really. In fact the work that most marked him in my schoolboy consciousness, *The Rime of the Ancient Mariner*, still recaptures for me the pen-top chewing, window gazing, minute-hand crawling tedium of grammar school English lessons. What's more, the guy only lived at Nether Stowey for three years, and for much of that time he was out of his head on opium, flitting around Germany or knocking about with his mate Wordsworth who had a house nearby. If he couldn't be bothered to take the place seriously, why should I?

I head off down the unclassified lanes, only slightly disturbed by the thought that my arguments for by-passing Nether Stowey could be used as a reason for never going anywhere. The reward for my philistinism is half an hour of fairly level cycling through pleasant countryside and pretty villages with barely a sniff of exhaust fumes. I look across to where the main road skirts the Quantock Hills – Sorry Mr Coleridge.

Bridgewater comes upon me suddenly. It's a cheery little town with its canal, river and pedestrianised shopping area, but I'm not moved to stick around. My plan is to rejoin the West Country Cycleway here, and I root out the map, thoughtfully printed on waterproof paper. It's immediately apparent that the cycle route out of Bridgewater meanders in an elaborate five mile arc around the town to avoid a mile of main road. This feels like a detour too far, and I opt for five minutes of fumes instead of half an hour of fresh air. These new cycle routes are grand, but they're not too brilliant at getting you from A to B. And there's an air of incompleteness about them that is frustrating. Maps are overlaid with dotted lines showing planned modifications currently under negotiation that, some time in the future, will offer greater directness or less traffic.

Back on the trail I overlook a turning, and only realise my mistake when I come up against a barred farmyard entrance complete with snarling dogs and disgruntled poultry. By now I'm thoroughly hungry and irritable, in need of my lunchtime fix. Cossington looks like a village that should have a pub but there's no sign of one. I stop to seek directions from two youngsters who are idling by the side of the road. They're keen enough to help but can't agree where the nearest pub is to be found, and fall to squabbling. I side with the more intelligent looking of the two (not an easy distinction) who believes that there is 'A Red Something' along the road towards Chilton Polden. He gives me convoluted directions which suggest that it's some way distant and that I will have to tackle a long hill before getting there. Less than half a mile along the road, at the top of a gentle incline I come to the Red Tile. It's two o'clock and the last lunch customers are just paying for their meals and waddling off to their cars. I have to ignore the delicious residual cooking smells and settle for two pickled eggs and a packet of crisps. The landlord makes a joke about me covering the rest of my journey on wind power, but I excuse him because his beer is very good.

There's just one other customer in the place – latish middle-age with the sort of flushed countenance and air of permanence that leads me to judge that he has been propping up the same bar for the past thirty years. But I'm wrong; he is a relative newcomer, as I soon learn from the life history he starts to relate. Twenty-seven years as a Royal Marines bugler – perhaps that's where he got the red cheeks – and settled here a few years ago just because it happened to be where he finished up. I do some rapid mental arithmetic and realise with a start that the guy's younger than me. I've happily let him slip into Methuselah mode while I play the part of skippy young lad on a bike passing through.

After chatting quite entertainingly about his past, his attention shifts towards what I might be about. He clearly believes that only a person in the last stages of dementia would consider cycling from

Exford, so I decide to make no mention of my intended final destination – that would be to invite ridicule on a serious scale – and confine myself to describing the meanderings of the West Country Way. He advises me not to follow it as far as Glastonbury. In his view this town is Somerset's answer to Sodom and Gomorrah. I'm bound to fall foul of muggers, buggers, jugglers and every other form of depravity within the repertoire of drug-crazed new-agers.

Well I always knew the place was a magnet for the vaguely unhinged, but I hadn't realised it was quite so interesting. Perhaps I'll go there after all. I had the idea it was populated by Neo-Arthurians: gentle people who hang up bunches of feverfew in their lavatories, name their daughters Guinevere, and spend countless happy hours with their dowsing rods plotting the course of ley lines – those invisible energy lines that, according to devotees, radiate out from Glastonbury to other centres of mythical power like some dark-age equivalent of the world wide web.

But as I bowl along through the glorious Somerset Levels, even I have to admit there is something magical about the place. You have this low lying pasture and reclaimed marshland, dependent for its dry-land survival on drainage ditches, pumps and artificially straightened rivers. And rising to the north, to the east and to the southwest, islands in this wide green lake, are ridges and low hills where the settlements are to be found, delightfully unspoilt villages with ancient roots. It's a landscape shaped everywhere by the hand of man, but at the same time there is a tangible wildness to it. Easy to see why it's the place of myth and legend, ghosts and fairies, Arthur and Avalon, King Alfred incognito burning the cakes. And who knows, within a hundred years, globally-warmed sea levels may return it once more to the marshes and meres and the mystical islands of its past.

I suspect that I'm not following the course of a ley line. There's a distinct lack of cosmic energy flowing through my body. Then again it could be the effect of the lunchtime beer.

Wedmore is a pretty village poised between ridge and wetland. There's been a settlement here since the Bronze Age, but the Saxon period was its finest hour. The village was at the centre of a royal estate and it was here in 878, after his final victory over the Danes, that King Alfred brought the defeated Danish leader Guthrum to agree the Peace of Wedmore, defining which lands should be governed by the Saxons and which by the Danes. As part of the surrender deal, Guthrum was compelled to adopt Christianity, which sounds to me like kicking a man when he's down. But, despite the religious mugging, there proceeded from this treaty a period of peace and tranquillity that allowed Alfred to unify his kingdom and establish a reputation for more than his bakery skills. It also resulted in a partitioning of the country that can still be seen in the place names and dialect words used today.

I buy a can of ginger beer and a Mars bar and stop briefly at a seat by a graveyard looking towards the Mendip Hills. An elderly man is busily tending his wife's grave. His actions are efficient, economical, borne of regular routine. Old flowers discarded, fresh water from the tap, new flowers installed, urn wiped over, traces of weed or debris removed from around the grave. And suddenly he has finished and he stands still and silent. I'm touched, and feeling like an intruder, watching from my seat with my Mars bar. And I'm thinking about being old and bereaved myself, trying to imagine what it will be like, and wondering whether the pain is any less if you can tend a grave in the warm afternoon sunshine overlooking the Mendip Hills.

Cheddar isn't particularly attractive. The settlement that has given its name to one of the world's most prolific cheeses should be a bit more imposing. OK, the gorge is attractive, but the village itself is just a bog-standard west-country nothingness with dreary pubs, tatty shops and rather too much traffic. Am I being too hard on it? No I don't think so. After all, the locals have been around long enough to make something of the place. Recent DNA testing on the 10,000 year-old skeleton of 'Cheddar Man', one-time resident of a nearby cave, has revealed that some of his descendants still live in the village.

I retire to the youth hostel which is tucked away at the back of a school. From the outside it looks rather poky, but it's actually quite spacious and pleasant – bright attractive dining room overlooking the garden, reasonable lounge, good showers and toilets.

I'm beginning to think it's time the word 'youth' was removed from our national hostels network. This evening there are very few customers to whom the term could reasonably apply. The place is full – a large group of walkers, one or two families and an assortment of individuals and couples. I guess the average age is around forty.

When I rejoined the YHA recently, it was with some trepidation. More than thirty-five years had passed since I had last been a member.

Would I feel out of place in an organisation dominated by young people? Would the spartan conditions I recalled from the sixties prove too austere for my pampered middle-aged expectations? Not a bit of it. My first visit confirmed that things have moved on. No longer are hostellers expected to bring their own sheet sleeping bags or assist with the cleaning. Long gone is the requirement for members to arrive on foot or by bike and stay a maximum of three days. Gone too the ban on alcohol – some hostels even have table licences. And the clientele? Well, many of them could be the same people I encountered in the sixties, but wrinklies now, like me.

And my experience was not untypical. I'm reliably informed that sixty-five percent of the current YHA membership is aged over forty-five. I wonder what youth hostels will be like in another twenty years. Will they have stairlifts, and zimmer frames for hire? In place of the ubiquitous bike shed, will there be somewhere we can leave our electric scooters? They will surely have to do something about the bunks. I'm finding the top berth a struggle at fifty-five.

Hostels are still cheap, but the differential between them and the less expensive B&Bs has perhaps been eroded. I find myself frequently weighing the relative benefits of the two. Bed and breakfast will offer a room on my own, often with en-suite facilities and, if I'm lucky, a mattress filled with something more yielding than gravel. If comfort's my main concern B&B wins hands down. But hostels have alternative strengths. I can turn up wet, muddy and travel stained and they won't bat an eyelid. I can wash out my clothes and generally get them dry by morning – albeit at the cost of infusing every garment with the distinctive *parfum de chausettes* that is a feature of every YHA drying room. I'm convinced that hostel wardens are issued with aerosol cans of the stuff. Even when there is not so much as a single crispy-toed sock to be found anywhere in the drying room, there is still a consistent treacly stench that smacks you in the face as soon as you open the door.

Then there are the benefits of the members' kitchen. If I really want to I can rustle up pathetic little meals for one, using saucepans large enough to put to sea in. I can rub shoulders with thin girls in cheesecloth kaftans, preparing more rice than I would expect to eat in a lifetime, and bearded men with the sort of BO that saps your will to live, who exist on Cup-a-Soup, tinned spaghetti and milk which they drink from the carton. And I can consume my sorry repast next to the silent couple who treat their food like an official secret, sheltering it with their elbows from the curious gaze of others. But mostly I don't do these things. If there's a chance of getting a meal that someone else has prepared, I'll go for it. It's not because I'm lazy or unable to cook – just that carrying the ingredients is such a fag, and there is always something left over that can't be easily transported but is too significant to be thrown away, and so has to be left on the 'please help yourself' shelf.

But of all the advantages of hostels, the greatest is the expectation of human interaction. People in B&Bs tend to be much more insular. In hostels I can run across others, single travellers or groups, people doing similar things to me – an assortment of the interesting, the eccentric and the downright loopy.

My room mates at Cheddar are a case in point. First up is an urbane middle-aged Irishman from Worcester, on a weekend recce of camper vans for sale. Now why would a man with £20,000 burning a hole in his pocket want to blow it on a camper van? Well, apparently they hold their value very well, they're less likely than caravans to engender death threats and, if you don't mind the noise of rattling cutlery while you're driving, you can use one in place of an ordinary car. One thing that puzzles me about camper vans. Why is it that ever since 1975 they have only been produced in white or that vile beige with hideous brown stripes down the side? They remind me of old-style Sainsbury's checkout assistants. Why can't they make them in a nice metallic blue or a restful green? They'd be so much less obtrusive parked up in fields or next to lakes.

Despite his mission, Mr Campervan is charming, interesting and amusing, but he is topped by the second tenant of Room 4. The Flying Dutchman is one mean cyclist. I realise at first sight of his gear that here is a man in a different league. Day-Glo bikewear, sweat-stained cap and pukka cycling shoes contrast sharply with my tee-shirt, flappy shorts and trainers. And as for his panniers – mine look like a couple of free carrier bags by comparison. I'm thinking that fifty miles from Exmoor is reasonable going. He has covered ninety from Okehampton and doesn't think it's anything out of the ordinary. He is three days from Land's End and expects to be at John O'Groats in twelve. For the second time today I'm coy about revealing my intended destination. Over dinner we talk about his other recent expeditions: a trip through the Atlas Mountains taking his chances on finding food and accom-modation at isolated villages along the way; a journey from Amsterdam to Rome on a recumbent bicycle; the road race from Paris to Brest and back again – 1200 kilometres in a maximum of ninety hours. Like the ex-marine bugler I met earlier in the day, he's just a little younger than me. But what a difference between them. Of course, we all know that age isn't a matter of simple chronology, but these two fifty-somethings demonstrate that neither is it a case of winning the health lottery. There's a large element that has to be down to the expectations you have of yourself. The Flying Dutchman is a pretty good advert for the assertion that it's not getting older that stops you doing things, so much as stopping doing things that makes you get older.

The fourth occupant of Room 4 is not deriving a whole load of benefit from being placed with three old geezers. He's about twenty-five, and one of the most painfully withdrawn people I have ever seen outside of an institution. He suffers from an almost complete inability to look anyone in the eye and, over dinner, he compensates for his extreme social unease by stuffing his mouth with tumble-drier sized quantities of food. The rest of us try to include him in the conversa-tion, and gently attempt to draw him out with innocuous questions about his travels and the places he has visited, but his one-word responses mumbled through churning steak and kidney pie don't invite supplementaries. Then, when he has given us a lengthy demon-stration of how to eat rhubarb crumble and custard without at any point closing his mouth, he suddenly leaps up and announces that he has more important things to do than sit around talking to us all night. And he leaves us there to clear up the debris of his meal and wonder what secret sociability button we failed to press.

The next leg of my journey presents me with a dilemma. It's all about how I intend to get past the largest urban sprawl that has con-fronted me so far. Phil Horsley's Land's End to John O'Groats cycle route, my latest flirtation, suggests a course through Bristol that skirts the coast and crosses the River Avon next to the M5, and is illustrated by an intricate zigzag sketch map aimed at avoiding the most major roads between Avonmouth and the Severn Bridge. An alternative meanders through the Mendips and Chew Valley and makes its entry to the town via the Clifton Suspension Bridge.

I go for the coastal route, but after seven miles I'm regretting it. Not only does it fail to spare me a hefty climb over the western end of the Mendips, the traffic on the narrow B3133 seems particularly heavy this Sunday morning. I turn off down minor lanes and make my way, hit and miss, in the vague direction of Clifton. I survive a couple of close encounters with Sunday morning horse-women – the sort who have grown to look like their steeds, and who threaten me with their riding crops because something about my aspect has caused their animals' eyes to roll – before being deposited back onto the main road which takes me through to Ashton Park and the Avon Gorge.

Clifton Suspension Bridge is one of those structures that always gives me a thrill. I can't imagine the Avon Gorge without it. But for all its absolute appropriateness, it might never been built at all, or at very least appeared in a substantially less pleasing form. In 1754 a Bristol wine merchant called William Vick bequeathed a thousand pounds to be invested until such time as it had realised enough to build a stone bridge. Seventy five years later the fund had grown to eight thousand pounds, but the cost of stone bridges had grown rather faster. Fortunately, iron bridges were now the thing, and a deal cheaper, so the trustees made a virtue out of necessity and organised a design competition to be judged by the world's most famous bridge builder, Thomas Telford.

Telford doesn't appear to have quite taken on board the requirement for judges to be impartial. He rejected all the entries and, in their place, submitted a design of his own. By all accounts this was so hideous that the embarrassed committee had to pretend they'd miscalculated the available funds and couldn't afford to build it.

A year later they ran a second competition with a different judge. A twenty-four year old engineer called Brunel submitted designs but failed to win. However, he wasn't prepared to accept defeat. He arranged a meeting with the chief judge and convinced him to change the decision.

Difficulties didn't end there. Work was suspended several times because of civil disturbance, shortage of funds and downturns in business confidence. The bridge became the longest running show in town, and was only completed as a memorial following Brunel's death in 1859 – thirty years after construction commenced and more than a century after the original concept.

So there you have it, the nicest bridge I know. Built for horse drawn traffic and pedestrians but now carrying four million vehicles a year. Not that everybody venturing onto it has been intent on making it to the other side. Quite a few have gone no further than the middle. One late nineteenth century would-be statistic called Sarah Henley was rescued by the fashions of the time. Her voluminous skirts apparently acted as a parachute and she landed in the river, injured but alive. Despite suffering a loss of dignity that must have been as painful as her injuries, she wasn't moved to repeat the experience, and died in her bed some fifty-five years later.

Chapter 5

Phil Horsley's sketch map of a quiet route through Bristol is impossible. I try to follow it, I really do, but I'm not up to the task. For it to make sense I need to match it against a proper map showing all the roads rather than just the disjointed fragments he presents me with. I attempt this by juggling the Horsley book and the road atlas sheets I'm carrying, but it's hopeless. I'm stopping every couple of hundred yards in an attempt to reorient myself. I decide to change my strategy when, at a set of traffic lights, a nine-year-old child winds down the passenger window of the car next to me and calls out 'plonker'. I point my bike in a rough northeasterly direction and hope for the best.

And so I make my fairly comfortable way alongside the main Gloucester road and out through Filton. Comfortable but for one thing, I'm starting to feel very hungry. The suddenness with which hunger descends is a phenomenon I've noticed particularly on the bike. Perhaps I'm more inclined to munch as I go along when walking, but this desperate, out of the blue urgency to eat something is a new experience. I crane for a source of sustenance. Nothing! Not even a newsagent along this stretch. Then – chung! My pedals lock and I skid to a halt. I look down and see that some form of package has inexplicably become entangled in my chain and gears. Of all things, it's a plastic bag containing half-eaten ham and tomato sandwiches. I spend several irritable minutes poking crusts, polythene and scraps of manky ham out of the links and cogs. And no, I'm not quite that hungry. I continue on my way, belly flapping, cursing the guy who couldn't be bothered to finish his lunch.

After much longer than I had imagined it would take, I finally make my way under the M5, over the M4 and I'm clear of Bristol. Now for the River Severn. There's a cycleway on the northerly side of the original motorway bridge, but getting at it means taking a meandering route through the lanes that link the little villages to the north of the M4. I've glanced at these places umpteen times as I've raced past along the motorway – a familiar mental snapshot between the grey slab of the Severn and the 'which lane?' choices of the M5 intersection. I'm surprised to find that they are delightful and worth far more than the blink of an eye – sleepy little villages preserving their postcard prettiness in spite of their ghetto-blasting neighbour.

Cycling across the Severn is an experience in more ways than one. First off, it's free, but easily worth the £4.40 that car drivers are paying for the privilege. Of course, you only pay when you are driving from England to Wales, not the other way around. Some say that's why there are so many Welsh living in England. For the cyclist there's the view you don't get a chance to savour when you're driving across the bridge. And there's a sense of delicious vulnerability – vehicles flashing past just alongside, the whole structure vibrating slightly. Even though I'm pedalling along inside a substantial caged corridor, I'm still feeling very exposed. Nothing but the cold waters of the Severn below me for a mile or so. I wouldn't fancy doing it on a windy day. The crossing also marks the opening of a new stage in my journey. It's the end of the West Country, the gateway to the Welsh Borders. I stop in the middle, and celebrate the occasion with a king-size Mars bar from the village shop in Tockington.

As I stop to get my bearings by the roundabout on the Chepstow side of the Bridge, a hitchhiker walks up from a side road and sticks out his thumb. He is the dirtiest hitchhiker I have ever seen in my life – absolutely black – his face, hands and clothes. He looks as if he has been immersed in tar. I can't imagine anyone, even the driver of the crappiest old wreck stopping to pick him up. I almost contemplate giving him a ride on my crossbar, so confident am I that he will be unsuccessful in any other efforts. But I don't, and when I glance back 200 yards down the road, I see a lorry has stopped for him. Perhaps he knows something about hitchhiking that I don't.

The road from Chepstow to Tintern is pretty but rather traffic-laden. The only alternative, however, is a steep detour out of the valley, bypassing Tintern. I'm not keen on the climb, and anyway, I tell myself, I want to see the Abbey.

It's certainly an imposing sight – stark ruins exquisitely positioned on a bend in the River Wye against the steep green sides of the valley –

but it's another of those treats best sampled from a distance. Close up there are just too many people. The car park is chocker and a stream of humanity drifts across the access road and winds its way around the gift shop, ice-cream stall, pub and tea rooms. Some intrepid souls even make it to the abbey entrance and stump up the fee for a closer look. Judging by the assorted accents, there are people who have travelled a fair distance to be here, but now they've arrived they're not quite sure what to do. They sit along the wall by the river licking ice cream cones and engaging in brief bouts of conversation about the neighbours back home.

Tintern Abbey had an active life of four hundred years until Henry VIII kicked it into touch with the rest of the country's monasteries and took into his coffers all that was worth having. And like the rest, it didn't take long before it was being treated as a free DIY store. Lead was stripped from the roof, stones were pillaged for other local building. But, unlike many of the others, this process stopped while a fair bit of the handsome architecture still remained in place. From the eighteenth century the ruins acquired the status of tourist attraction and were visited by influential literary and artistic figures such as Wordsworth, Coleridge and Turner.

I join the ice-cream lickers on the wall for a diminutive rum and raisin and then follow the path along the river side of the abbey to see how much of the site I can take in for free. How much? Well, enough to get a feel for the dimensions of the thirteenth century great church, the most striking of the remaining buildings, and to fire off a few photos. Ignoring the little voice in my head that says 'cheapskate', I ease myself back into what is becoming a rather painful saddle and continue on my way.

The village of Tintern itself is less heavily polluted with tourists than the area around the abbey, and is the more attractive for that. It's the usual mix of craft and gift shops, cafés and pubs, but there are some attractive buildings and sympathetic restoration. I particularly like the old station – a relic of the Wye Valley Railway which fell to the Beeching axe in the 1960s – a little to the north of the village. It must have been one of the most picturesque railway stations anywhere in the country and the buildings have been restored to make the most of its enviable setting. A railway coach has been brought into service as a gift shop, the waiting room does duty as a café and the signal box hosts art exhibitions. Add some pleasant grounds, picnic and play areas, and it's a thoroughly nice place for a stop. Just a pity it can no longer function as a railway station.

At Brockweir I leave the main road, cross the river and start the slog up the side of the valley. It's a hell of a climb, the toughest since Exmoor, and I'm soon cursing noisily. My thoughts flit to images of cyclists tackling the mountain sections of the Tour de France – little lycra backsides bobbing away as the machines eat up near vertical inclines. Not a lot in common with my laboured efforts. The thing I'm riding may be called a mountain bike, but it lacks a mountain rider.

But it's worth it. The view from the top – a limestone plateau 800 feet above the valley floor – is lovely, and I have the reward of a gentle, almost level run along to St Briavels, my destination for the night.

The youth hostel at St Briavels is a genuine twelfth century castle. At least, that's when the thing was originally built. The oldest bit still standing is the twin towered gate house which dates back to 1293, and in the centuries that followed there was a hotchpotch of building and rebuilding that saw off all the original structure. But it still has to be a cut above your bog standard hostel. It's not often that you can pay eleven pounds to stay in a place that was used as a hunting lodge by King John.

Sadly some of the facilities seem not to have been updated since medieval monarchs and earls chased deer around the neighbouring woods. The showers are a particular disappointment, and my enquiry about the drying room reveals that they have one, but that it is no good for drying things. Still, how can I complain when I have a bed in the circular porter's lodge rather than the dungeon, and am able to look out through tiny slit windows to the castle entrance and the pretty Norman church opposite?

My roommates this time are a couple of amiable lads, Adam and Doug, who have just finished their A'levels and are taking a break from shelf stacking at Tescos to walk some of the Offa's Dyke path. Doug has a terrible cold and doesn't feel much like walking, but he is hoping the fresh air will bring the relief that paracetamol and Lockets have failed to provide. The fourth person in the room is a manic twenty-something South African whose main aim in life is to run naked across as much of the earth's surface as possible. It's a project that had its origins back in Johannesburg, streaking around the block in front of bemused neighbours, and not always making it back to his front door ahead of the police. Now he has gone global with a missionary zeal and he lists for us some impressive credits – stark naked through London, Paris, Madrid, Rio de Janeiro. He calls up all his skills of persuasion in an attempt to convert us to his cause, and even offers an immediate taster – out of the hostel, past the church, down the lane to the river (a distance of two miles) skinny dip and then run back up again. There's an tantalising lunacy about the idea and I'm almost flattered to be included in the plan, but I'm conscious that, bringing up the rear, I would be the one savaged by farmers' dogs or picked up by the police as I plodded up the hill glistening in the moonlight. I plead old age and Doug pleads his cold. Only Adam is left without a convincing excuse.

There aren't many people staying at the hostel on this Sunday night. The weekenders have departed and apart from my roommates there are just five others. I meet them in the dining room – a family of four from California and a middle aged woman from North Carolina. The Californians are nodding off into their soup, having driven straight here from Gatwick, jet-lagged after a ten hour flight. They tell me how hard they found it to drive on the left, the first time they've ever had to do it, and I shudder on behalf of all the other road users between here and Sussex who have unwittingly shared the highway with them.

It's the first trip outside the States for the woman from North Carolina. She's making it to demonstrate her independence to herself and her family. Around Britain by public transport, now there's courage for you. She hasn't been here long enough for the novelty to wear off. She still regards late, dirty trains and unsynchronised bus timetables that leave travellers stranded for hours on end outside dreary stations as examples of olde worlde quaintness. She's in her late fifties and seriously overweight – the result, she tells me, of a back injury, although I have a sneaking suspicion that eating may have had something to do with it. Certainly she has no trouble putting away the microwaved stodge served up under the guise of an evening meal (perspicacious readers may discern that this hostel would not win my prize for culinary excellence.)

She's one of those people who have taken the decision to be old because of the opportunity it offers them to hand down grandma-like certainties to others. She clearly thinks I'm much younger than her, despite my efforts to convince her otherwise, and after a while I fall into role, deferring to her as if of another generation. Once again, I'm being assessed by my activities rather than my wrinkles.

Our conversation is transferred from hostel dining room to local pub a hundred yards away. We've barely sat down when we're joined by a benign drunk with a damp and extremely smelly dog in a woolly hat (that's the drunk not the dog). Here's another person who likes to talk and he quickly asserts his supremacy over my American companion. He's been drinking here for fifteen years but must have bored the arses off the other locals, or they him, because he has no inclination to join in their predictable banter. Despite advanced inebriation he launches into a well-informed history of the area. Somehow the conversation turns to spirit residents of the village and he treats us to an entertaining and, with the aid of the booze we are all liberally tipping down our gullets, not entirely implausible description of ghostly events at this very pub – unexplained noises, a sense of presence at times when nobody else is around. He himself has seen a small hooded monk-like figure walk through the main bar from one end to the other and out through the external wall, and on another occasion a female figure, again much smaller than a modern person and clad in simple medieval garments.

My American companion is more scathing than I am, suggesting that the only spirits around are the ones he has consumed. I'm a little more kindly, if only because he spins a good story – better than listening to tales of dysfunctional family life in North Carolina. He professes not to care about our sceptical comments, but I can tell he does really. He's the pub's champion ghost-spotter and as far as he's concerned that's a talent every bit as prestigious as being the best darts player or yard-of-ale drinker. There must be plenty like him propping up the bars of old inns around the country. It makes you wonder whether there could be a hitherto untapped opening for a new form of inter-pub competition: 'Bushy Ales Spectral League, The Star v The King's Head, next Thursday 8pm. Bring your own poltergeist.'

And if there are to be the ghosts of long-dead monks, then this has to be the place for them. The very name of the village, St Briavels, owes its origin to a fifth century bishop who founded a religious community here. The Norman church is thought to stand on the site of a much older place of worship.

But why would these monks want to march through the public bar of the George? Well, according to our informant they were on their way from a nearby chantry to the church, and the room in which we are sitting wasn't there then, being a relatively recent extension to an older building. All quite feasible I suppose and, to back up his theory, the Ghost-spotter General shows us a stone slab engraved with a Celtic cross in the wall of the bar – a relic of the chantry ruins used as building material during the extension.

I'm minded to ask whether either of the ghosts asked if they could have their chantry back, but one look at his serious face dissuades me.

Next morning I'm off through the coal mining fringes of the Forest of Dean and then plunging down into the valley once again to make the acquaintance of Monmouth. It's easy to see why this town has had such strategic importance over the centuries, sitting as it does at the junction of natural routes between Wales and England. It has some attractive and distinctive buildings – most particularly one of only three remaining fortified bridges in Europe.

Monmouth is also proud of its connection with three historic figures – Henry V, Admiral Nelson, and Geoffrey of Monmouth. What connection would that be? Well, the first was born here but never lived in these parts after the first few weeks of his life. The second never lived here at all, but the Monmuthians were full of admiration for him and built a naval temple in his honour. The third? Surely Geoffrey of Monmouth came from here. No he didn't. Brittany actually, but he did spend a number of years at the Benedictine priory in the town before moving to Oxford where he produced his *History of British Kings* – an account of Dark Age British politics including the exploits of various legendary monarchs. If you were paying attention earlier you will remember that we have Geoffrey of Monmouth to thank for the King Arthur story, including the connection to Tintagel and Avalon.

Leaving Monmouth I'm caught out yet again by my unwillingness to waste time stopping, putting on my glasses and peering at the map. If I could seek one bodily modification that would make life immeasurably easier and help ensure the survival of the species, it would be drop-down, non-misting reading spectacles integral to the forehead. Just think about it – ninety percent of us need reading glasses by the time we're fifty. It's surely not too much to expect that in the course of human evolution our versatile bodies could have developed some compensatory adaptation to deal with this problem. Far from it. The only modification I can detect as my body moves into its second half century is the production of vastly increased quantities of ear hair. Where once there were a few downy wisps well inside the orifice, there now sprout obscene tufts like the pampas grasses you see dominating bungalow front gardens. This disgusting excrescence grows at such an alarming rate it has to be strimmed back every three or four weeks. I cannot begin to conceive what biological purpose is served by such sudden growth, unless it's to provide us with something to comb over in the event of advancing baldness. 'Oh come on!' I hear you say, 'Whoever heard of ear hair comb overs?' But you'd be surprised. I have it on good authority that the world record length for ear hair currently stands at twenty-two inches. By my reckoning that's enough to go from one ear to the other across the top and back again.

So anyway, leaving Monmouth I should be taking an unclassified road off to the left but I miss it and am well out of the town before I realise my mistake. Never mind! There's another one up ahead and it links with the original route a couple of miles on. Pity the map doesn't show hills. My alternative route takes a course that's as tough as any I've experienced. Far below I can see the lane I should be on, meandering alongside the River Monnow, but still I keep climbing. Eventually it gets so steep that even standing on the pedals and pummelling the last of my eighteen gears I can't manage it. I get off and push, cursing foully to any birds and hedgerow creatures within earshot.

The swearing doesn't help, just raises my blood pressure to the point that it sings a merry little tune in my head. I'm told I should be perfectly capable of learning to control my anger and frustration when faced with unexpected challenges and stubborn obstacles. It's just a matter of giving myself positive affirmations, setting calmness targets and accepting that traffic lights, inkjet printers and the cellophane wrappings on CD cases aren't really employed in a global campaign to enrage me. But I suspect I'm hooked on getting steamed up, and that I rather enjoy the blood pressure buzz I get from cursing and thrashing some innocent inanimate object, so I probably won't stop until I burst a gasket. At least I don't get quite so steamed up with people, so that's a good thing. Or is it?

The descent, when it finally comes, is exhilarating to the point that I'm quickly back to a positive frame of mind. And from then on the journey is a delight – almost traffic free minor roads along the valleys of the Monnow and the Dore – occasional stiff climbs but nothing too extended. I bowl along through rich countryside with substantial farms and prolific orchards. The little towns of Skenfrith and Grosmont are worth a visit, with their attractive pubs and dinky castles built in the thirteenth century to keep the Welsh at bay. Off to the left are the Black Mountains. I pass signs welcoming me to England and others welcoming me back to Wales.

At Abbey Dore I consume a none too inspiring packed lunch courtesy of the St Briavels Youth Hostel and take a look around the parish church of St Mary's. It's massive – an architectural cuckoo in this cosy community. The village name is the give-away. St Mary's is part of a former Cistercian abbey, another victim of Henry VIII's merry men. It fell into the hands of the Scudamore family following the dissolution of the monasteries, and was used as a stone quarry for a hundred years until the first Viscount Scudamore, perhaps in a fit of conscience about the actions of his ancestors, chose to restore it. And so what you have is a truncated medieval cathedral, wildly oversized for current use, furnished internally with ornate seventeenth century carved wood that contrasts sharply with the simple lines of the original stonework. It's a striking but decidedly odd hotchpotch.

I continue towards Hay on Wye, the town of books, but turn off just before I get there. It's an interesting town to visit once, but I've visited it once and I'm not keen to go back. A bookshop for every sixty-three members of the population – you've got to be joking!

I can't understand why so many people delight in spending hours browsing bookshops. It seems such an inefficient way of finding what you want. Disregarding the English language titles published abroad, the database for British Books in Print alone contains more than a million titles, and 100,000 new ones are released each year. How many does your average bookshop hold? Ten thousand maybe, and that's likely to include multiple copies of the popular stuff. Unless you're after a bestseller or are pathetically easy to please, your chances of walking into a bookshop and finding exactly what you want are pretty limited. And remember too that bookshops make a practice of employing people whose minds work differently from the rest of us. It's a well known fact that they only take applicants whose CVs have been written in green ink with assorted calligraphic pens. If, by strange chance, the book you are after is in the shop somewhere, you can be quite sure it won't have been shelved in the place that any reasonable person would expect to find it.

I reckon I've marched chuntering out of more bookshops than any other form of retail outlet. Maybe you think I'm a philistine, but I don't care.

So I head away from Hay in a northeasterly direction, crossing the Wye at a rickety toll bridge near Whitney where a bored-looking man in a booth charges me five pence for the privilege. I tell him that five pence to ride a bike across a piddling bridge like this is a complete rip-off. On a yard for yard basis the Severn Bridge should have cost me seven pounds fifty. He hands me my change with a shrug.

I'm feeling really tired, and resolve that I'll end the day at the next likely looking place. There are no youth hostels in this neck of the woods, so it will have to be a B&B or a hotel. Eardisley is coming up, and it's an attractive enough village, but I can't spot any potential source of accommodation other than a couple of dreary looking pubs on the main A4111. I continue along minor roads and am about to sail through the little village of Almeley when I notice a B&B sign on a fine Georgian house opposite the church.

This will do. I prise myself out of the saddle, lean the bike against the garden wall and creak my way towards the door. A powerfully built man with a one-time broken nose emerges from the side garden before I get there. 'Yes there is a room free,' and 'It's good to see a lone cyclist.' He offers an enormous paw in welcome and chats enthusiastically about the joys of cycling in Herefordshire, before handing me over to his mother-in-law, an energetic lady called Jo, who shows me a lovely panelled room with glorious views and private bathroom. I'm bowled over with the place. After three nights in youth hostels, the comfort hits me like a shot of opium. But more, the people are so genuinely friendly. I'm instantly at home.

While I sort myself out, Jo makes me a stunningly good pot of tea, chucks my dirty washing in the machine and phones the local pub in response to my question about nearby eateries. 'They don't normally serve food in the evening', she tells me, 'But they'll put something on if I give them a call.'

The B&B is a fairly recent venture, run by Jo and her daughter Gwenda who also manages to fit in a job as a PE teacher. Her husband

Ken, the chap I met as I arrived, is a former army officer who now charges all over the country running leadership programmes and all sorts of other motivational activity. That's when he's not acting as jungle and desert survival specialist on reality TV programmes – one of which involved Gwenda and eleven of her cronies living on their wits in the jungle of Brunei. And Jo too is something of a survival expert, having single-handedly run a business in Uganda after her husband was murdered during the worst days of the Amin regime. But none of them are remotely boastful or anxious to talk up their exploits. There's something about them, and the two children who greet me politely before disappearing off to other activities, that gives a real vitality to the house. This is clearly not your typical B&B where people slip around like shadows and whisper in the dining room.

The pub is not exactly humming when I arrive just after seven – in fact my appearance doubles the clientele – but once again I'm made to feel welcome. Martin, the barman and one half of a landlord duo, is regaling the other customer with an account of the village rounders match the previous day – two carried off injured within thirty seconds of the start. He draws me into the conversation and calls to his partner to start cooking my dinner. He hopes I won't mind eating it in the bar – the lounge has been booked for a meeting of the neighbourhood watch committee. I'm intrigued. This little village seems about as far as one can get from the crime spots of Britain. What can there be to occupy the attention of a neighbourhood watch group? 'Don't be fooled,' says the other customer. 'Criminals like this sort of place. They drive over from Birmingham to rob houses while the owners are away.'

My meal arrives and it's tremendous – a beautiful rare steak with an excellent sauce and perfectly cooked vegetables. No microwaved ready meal here. I'm happily tucking in when the neighbourhood watch group arrive. They're a rather glum lot in tired fleeces who order up a round of orange juices and halves of shandy before disappearing into the next room in a haze of tobacco smoke. I idly wonder whether it's wise for them to meet en masse in this way – could be some easy pickings around the village tonight. Or perhaps they've thought of that. For all I know they may have sentries posted at the edge of the village, primed to raise the alarm if any white vans with Birmingham number-plates appear.

I arrive back at the guesthouse in benign mood – something to do with only being charged a tenner for my meal and two pints of beer – to find Ken and Gwenda sitting at the kitchen table eating beans on toast and drinking white wine. Out comes another glass and I'm invited to pull up a chair. The beans? They've been so busy, no time to prepare anything else.

I leave Almeley with a warm feeling. This is a place I will happily return to. And it's great easy riding for the first few miles through lovely countryside with apple orchards and black and white villages. Pembridge is a particular delight with its early thirteenth century octagonal bell tower and half-timbered Tudor buildings. I note too that it also has what is claimed to be the oldest New Inn in the country. After Staunton the character of the landscape changes, back to hills once more, but I'm on unclassified roads all the way this morning and there's hardly any traffic. The hard climbs are so much more tolerable, therapeutic even, when you're not breathing in the shit from fifteen year old Maestros with dodgy rings, or being blasted into the hedge by some tattooed nipper in a white Transit.

I come to a village that has fascinated me since I first saw it on the map. Brampton Bryan – I love the name. It's been there, grinning at me, right at the top of the sheet I've been following all the way from the Severn Bridge, so passing through assumes a special significance – a fresh map, a step into the unknown. I stop at a convenient seat by the church and consume some snacky goods. The place is a ghost town, not a soul to be seen, nothing moves. Everything is so well kept, but there are no people. Have I arrived on the day of the annual village outing, or has there been a new outbreak of the Black Death? Come to think of it, I've passed through other places that were similarly devoid of life. It's only because I have stopped that I'm noticing it. There must be hundreds of weekday villages like this, the length and breadth of the country. The inhabitants are either at work thirty miles away, in school or at a pensioners' day centre. It's only the picture postcard tourist traps and places with proper shops and markets that have people cluttering them up.

And so I delve into my bag for the next map sheet and – Hey! If I thought Brampton Bryan was a good name there are some even better ones here. There's a place just down the road called New Invention and what about Clungunford. It must be nice to live somewhere with a really off-the-wall name. Earlier this year when my wife and I were house hunting, an estate agent sent us details of one in a road called The Pitts. It wasn't a particularly good house, but I was seriously tempted to buy it, just so that I could sit in the garden and say 'This place is The Pitts.' But I had to concede that even I might tire of this eventually. No doubt that's what happened to the residents of Shitterton, a one-time hamlet near Bere Regis in Dorset. Generations of yokels had lived as happily as pigs in Shitterton, but in the late sixties some new houses were built there and the sensibilities of incoming owners were offended. The H was removed and a little bit of Dorset character was lost.

The sudden hunger comes upon me with a vengeance, and there are some angry clouds heading this way. My map shows that the village of Lydbury North (there doesn't appear to be a Lydbury anything else) has a pub and I'm looking forward to a comfortable lunch while, hopefully, the rain passes over. The pub is there all right, but it's closed – a sign on the door says it's only open evenings and weekends – another manifestation of the ghost village syndrome. I grit my teeth and pedal on.

Bishop's Castle has shops, a livestock market and a choice of pubs and cafés, but no castle – well, only the last traces of one. There are no bishops either, but in the Middle Ages they owned the castle and, in a stroke of quite startling originality, this gave rise to the name of the town. I say town, but with a population of just 1,500 it barely qualifies for that title. Until 1967 it held the distinction of being the smallest borough in England, and prior to 1832 returned two MPs to Westminster. By the rotten-borough standards of some early nineteenth century parliamentary constituencies it was a shining symbol of democracy with an electorate numbering a staggering 200.

The sudden surfeit of eating places leaves me in a ferment of indecision. I walk up and down the main street pondering the relative merits of this pub or that café. But the abrupt onset of rain drives me into the closest pub to hand, where the landlord takes aeons to serve coffee to four nattering pensioners before attending to my order.

The big upcoming event in Bishop's Castle is to be the Michaelmas Fair. The beer mats on every table announce a weekend of fun and entertainment for all the family. To get us in the right mood there are anagrams on the back of every mat, ramming home the attractions of the Fair. Unscrambling SCRIDS MEN ROAR (clue: rowdy hoppers with bells on) does nothing to increase my desire to attend. It's not that I'm dancist or jinglophobic. If nine men want to hang bells on their legs and dance around in a circle waving their hankies and knocking their sticks together, that's their affair. It's just that I don't believe innocent members of the public should have to witness them at it.

The rain has almost stopped when I tear myself away from the beer mats. Ahead is what the cycle guide describes as a hefty climb along the side of a range of hills ominously called The Long Mynd. It's over these that the brooding clouds seem at their heaviest and I'm not looking forward to it. I could make a detour and ride around the hills, but it would make my journey longer and, anyway, towards the top of the climb there's a little youth hostel where I could spend the night. So here goes.

In fact it's very pleasant, none too strenuous and the rain continues to hold off. I don't know why I take such notice of guide books. I'm sure they must be written by people like me who have good days and bad days, and take dislikes to some places for no good reason. In no time I'm at the youth hostel. Far too early to think about stopping, they won't be open for another two hours. I continue to the top from where I'm able to gaze across the North Shropshire and Cheshire plains, laid out like a clichéd patchwork quilt. I focus on Shrewsbury as my destination for the day. It's a town I've never visited and it's more or less in the right direction.

The Shrewsbury Youth Hostel is in a Victorian ironmaster's house, some way from the centre and set back from a busy roundabout. 'Yes there's plenty of room,' says the assistant manager. 'There are fifty-four beds, and so far today you're the only person who wants to stay here.'

I catch the weather forecast on the early evening news. Gales and heavy rain are set to sweep in from the northwest tomorrow lunchtime and are expected to continue for several days. I had hoped to finish this stage the day after tomorrow somewhere around Preston – handy for a train back and within easy reach of the Lake District for Stage Three. But this has been an enjoyable trip so far and I don't want to spoil it by spending the final day soaked to the skin, battling against a northerly gale. I decide that I'll make a bolt for Crewe tomorrow morning and finish the stage there. It's surely one of the best places in the country from which to catch a train, and there are some handy canal towpaths that will see me through to Lancashire when I return.

I take a walk around the town centre looking for somewhere to eat. I've never seen so many pubs within such a small radius. But, even though my stomach is flapping against my backbone, I'm feeling choosy. If this is to be the last night of the current stage then I want to mark it with something decent in my belly – a couple of good pints and some proper food in amiable surroundings. Shouldn't be too tall an order. The place is full of character after all.

Well, either I've chosen the wrong bit of town or things are not as they appear. I sound out umpteen pubs and all are found wanting. In one the average age of the clientele appears so low that I'm afraid, if I remain, I may fall under suspicion as a would-be child abductor. At the next, my enquiries after food draw a vacant look from the barman, followed by a gesture in the direction of the dry roasted peanuts. In yet another it is the food itself that sends me scurrying away from the buffet counter – glutinous chilli adhering to the metal sides of the serving dish, crispy edged lasagne that looks as if it has sat there since a week last Wednesday, wizened turd-like sausages waiting to be coaxed back to respectability with dollops of, no doubt, lumpy mashed potato. At last, in a side street away from the main drag, I come upon a most agreeable looking place – old, quiet, tasteful. The board outside shows some appetising stuff – none of the usual crap – there are real ales and (Hey!) a sign indicating that this is a no smoking pub. I stumble in and am warmed by the pleasant smiles of the small group of customers clustered around the bar. The barmaid smiles too.

'I was hoping for some food.'

'Oh, I'm awfully sorry! The chef's on holiday. I can manage a pork pie.'

I retrace my steps to the least unappetising of my previous hits and settle for a surly looking trout with dried up chips and ball bearing peas. Next to me, a strapping blonde woman from Scotland holds a loud, long and, at times, embarrassingly frank, mobile telephone conversation with a man of her intimate acquaintance. When the exchange finally comes to an end, she turns to me.

'Never date a man who thinks with his testicles.'

I solemnly promise to apply her advice, and allow myself to be drawn into further discussion, wondering whether there may be more handy hints on offer. But the brain/testicle issue is closed: she rapidly moves on to the subject of international terrorism and asylum seekers. It's one of those conversations you long to be airlifted out of. Her entrenched views are founded on very limited information but it swiftly becomes apparent that argument is futile. I resort to the occasional unassertive mumble as she sets out her simplistic recipe for global order and security. The volume of her delivery is particularly disconcerting and I'm acutely conscious that other diners are listening to us. I briefly consider the feasibility of scrawling a message on my napkin, disassociating myself from the views being expressed, but conclude that I wouldn't be able to hold it up for others to read without my companion noticing.

My morning dash for Crewe starts badly. Never one with much of a memory for numbers I head out of town on the A458 rather than the A528. 'Funny, this doesn't seem to be going the right way at all, and I'm sure Welshpool isn't in Cheshire.'

I stop to consult the map and realise I've left my glasses back at the youth hostel. My hope of getting to Crewe before the rain is beginning to look a little shaky.

But once I'm away from Shrewsbury and off the main road, the miles peel away quite merrily. There are advertising placards along the side of the road bearing the slogan 'Farmer's Own Seed'. Well, I knew that agriculture had been hit hard over recent months, but I never realised it had come to this. And who said that farmers were a dying breed?

Whitchurch is a place to come back to. It's a very attractive little town and I'd like to look around, but the wind is getting up and clouds are rolling in. Reaching Crewe without donning my waterproofs has shifted from vague hope to total obsession. It's as if I've become a Triffid – me versus the weather man, a fight to the death. But I'm not yet mad enough to take to the main road. I press on through quiet lanes between Whitchurch and Nantwich. Then I go for it, all or nothing, a final burst, head down, alongside the busy Crewe road.

The clock shows half past one as I wheel my bike into the ticket hall at Crewe station, the first three spots of rain on my cheek.

'I'd like a single to Southampton, and I'm taking a bike. Do I need to make a reservation for that?'

'You most certainly do sir. When do you want to travel?'

'This afternoon.'

'That's out of the question sir. I can't do you a bike reservation for today.'

'But I've done it before – last week in fact – the bloke just checked on his computer that there was still bike space on the train and made the reservation, fifteen minutes before the train was due.'

'I can't issue you with a reservation sir because, if I do, we will be legally obliged to get you to your destination even if that means we have to pay for the cost of a taxi to get you there.'

I reason that I should let pass the question of how I'm going to get my bike into a taxi, and try to confine myself to the world in which most of us live.

'Can't you check on your computer. Surely that will show you whether the available space has been taken up or not.'

'It may show that there is space, but the guards might have taken on bikes at previous stations.'

'But if there are bikes on the train that aren't shown on the computer, that means they don't have reservations, and you told me I needed a reservation in order to travel with mine.'

'Yes.'

Move over Joseph Heller, we're into crazy land here.

I glare at him – chubby face, neat haircut, regulation shirt and tie. I can see that he was one of those fat boys with sloppy mouths and breasts who got beaten up at school even more frequently than the skinny ones like me. And now he's getting his revenge. He's young, early twenties perhaps, but he carries the flag for elements of public sector culture from way before his time. It must be a matter of social initiation, a set of attitudes handed down from one generation of employees to the next. And it's unrattled by changes of company ownership, scarlet waistcoats, customer service centres and Investors in People Awards. At its roots the railway system is still provider centred and, until that is tackled, we will never have a decent rail service. I'm sure there must be people working for the rail companies who want to serve the needs of the travelling public, but there are still too many who think, 'Bollocks to the public, this network exists to keep me in work.'

My patience snaps. 'Look Mate! I've just cycled from Devon. I'm tired, I'm hungry and I want to go home.'

'Oh really sir. Are you doing it for charity?'

In the end he sells me a ticket for myself but says I will have to take a chance on finding a train that has room for my bike. And if that space is filled by others who get on at later stops with bike reservations, then I'll have to get off.

The train arrives about an hour late. It has a guard's van that could accommodate a centurion tank – completely empty.

And, but for my solitary bike, mournfully twiddling its pedals in the corner, there's still not so much as a matchstick in there five and a half hours later when I get off.

Chapter 6

When I originally anticipated ending the second stage at Preston, I had it in mind to walk northwards from there along the canal towpath as far as Carnforth, and thence by lanes and footpaths to the Lake District. But I finished at Crewe, way down in Cheshire, and I'm not fancying three days plodding past Manchester. I want to get to some wild walking country quite quickly. Of course, I could head in a north-easterly direction and pick up the Pennine Way after a couple of days, but everything I've read recently about this most famous of long distance paths suggests that it's walked to death. Processions of woolly-booted wanderers lining up to paddle through thick black ooze or scar still further the brittle moorland tops.

So I decide to return with the bike and pedal the by-ways of Lancashire before donning my boots for a pleasant slog through the Lakes. But this raises a new kit problem – how to carry both cycling and walking gear on the bike, and what to do with the bike once I am ready to start walking. After a bit of experimentation, I find I can secure my scrunched up rucksack, containing items exclusive to walking, onto the pannier rack of my bike. It overhangs a bit, but not enough to make me a figure of touring ridicule. I compromise again on clothing and equipment, such that I will be far more a walker on a bike than a cyclist on the moors. The question of what to do with the bike when I reach the Lake District is more problematic, as I would quite like to hop on it again for the stretch between Carlisle and Glasgow. So it's a case of a walking sandwich between two slices of bike. In the old days Red Star Parcels would have been the answer. You could leave a bulky item at the Red Star depot at one railway station and pick it up from the destination depot some days later. But Red Star finally bit the dust a couple of years ago and there doesn't appear to be any courier firm that offers a similar service. Indeed, some of those I phone, asking if I could drop off a bike at their Lancaster depot and pick it up a week later from the Carlisle depot, are utterly uncomprehending. It's almost a case of, 'Why would anyone want to do such a thing?'

Arnside Youth Hostel proves to be my saviour. They have no problem with me arriving as a cyclist and departing as a walker, leaving my bike in their cycle shed for a few days. Of course, I'll have to come back to pick it up, but it doesn't take long on the train.

So it's back to bloody Crewe again, but this time there's no fuss about the bike and the train is on time. What's more, everything about it is clean – compartments, toilets, buffet, the lot. Things are definitely looking up. On the leg from Birmingham, I'm even in a compartment that is labelled as a quiet zone. 'Please refrain from using mobile phones and creating unnecessary noise.' It's like a bear garden. Every conceivable ringtone jingle, and people holding intimate conversations across the ether in voices a mere decibel short of shouting. Opposite me is a young bloke who smells of stale fags and sniffs constantly. He jiggles his leg irritatingly and incessantly as he recounts to an invisible friend the events of his just-completed holiday:

'It was real, man. I was screwing a different one every night …You Prat! …Yeah! …When we come away most of um were crying … The lads, they didn't want to leave … On the coach to the airport … I wasn't … Course I wasn't … Prat! I'm fucking knackered now though … Didn't get any sleep on the plane.'

Across the aisle are two ladies from Cornwall – off to a flower show in Glasgow. They've been on the train since Redruth and are surrounded by thermos flasks, mountains of sandwiches, library books and enough magazines to stock a small branch of WH Smith. They have discovered that two other ladies three rows further up the compartment are bound for the same show and they are craning around their barricades comparing notes on the attractions they intend to visit.

'We're going to the demonstration on Friday by that Dutchman. What's his name? Van der something or another. Are you going? He's supposed to be really good.'

From somewhere behind me, come the indignant tones of a woman in the middle of a mobile phone row with her partner.

'What? Am I supposed to be a mind reader now? How am I expected to know what she's thinking? … Oh come on … There's nothing wrong with them. They're just as good as the ones Kelly had … Superdrug … They were, yeah, but I'm trying to save her money … Well, I'd like to see you wasting your lunchtime running round town after her. Whose mother is she anyway?'

If this lady and her partner were sitting together on the train they would glare and whisper, but stick a cellular radio frequency or two between them and all inhibition is cast to the wind. She's prepared to air her dirty washing in front of a whole compartment, because for the duration of the call she isn't physically with the rest of us at all. She's in a private space somewhere else. Picking up a mobile phone has the same effect as getting into a car, we throw a bubble of protective territory around ourselves – territory in which we can happily engage in behaviour that would otherwise cause us severe embarrassment. Just as we can sit at the traffic lights picking our noses and swearing at other innocent road users, so too can we parade our most intimate exchanges in front of all and sundry while we remain in mobile-land.

As you approach Crewe station from the south you pass a locomotives' graveyard. Clapped-out old things bearing the sort of livery last seen in the 1970s – orange and black, blue and white – a sort of railway equivalent of loon pants and tie-dyed grandad-vests. They sit grubby and forlorn, broken-windowed and cobwebby, giving the lie to the term 'rolling stock'. Is their scrap value so low that it's easier just to leave them in a siding until they finally rust away, or is somebody deliberately hanging onto them in the hope of a retro-revival?

The best thing about Crewe is that it's quick to get out of. The town itself is a dump, but it's surrounded by some rather nice Cheshire countryside. In no time at all I'm bowling along quiet lanes with the smell of cow-shit in my nostrils. There's a tangle of easy and peaceful unclassified roads between Crewe and Middlewich but I suspect that the person charged with their signposting received his training in the Secret Service. One or two junctions are labelled, but that only serves to add mystery to the majority that aren't. I navigate by guesswork, figuring that as long as I stay within the triangle formed by the main railway lines I'll be OK. A resurfacing crew is putting down new chippings on one empty stretch and I stop to ask if I'm on the right road. But the man with the Stop/Go lollipop isn't sure where the lane leads – rather surprising in view of the fact that he and his colleagues have obviously been working on it for several days. For the next three miles it's fresh chippings all the way and not a single car. I rattle merrily along, exceeding the ten miles per hour speed limit by fifty percent.

At Middlewich I'm into salt country. Huge deposits were laid down in times when a prehistoric sea covered the Cheshire Plains. As the sea retreated it left salt water lakes that gradually evaporated and, over millions of years, the resulting deposits were thrust below surface rock. They've been extracting the stuff since Roman times. Of course, everyone knows that Roman soldiers were paid partly in salt and that this is the origin of the word 'salary'. As a form of currency, I guess it had its advantages – a valuable commodity with all manner of uses, easily carried by your average foot soldier. But what served as a reasonable means of remuneration in sunny Italy must have had its drawbacks in dreary old Britain. A legionnaire caught in a sustained downpour might well have wound up with nothing more to show for his labours than well seasoned legs. No wonder they didn't like coming here.

Did you know that it's only in the last hundred and fifty years that salt has become a low cost commodity? So prized was it previously that from Elizabethan times until the early nineteenth century salt taxes were levied, and thousands of excise men deployed to prevent bootlegging. The seventeenth century equivalent of white-van-man with his smuggled cigarettes was white-pony-man with his bag of illicitly produced salt. At their peak, salt taxes were bringing in one and a half million pounds for the Exchequer – a sum sufficient to pay and equip a decent-sized army of the time.

Between Middlewich and Northwich I take to the towpath of the Trent and Mersey Canal. There's a heritage boat rally starting today and narrow boats have been arriving from all points of the compass. There are dozen upon dozen of them double-parked along the canal bank, some from as far afield as Oxford or Newbury. All the boats are crewed by similar types – middle-aged home-knitted males with beards, bellies, a dog or two and sturdy, obedient-looking wives. Being a narrow-boat wife must be a thankless existence. On every boat I encounter, it's the man who stands sternly in control at the tiller. So it doesn't take much to work out who has to jump off to secure moorings, open and close lock gates, and fend off other boats with the mop. They're all extremely spick (the boats that is, not the wives) with fresh paint and flower pots, neat galleys and carefully stowed equipment.

These are most certainly not your holiday variety of narrow boat, but permanent, bijou mobile dwellings.

I imagine it's quite an undertaking to shift permanently from a standard house into a space forty feet by six without benefit of lofts, garages or junk rooms. I mentally check off the things I would have to do without – the exercise bike, unused for the last five years, those jackets I kept in case they come back into fashion, the hi-fi with the 1980s chipboard speakers, the stainless steel monstrosity that calls itself a cappuccino maker – we don't even like cappuccino. After ten minutes of this activity I'm having difficulty identifying a single item among our current household clutter that we would have the remotest difficulty living without. I resolve to talk to my wife, as soon as I get back, about the possibility of us moving into a narrow boat. I wonder how she'll get on with the lock gates?

The towpath is hard compressed gravel at first, with bone-shaking cobbled inclines where the level changes alongside locks: horse-friendly maybe, but not conducive to the procreative prospects of cyclists. Recent research has revealed that hard bicycle saddles are associated with an eighty percent reduction in male sexual potency. My saddle is about as comfortable as a plank and, in combination with these cobbles, it's perhaps fortunate that my reproductive period is behind me. But hang on a minute! Back in the nineteen twenties and thirties everyone rode hard-saddled bikes over cobbles, and families were much larger than they are today. Maybe this research isn't as solid as it claims to be.

It's amazing just how much health related research there is going on at the moment. Hardly a day goes by without something we all thought was good for us being exposed as disastrously bad, and something we had always considered harmful being revealed as beneficial after all. Hard to know what to think. Take sunshine, the villain of the past twenty years. I read a piece earlier this summer suggesting that it has more benefits than problems. And as for things that prevent stomach and prostate cancer. Would you believe eating pizza and masturbation? Yes honestly, I read it just the other week. Not that the researchers are recommending both at the same time, of course.

As I leave Middlewich behind the towpath turns to very tufty grass and, in places, thick mud. There's the original stone edging to the canal itself, about a foot wide and temptingly smooth riding. And as I slither and bump on the rough ground I tell myself how much easier it would be along the edge. For a moment I almost convince myself, but then up pops a startlingly vivid picture of me pitching headlong into the green waters of the Trent and Mersey with all the clothing and equipment intended to see me through the next couple of weeks, and this after no more then an hour from starting out. I visualise myself, turning up at the door of some Cheshire B&B, limp and sodden, runnels of brown mud marking my passage from the gate. 'I was wondering whether you had a room for the night?'

I continue to bump and slither, but for all the discomfort it's jolly pleasant countryside. I can faintly hear a main road rumbling somewhere out of sight, but otherwise I could be miles away from the hustle of traffic. There are herons guarding each bend, turning themselves from graceful statuettes to ungainly pterodactyls as they slowly take to the air on my approach. Low hanging branches swipe me in the face, foiling my attempts to avoid them.

I try to conjure an image of the gangs of navvies who sweated, dug and blasted their way though this lush countryside at the end of the eighteenth century. They must have thought they were building an artery of commerce that would remain for a thousand years. After all, the roads of the time had been going for longer than that. But the canals were redundant in less than a century with, indignity upon indignity, railways thundering past within spitting distance of them.

In addition to serving the salt industry – coal coming in, salt going out – the Trent and Mersey Canal offered a waterborne route through the Potteries, and one of its main backers was Josiah Wedgewood whose raw materials and delicate finished products had previously to be carted along dreadful roads between his works at Stoke and the nearest navigable point on the River Weaver at Winsford. He tried to persuade the Weaver Navigation trustees to accept a junction between the new canal and the river but they, frightened of losing business, refused and did everything in their power to prevent the canal being built. There was even a clause in the 1807 Weaver Navigation Act forbidding the transfer of any goods other than salt between the two waterways, despite the fact that they pass within fifty yards of each other. This mutual suspicion and cut-throat competition was not at all unusual, and when the railways came on the scene, their owners continued in the same vein, often buying up adjacent canals, simply in order to eliminate them as potential competitors.

There's one other cyclist along my bit of canal bank this sunny afternoon – a shaven headed youth who passes me pedalling wildly, only to stop fifty yards further on and peer long and hard at his wheels. As I draw level he says to me,

'Bloody fonz is a problem.'

I smile and agree despite being unacquainted with this particular cycle component.

He comes past me again and stops once more.

'Pissing fonz!'

We continue like this for a mile or two, passing and re-passing each other with further invective directed at the problematic fonz. I sympathise with him, but am loath to display my ignorance by asking exactly what the thing is.

Every so often I meet a boat chugging in the opposite direction. The people on board wave to me and exchange cheery greetings. The exception is one emblazoned with the legend 'Trafford Youth Services' which is skippered by a poor distracted sod who is trying his best to motivate a group of apathetic adolescents. The youth at the controls keeps revving the engine horribly and veering wildly from one side of the canal to the other while, at the prow, one of his colleagues is thrashing over the side with a fishing net. His action suggests an attempt to stun rather than net any unfortunate fish within range. As I draw level, somebody chucks two life belts into the water.

A little further on there's one of those heritage boards alerting me to the presence of the Lion Salt Works. With the aid of illustrations, the board informs me that production started in the late eighteenth century, around the time the canal was built, and continued until 1986 – the last open pan salt mine in the country. Now the site is being restored and has a museum staffed by volunteers. Well, I'm not in a hurry, I tell myself, worth taking a look. I wheel my bike through the gate. The place has about as much life as a turkey farm on Boxing Day. Not a soul in sight: just a bunch of ramshackle buildings. It seems that volunteers are in short supply on this Wednesday afternoon and the restoration project still has some way to go.

That's most certainly not the case with the next restoration project I encounter about ten minutes later. The Anderton Boat Lift is an all-singing, all-dancing humdinger of a project with no expense spared, from the electric visitor buggies to the glorious spanking new toilets. The original lift was the world's first, and was testimony to the foolishness of the River Weaver trustees in rejecting a link with the canal back in the seventeen seventies. Come the second half of the nineteenth century the ban on transfer of goods between the two waterways had been abandoned as detrimental to both. But almost as nonsensical was the costly and time consuming palaver of unloading bulky cargoes and dragging them up ramps or down chutes before reloading them on the second waterway. So the lift was built in 1875 to raise boats the fifty feet between the level of the river and that of the canal. It's an impressive structure, originally operated by hydraulics and converted to electric power early in the twentieth century. But it had to be abandoned on safety grounds in 1982 and for twenty years stood rusting and unused. At a cost of seven million pounds it has now been completely restored, complete with the original Victorian mechanism, and has reopened to boat traffic just a few weeks ago. The secret? Well, three and a half million of lottery money may have had something to do with it, plus a high profile public appeal and a lot of support from the relevant authorities. British Waterways are clearly very proud of what has been accomplished and have erected a semi-permanent tent with a constantly running video display and a stall selling Kit-Kats, Coke and little model barges. The electric shuttle cart to bring visitors from the car park is perhaps a little over the top considering the distance cannot be more than two hundred yards, but plenty of people are taking advantage of it. Indeed, the expressions on their faces suggest they are considering it a rare treat.

For not so small a fee you can take a boat trip down the lift, make a quick circle around the River Weaver and back up again. When I arrive a trip has just started. A handful of bright-faced visitors are expectantly peering out from the modern craft as it waits at the top for the lift to descend. I amble down to the bottom, look around the exhibition, buy a Kit-Kat and a Coke but not a model barge, and wander out to the seats overlooking the river. Still the trough containing the trip boat doesn't appear to have moved. After much longer than my patience could have endured had I been paying to travel on it, the lift inches downwards accompanied by such a cascade of water that I'm concerned the trough will be empty by the time it gets to the bottom.

I return to my bike to find that the front tyre is completely flat. Further investigation reveals that three enormous thorns have speared their way through the hefty all-terrain tyre and the inner tube. Realisation dawns. Fonz! Shit! I spend an interesting twenty five minutes repairing the damage only to discover, when I pump up the tyre again, that there is a fourth thorn I had missed.

Beyond the boat lift the canal bed is completely dry. Workmen are renewing its lining. After several miles of meandering green water, it's quite a shock to come upon this sudden brown bottomed channel – like catching the poor thing with its trousers down. The tow path is closed too, so it's back to the lanes for me. There are plenty of them to see me through to Stretton, where I cross the M56 – my first motorway since Bristol.

There's a four star hotel in Stretton and a couple of B&Bs. It's half past five and I don't really want to go much further.

'Bugger the expense,' I tell myself, 'Tonight I'm going for the four star hotel.'

No I don't – that was a joke – you weren't fooled for a moment were you? In truth I jiggle around at the traffic lights eyeing up the two B&Bs which are positioned on either side of the junction, trying to work out which is likely to offer the best combination of cheapness and comfort. The Old School House wins. It's set back slightly from the busy road, whereas the Beehive Guest House appears almost close enough to be counted an obstruction. I park the bike, march up to the door of the Old School House, ring the bell and put on my best winning smile. Nobody comes. I knock, ring again, cough, hurrumph, scuffle my feet, knock again. And when I am quite sure that the winning smile has faded completely and has no chance of returning, I go back to the bike and head for the Beehive Guest House.

The landlady, who also runs the shop and post office next door, is cheery and accommodating. She shows me to a comfortable room and asks if I'm doing the Land's End to John O'Groats in a manner that suggests the majority of her customers are engaged in this everyday pursuit. I'm startled – it's the first time since Land's End that anyone has immediately twigged what I'm up to. I suppose it's less than likely that a B&B next to a busy road junction on the outskirts of Warrington would feature on the itinerary of a leisurely cycling tour around Cheshire, but to assume Land's End to John O'Groats! Her accuracy unnerves me to the point that I readily admit for the first time my intended destination. And it isn't just a lucky guess on her part. It seems that among the regular clientele of company reps at the Beehive Guest House there really has been a steady trickle of end-to-enders. She enumerates them for me:

'I had a walker through last week. He was an old chap who'd done it once before. He had a friend following along in a camper van. Then there were the two cyclists. That must have been a couple of weeks before. And earlier in the year there was this chap who was making a recording of his journey for Channel 4.'

I'm astonished. I have to go and sit down in my room for five minutes to recover. Of all the possible routes and available accommodation, end-to-enders appear to be drawn to this place. What mysterious force is responsible? And, I wonder, did all the others try the Old School House first?

Across the road there's one of those characterless mock-gothic pubs that have their food menus printed in glossy colour on fold-out laminated card, with overblown descriptions – 'A tender, succulent half roast chicken served with a generous scoop of crispy French fries and pan gravy' – and colour photographs to give the terminally stupid an inkling of what chicken and chips looks like. I hate these things. They indicate an establishment that is resolved to turn out the same synthetic, portion controlled crap month after month, year after year.

But there's one thing that annoys me even more about pubs like this, and that's the inability of staff to serve you a drink and ask for your money straight away. You order something unremarkable like a pint of ordinary bitter and you can see from the mini blackboard at the back of the bar that it's going to cost you £1.90. You even have two pound coins ready in your hand, but the barman can't pour your drink and say 'That'll be one pound ninety please.' He doles out the same stuff all night every night, but each new order is a voyage of discovery for him. He has to go over to something that looks like a computer game and search around on a touch screen for the item you've ordered. When he finally finds it, he jabs with his index finger like one of those benighted minor celebrities they use to release the balls on the national lottery, and he turns to you with a look of blank astonishment and says, 'That'll be one pound ninety please.'

Back in the dark ages when I worked in bars, you were expected by customers and employers alike to memorise the prices of all the stuff you were flogging and to maintain a running total of every order in your head. It could be a bit hairy when you were dealing with a round for twelve people who kept changing their minds about what they wanted, and the Guinness ran out half-way through, but I'm sure it gave us an advantage at cards and it was so much quicker. You could present them with the total the instant you handed over the last drink. When thirsty customers are hanging over the bar waving ten pound notes at you, it's speed they appreciate.

The couple opposite me are having a secret affair. There's an air of snatched forbidden moments about them that says this cannot be anything else. It's seven forty five and they're still in their office clothes. He has five different coloured pens in the top pocket of his jacket.

They order two puddings – no starter, no main meal. A case of clandestine lovers getting their just deserts I suppose. But then, if you've got to go home and make a stab at eating the dinner that's been left to keep warm for you, I guess it's the best policy. He stretches theatrically, and somehow when his arm comes down it's draped loosely across her shoulders. He's behaving as if the arm doesn't really belong to him, but he's embarrassed by its sauciness nevertheless. Puts me in mind of my own clumsy adolescent attempts at making physical contact with the opposite sex. I'm surprised to see the ploy still being used, particularly by a man the wrong side of forty.

My concerns about the proximity of my B&B room to the road prove unfounded. Vans and lorries lumber by so close that I would have no difficulty stretching a hand from my window and writing 'Also Available in White' and 'Please Clean Me!' on their sides, but the double glazing is effective and even the slight stirring of the foundations as a particularly large vehicle passes has a soporific effect.

So the next morning sees me, refreshed and invigorated, cycling through the centre of Warrington. The shopping centre – scene of the IRA bombing outrage in 1993 which killed two young boys and sparked a wave of national revulsion – has been transformed of late with smart pedestrianised areas, water features, street sculpture and attractive malls. But it's deserted. Maybe it's the time of day or the day of the week, but there's all this stuff waiting to be bought and no-one to buy.

Even though my route has deliberately avoided the major urban areas, I've been struck by the sheer number of shopping developments I've passed along the way. Shopping may have become the number one leisure preoccupation in this country, but without a massive procreation campaign I wonder whether we've a hope of producing enough shoppers to keep pace with the ever burgeoning number of outlets. As each new development is opened, it simply sucks the life out of another further down the food chain – one that is judged by its fickle customers to be too old, too tired or too inaccessible. But the crazy thing is that the new developments are made up of just the same enterprises that previously inhabited the old centres, and they're selling exactly the same stuff, just doing it in rather more glitzy buildings. Meanwhile the older centres, deserted by the big names, are inhabited by 'nothing over a pound' shops and the sort of outlet that sells Elvis Presley mirrors and Christmas decorations all year round. And they're haunted by young men carrying clipboards and wearing ill fitting shiny black suits, who insist, despite all evidence to the contrary, that they only want to talk to you for market research purposes and not to sell you anything like double glazing or roadside assistance.

I like to think that one day we'll wake up to the stupidity of our spending culture. It's a con on a scale to rival world religions that leads us to queue up in our millions, ready to shell out hard-earned cash in order to replace perfectly serviceable items with others offering, at best, marginal improvements or superficial style changes – purchases which defy even the most liberal interpretation of the word 'need'. Yet we continue to do it under the sad misapprehension that somehow contentment will follow.

And this mindless squanderbuggery is actually feted as a cornerstone of western values, without which our economy would collapse and our jobs and lifestyles with it. The health of my pension fund depends on people going into that wretched sports shop over there and buying trainers at seventy-five pounds a throw from assistants on the minimum wage who, in turn, are supported in their wealthy wasteful western existence by far eastern sweatshop workers who make the things for ten pence an hour, and for whom the shop assistant's minimum wage or my modest pension would represent undreamed of wealth. What sort of foundation is that on which to base our values?

And as I climb down from my soap box I know with absolute

certainty that I'm bound to continue playing my part in this ridiculous exploitative charade. I remount my heavy uncomfortable bike noting, momentarily, that perhaps I'll buy a lighter, shinier one after this trip.

North of Warrington I take to minor roads through dreary South Lancashire, taking in such places as Newton le Willows, Haydock and Billinge. Newton is particularly desolate. The Vulcan Locomotive Works – proud producer of engines from the very start of the railway age – is reduced to a shadow with boarded up buildings and a miscellany of Johnny-come-lately small enterprises of the sort that are drawn to the corpses of obsolete factories. The only businesses that appear to be thriving in this town are hairdressers and tanning studios. One of the latter has a sign advertising 'vertical sunbeds' – the two words are contradictory, aren't they? Why would you want to get a tan standing up? Is it so you don't have to lie in other people's sweat?

And every house has a burglar alarm. I've never seen so many in one small area. Even tiddly terraced two-up two-downs are wired against intruders. Either these modest dwellings harbour more wealth than could possibly be deduced from their stone clad facades or there are some pretty hot alarm salesmen around.

Moving north I encounter the first signs of mining activity since Cornwall - equally redundant but much less picturesque. The only evidence of any significant new employers comes in the form of hanger-like distribution centres for mail order books and supermarket companies. It's all very depressing.

Things look up a bit when I get to Upholland, or 'Historical Upholland' as it says on the town sign. Well, the place clearly has a lot of history, with a past that stretches back to the Norman Conquest. The churchyard, I discover, contains the grave of Lancashire's last highwayman, one George Lyon who was publicly hanged for his crimes at Lancaster in 1815. Quite how he made it back here, I'm not sure. Certainly Upholland was his home town and that must count for something, but I always thought that the bodies of executed felons were treated to nothing more than an unmarked grave by the prison wall. Not that it would have bothered George Lyon one way or the other.

I'm moved to make a detour into Wigan to see Wigan Pier. I remember picking up Orwell's book for the first time as a teenager. Perhaps it was something to do with the title, but I honestly thought I was in for a funny book. And for most of the first chapter I wasn't disappointed. I creased myself with laughter at descriptions of the grim boarding house where the writer stayed, four men to a room, with a landlord who planted dirty thumbprints on the tripe and routinely combined breakfast preparation with chamber pot emptying. And then, as I embarked on chapter two, the truth dawned – Orwell wasn't writing comedy, but bleak commentary on blighted lives and rank social injustice.

Well it's all changed now. There's not a lot to point to Wigan's austere industrial past, and the area they call Wigan Pier is as twee as any tourist venue I have encountered on the trip so far. Restored warehouses on the banks of the canal play host to the imaginatively named 'The Way We Were' museum' and a theme pub called 'The Orwell', all dark wood and shiny fittings. The poor man must be squirming in his grave. Moored alongside are narrow boats with perspex roofs, loading up with crocodiles of school kids for a half hour trip along the Leeds and Liverpool Canal to catch a flavour of the industrial past.

The fame of Wigan Pier wasn't started by Orwell; he just spread it around a bit. It first entered public consciousness as a music hall joke around the turn of the century. The word 'pier' had long been used for any structure built out over water, from which the loading of boats could take place, and along the Leeds and Liverpool canal there were dozens of piers like the one at Wigan. But with the upsurge of mass seaside tourism in the late nineteenth century, the word had been commandeered by the pleasure piers of Blackpool, Morecambe and other resorts – a structure on which you could put to sea without leaving the land, catch up with the latest in light entertainment, and find out what the butler really saw. So the incongruous notion of such a pier in Wigan, at the gloomy heart of industrial Lancashire and twenty miles from the sea, had them wetting their pants in the aisles. The irony of the thing is that now Wigan looks a lot less wretched than parts of some seaside resorts with which it was being so unfavourably compared back then.

And what about Wigan Pier itself? Well, the area now known as Wigan Pier is not the pier at all. The real thing is on the opposite bank of the canal and, but for a modest sign screwed to a barbed-wire-topped brick wall, you could walk past without noticing it. All the pier consisted of was a length of slightly raised railway track running to the canal edge and a small platform that extended a couple of feet over the water. It was just the end of the line for a simple railway transport system built in 1822 to bring coal from a couple of local pits to a point where it could be loaded onto barges. A hand-winched device called a tippler was used to lift and tip the trucks, emptying the coal into the waiting boats. For all its simplicity, Wigan Pier was busily occupied – handling up to a thousand tons of coal a week at its peak. But by the time Orwell put it on the literary map, the pier was already redundant. The collieries it served were closed in 1929 and the railway line and tippler sold off for scrap, netting the receivers a grand total of £34.

As I cycle out of Wigan, there's a strong smell of peppermint. A prominent sign tells me it comes from Uncle Joe's World Famous Mint Ball Factory, an unassuming building just at the back of the station. It's at times like this I become acutely aware of the sad limitations to my knowledge and experience. How is it possible that, in more than half a century on this planet, I have never previously heard of Uncle Joe's World Famous Mint Balls? If I'm to have any hope of fulfilment during the pathetic remnants of my life, I must surely make a point of sampling them at the next available opportunity.

The minty smells bring on the inevitable urgent cycling hunger and I'm lured by a pub sign that promises a warm welcome at the Crook Hall Inn. It's just off the main road next to the canal and the sign offers a beer garden and bar food. Yeah, this looks like a pleasant stopping place. I park the bike around the back and make my way up the steps to the bar. It's curiously quiet – just two or three people lurking in shady corners – and the warmth of welcome does not quite match up to the road sign promise, but I slip into my normal routine of ordering a pint before asking about food and give the wrong answer when asked whether I intend to drink inside or out. The flimsy plastic glass is already three-quarters full when I'm minded to pursue the true purpose of my detour.

'What have you got in the way of food?'

'Erm, I don't think we're doing food today. He's gone out.'

She calls over her shoulder to her fellow barmaid. 'Has he gone out? Tony?'

'No he's out the back.'

'Is he doing food?'

'No, I don't think he is.'

'No he isn't, sorry.'

I rise well up in the stirrups of my high horse and in a manner that swings between pomposity and obscenity treat the unfortunate woman to my views on establishments that mislead members of the public with unfulfilled promises such as 'Warm Welcome' and 'Bar Food'. Then, not deigning to boost the pub's takings by purchasing a bag of nuts, I march out to the garden with my plastic glass of flat beer.

A scrawny unshaven man in a baggy tracksuit is pushing his three-year-old daughter dementedly on a swing made of a tyre on a chain. Her bottom is hanging right through the tyre and almost scraping the ground. Any moment, I think, there's going to be a nasty accident. As I watch them a fly goes in my eye, right inside, and I mess around trying to get it out until I'm not sure whether the pain I still feel is the original foreign object or the result of ten minutes dabbing and poking.

Tony, the absentee landlord, is in the garage making a new bench seat for the garden out of timber off-cuts. I have to acknowledge this as a worthwhile activity, if less valuable than food preparation; the existing benches are rickety to the point of imminent collapse.

I appoint myself an undercover inspector for the Good Pub Guide with immediate effect and, in this new role, complete my assessment with a visit to the gents. They fail to lift the establishment out of the 'no star' category.

Once I'm past Appley Bridge there's a sudden startling change in the scenery. The post-industrial dereliction gives way to rolling fields with dry-stone walls and lovely quiet lanes. After the dreary landscape just past it's very welcome and I feel I can legitimately reassume the status of tourist rather than some sort of cycling oddity.

Just beyond Eccleston is a nice little sandstone church by a stream. One of the most valuable pieces of knowledge I've acquired on this trip is that churchyards are reliable places for a sit down. There's always a bench seat or two dedicated to a deceased parishioner, and generally congenial surroundings in which to eat one's grub – even something to read while you rest, albeit gravestone inscriptions can tend to lose their fascination after a while. I become weary of those describing people who 'fell asleep with Jesus' or who are 'reunited in heaven'. I'm much more favourably inclined towards the sort of epitaph that hits the nail on the head rather than pussyfooting around the subject of death and the hereafter. The grave of Harry Edsel Smith of New York is the sort of thing I would like to see more often :

Born 1903 Died 1942
Looked up the elevator shaft to see
If the car was on the way down.
It was.

Or a little closer to home:

Here lie I, Martin Elginbrodde;
Have mercy o'my soul, Lord God;
As I wad do, were I Lord God;
And Ye were Martin Elginbrodde.

It was a great disappointment to me to discover that you can't actually visit Mr Elginbrodde's grave and read this wonderful inscription. In fact, he never had a grave. Didn't have much need of one, being an entirely fictional character from the pen of nineteenth century Scottish novelist George McDonald. That's a bit of a bummer, isn't it?

I have been invited to stay overnight at the house of a cousin in Preston, so I stop off at a supermarket to buy a bottle of wine that will form my token thank you. As I walk towards the automatic doors, a starling falls from the sky and bounces off the turban of an elderly Sikh gentleman who is just leaving the shop. I'm serious, it really does. We both express surprise and concern but that clearly isn't enough to prevent the creature dying at our feet. One of the shelf stackers is sent out to dispose of the corpse, which he does with the aid of a red and white carrier bag.

I mention this little incident because I've read in the paper only this week that, according to the British Trust for Ornithology, those two most common of British birds, starlings and sparrows, are rapidly declining in numbers. And it's not just in the countryside where new farming methods may be to blame, but in the towns as well. Quite what's going on the experts aren't sure. For generations these birds have thrived in the most inhospitable of urban landscapes and now here they are, keeling over and falling to earth on supermarket fore-courts. My theory is that they're dropping dead from sheer exhaustion through trying to pursue a 24/7 existence – victims of the same relent-less modern lifestyle that turns us into clapped-out wrecks in our mid-forties. No longer do they tuck their heads under their wings when the sun goes down and spring back to joyful life with the first fingers of dawn. These days they're up and twittering at all times of the night. I hear them when I'm lying awake worrying about with-profit annuities and guaranteed income bonds at three in the morning. It's the street lights and constant traffic noise that does it. Poor things! Perhaps we'll have to start hanging up bacon rind steeped in Prozac.

The rain starts just as I climb onto my bike the following morning. It's that steady, pitiless straight-down variety that feels as if it's set to continue to the end of time. I make my way via back roads past Garstang and on towards the estuary of the River Lune. If it weren't for the rain, this would be a comfortable and pleasant ride. But it's amazing how quickly the spirits start to flag when you're soaked through by mid-morning and have nothing to look forward to but more of the same until late afternoon. At Cockerham I eat a bar of chocolate in a bus shelter, staring gloomily out at the empty road, as complete a picture of self pity as could be found anywhere in the Northwest.

From Conder Green there's a cycle path that runs for five miles along the estuary to Lancaster. It's a pretty route but, as I soon discover, extremely muddy. Not the normal sticky brown mud, but a sloppy black mixture an inch or so deep that flies in every direction as I pass through it. Slowing down doesn't help. At whatever speed I choose to travel, it defies my mudguards, coating the frame, wheels, panniers, handlebars and every inch of me, front and back, deeply and evenly. At intervals along the river there are seine fishermen; curious figures in chest-high waders, up past their waists in water and mud, patiently manipulating their ungainly nets. It seems such a committed way to fish – getting right in there with them. I nod to them rather enviously as I pass. They're a lot dryer and cleaner than I am.

Self consciousness starts to set in as I approach Lancaster. It had been my intention to take a look around this attractive town, but in my present condition I resemble a landslide survivor rather more than a casual tourist. I avoid the town centre, crossing the river by the nice new footbridge and then following a, mercifully tarmacked, cycle path that takes me unobtrusively past the backs of houses into the centre of Morecambe. It's raining even harder now but it doesn't seem to have shifted much of the mud that coats me. I had considered the possibility of visiting an aged aunt who lives in a Morecambe rest home, but I figure that my appearance might lead the staff to call the police.

So my first contact with the residents of Morecambe comes in the form of a young woman in a flowered skirt, anorak and slippers, standing trackside of a railway pedestrian crossing gate and effectively blocking my path. Her dull blonde hair, betrayed by two inches of dark roots, is plastered to her face in damp streaks and she leans on a push chair in which sits a small jammy-faced child. She's angry. So much so that she's oblivious to my presence or to any threat from approaching trains. And she's venting her wrath on a thirteen-year-old in incredibly baggy jeans and a hooded tracksuit top who skulks and fidgets in the road some thirty yards further on. She yells at the top of her voice:

'And you go back and tell him I'm not getting fined a thousand fucking quid for him.' She crosses the railway track and walks back, crosses again and walks back once more, bound up in her individual rage. I wait patiently, looking for my opportunity to get past her.

Morecambe as a town is a bit like her. Shabby, inappropriately dressed and with a sense of brooding resentment at the injustice of its situation. But, like her, I suspect it could still be pleasant and attractive with a bit more care and attention.

It wasn't always this way. In the late nineteenth and early twentieth century Morecambe rivalled Blackpool as the premier resort of the Northwest. In very large measure this was down to the Little North Western Railway line opened in 1850 which provided a direct link with the industrial towns of the Yorkshire West Riding. If Blackpool served the mill workers and miners of South Lancashire, Morecambe was the leisure destination of choice for their counterparts across the Pennines. It was known variously as Leeds-on-Sea and Bradford-Super-Mare. With a huge annual influx of visitors, the town flourished and became quite unrecognisable from the early nineteenth century fishing village it had been. It was host to top entertainment venues: ballrooms, music halls, cinemas, concerts at the Winter Gardens, a major fairground, two piers and the largest swimming pool in Britain. It was the first place to produce seaside rock, and even outdid Blackpool with its illuminations.

But just as the railways were largely responsible for its growth, so the switch to other modes of holiday transport signalled its decline. Dr Beeching wielded his axe at just the same time that cheap package holidays started to lure a new generation of northern tourists to sunnier climes, and growing car ownership meant that holidaymakers could set their horizons beyond the excursion specials from Leeds Central.

So the Morecambe of today is a town whose grandeur has very much faded. Boarded-up shops, pubs and amusements feature heavily along stretches of the seafront and some of those that are open for business seem to represent a triumph of optimism over common sense. Here and there, small posses of elderly holidaymakers peer from rain-streaked café windows. The mainline station that once deposited thousands of trippers directly onto the promenade is now a pub – an attractive one I have to admit. Amazingly, there are still several hundred hotels and guest houses in Morecambe – there were more than a thousand in happier times. They have the usual cheery or prestigious names – Balmoral, Marina, Sunnyside, Prospect – but a number have been reduced to advertising exceptionally low rates on boards outside their premises. A list of local holiday hot-spots underlines the decline. After detailing the four premier attractions – Ten Pin Bowling, Bingo, The Megazone Laser Shooting Gallery, and The Wacky Warehouse, the list goes on to offer Heysham Power Station – 'A free day out with a difference: including guided tours, exhibitions, interactive quizzes and much, much more!' It's an odd thing, isn't it? Whenever a list ends with that phrase 'much, much more', you know with utter certainty that there isn't anything more to speak of.

But I mustn't be too harsh – this could so easily have been the town of my birth. I was certainly conceived here, and would have entered the world here too had my mother not decided, halfway through her pregnancy, that she couldn't bear sharing a house with my father's relatives any longer, and persuaded him to move. She had New Zealand in mind, but he'd been there already and so they went to Leeds.

There were no Lancashire roots to my family. In fact it was personal disgrace that led both sets of grandparents to fetch up next to Morecambe Bay shortly after the First World War. My paternal grandfather earned himself a year in Armley Gaol when, as a Leeds subpostmaster, he took it into his head to start forging signatures on postal orders. His motives were never made specific but there were family rumours of an illicit affair and a second home. As he was almost sixty at the time, I'm not sure whether to admire his stamina or condemn his stupidity. His outraged wife and grown up daughters took the latter course and decamped to Morecambe to escape the shame and to run a seaside boarding house.

The surviving photos of my grandfather, taken after he emerged from prison, show a teeny, white-haired man with a permanently apologetic expression. One gets the impression that his formidable wife made him pay for his misdemeanours at least as heavily as did the criminal justice system. He didn't survive long, popping off a year or so after his release following the excitement of a visit to a seaside boxing match.

My maternal grandfather's angle of descent was less steep but more sustained. He was a teacher with a weakness for the bottle, in an era when this was considered a CV no-no rather than the essential survival tool it is for today's educational professionals. It saw him sacked from a succession of posts that ran from Hertfordshire to the Orkneys. After the last of these disgraces, the family settled in Lancaster where my mother was sent out to work at an early age because the money for her continued education had gone on whiskey and removal expenses.

Before leaving Morecambe I light on the idea of phoning my mother from a weather-lashed shelter on the promenade. I think it might cheer her up to get a call from one of her former stamping grounds. It doesn't. She immediately starts to worry that I'll take it into my head to walk across Morecambe Bay and be swallowed up by its infamous quicksands, or be cut off by the tide that, she tells me for only the hundredth time in my life, comes in as fast as a man on a galloping horse. My mother's capacity for worry is prodigious. I've never met anyone who can run her close. She always keeps a worry or two in readiness as others keep handkerchiefs tucked in their sleeves. And if there isn't an obvious source of anxiety immediately to hand, then she'll sure as hell find one. Take something like a simple meal in a restaurant. You'd think this would only be a source of worry if you had some sort of dietary problem or lacked the wherewithal to pay the bill. Not a bit of it. My mother doesn't need prompts such as these. She'll agonise over the menu – what's everyone else having? How can she ensure that her choice doesn't mark her out as greedy, extravagant or ignorant? If there are significant quantities of liquid involved, will it mean a visit to the lavatory? And if so, can you be heard when you're in there? What will the other customers think? And she'll spend the meal consumed by anxiety about who's going to pay – how can she make certain that it's her? What if somebody else jumps in before she can get her purse out? What future gesture might she then make to repay their generosity? And assuming she does manage to pay, how much should the tip be? Too little and be thought mean, too much and be thought stupid. Should the tip be handed to the waiter with all the dangers of ostentation, or furtively hidden under a plate and possibly missed altogether? For my part, I'm inclined to watch silently as she worries her way through the meal, unable to enjoy it. You see, the thing that worries me, I mean really worries me, is that the older I get, the more like her I seem to become.

A few miles north of Morecambe is Carnforth. My guidebook tells me it's a Mecca for railway enthusiasts and boasts a museum called Steamtown where men of arrested development can video each other going into orgasm at the sight of very ordinary steam engines and carriages. If they're up for the really big thrills they can even ride on a miniature railway, sitting with their knees up by their ears while sympathetic bystanders caution their children not to laugh. I'm relieved to discover that that my book is out of date – the place having been closed down a couple of years ago.

However, I do stop to take a look at the station, something of a film buff's Mecca, having been used as the location for the 1945 classic *Brief Encounter*. The director, David Lean, said he chose it particularly for the subways between its platforms: so much more becoming for Celia Johnson to run down a gentle slope to catch her train than to scamper across some rusty footbridge. The truth, like so much in wartime Britain, was more a case of him being allocated Carnforth than choosing it.

The station is in the process of being restored to its 1940s state, but there's clearly some way to go with the project. I half close my eyes and try to recapture the tight-lipped black and whiteness of it all, but I can't. In spite of the blurry vision it's just an ordinary little station, indistinguishable from hundreds of others around the UK.

Just past Carnforth I judge that the rain is about to stop. I even undo my jacket a little and start to contemplate the possibility of a café in the next village – chance for a sit down and a cup of tea. I'm still pretty muddy, but I figure that if I can get my sodden outer garments off before entering, I might just about pass muster – as long as the chairs are plastic and the floor isn't carpeted. But then it really starts to piss down again – stair rods, fishing rods, drain rods even. It's the sort of rain that has drivers pulling onto the last visible remnants of land and sending up distress flares. Representatives of the local fauna line up in pairs, paw in paw. It's not the best of times to appreciate the scenery, but even peeping out from under my sopping hood I can see that this is an attractive little corner of northern Lancashire: one I would like to return to if it's ever reclaimed from the deluge. And there's one more positive outcome – at last I'm washed clean and rendered wholesome in the eyes of the Lord.

From Silverdale there's a tough climb over Arnside Knott before I gingerly descend into the village, an hour early for the youth hostel, and drag my dripping frame into a tea shop with a composite floor.

My earlier musings about the average age of youth hostel clientele have really come back to haunt me at Arnside. As I wait to check in, very cold now and still dripping, there are three Australians in front of me. All of them have surely surpassed their three score years and ten, and it appears they have chosen to use the time remaining to them on this earth completing the straightforward hostel registration procedure. After five minutes fidgeting behind them, damp and uncomfortable, desperate for a shower and a drying room, I'm mouthing obscenities and doing a passable impression of that Edward Munch picture of the man on the pier. And just when I think they must have finished – when they've paid their money, collected their room keys and their sheet sleeping bags, and been treated to a thorough verbal rundown of the hostel facilities – one of them decides she might like to buy something. She pores over the few souvenir items on sale with all the intensity of a Hatton Garden diamond merchant, and eventually settles on a tea towel with pictures of the Lake District and three of those postcards with multiple views on each. She pays for them in painstakingly counted-out copper. I want to knife her very badly.

I christen her Dame Coco for the combination of her voice and her garb. The former bears an uncanny resemblance to that of Dame Edna Everidge, while the latter is less Coco Chanel than Coco the Clown. It's unkind of me to say so I know, but she really is one of the most oddly attired people I've seen in a while. She's wearing a red tartan jacket, three sizes too large for her, a bright green polo-neck, baggy brown and green check trousers disappearing into short boots and the most amazing blue and white hand-knitted tam-o'-shanter. She's accompanied by a man with a white Amish-style beard hanging off the bottom of his chin and one of the largest beer guts I've seen outside of the England Supporters' Club. He's clad in a sweat shirt advertising his country of origin (as if this were necessary) khaki shorts, knee-length off-white socks and sandals. Atop his great brown bald head is another of the weird tam-o'-shanters. This one's yellow. I suspect they have been acquired at some Scottish craft stall, but they have the appearance of objects knitted by a particularly spiteful granny – the sort who takes sadistic pleasure in producing the most bizarre items of clothing for her grandchildren in the sure knowledge that terrorised parents will insist they be worn for fear of offending the old biddy. The third member of the trio is clearly married to Mister Yellow Hat, but she doesn't seem to go with him at all, not least because she is completely tam-o'-shanterless. She is tiny, five foot at most, with a tight knotted perm, a darker shade of black than nature could ever produce, troweled-on make-up, a flowered skirt to her ankles and little beige shoes. She says nothing at all, but constantly peers around in every direction, squinting as if unaccustomed to the light and smiling benignly. The impression is of a minor character, a small nocturnal animal, from a children's story book I once read but have long forgotten.

At last the three move away from the reception counter and I'm able to take their place. I'm a little speedier than they were on the check-in formalities and when I head for the stairs I find that they are still only half way up, effectively blocking my progress. I make it eventually to my room, remove my sodden outer garments and take them down to the drying room in the cellar. They're in front of me again on the narrow stairs. I drop into the members' kitchen to make a cup of tea, and discover that they've arrived there first and are monopolising the kettle. I go back upstairs, and once more they're ahead of me. I gather up some washing and head for the laundry, only to find them feeding coins into the only available washing machine. They are like those very slow-moving lorries that always contrive to be in front of you just as the empty dual carriageway turns to single lane traffic. I cannot begin to understand how they manage to time it so perfectly. By the time dinner is served at seven o'clock, my one aim in life is to gun them all down in cold blood. And guess what? We're sharing a table.

Even before we get to the end of our soup I'm no longer quite so keen to witness the three of them being slowly boiled in oil, and as we scrape the last crumbs of pudding from our plates we're already into exchanging email addresses. This is the youth hostel equivalent of giving out business cards. It doesn't signal any firm intention to communicate in future; just a way of acknowledging that the other person is basically sound and has a right to a continued existence on this planet beyond the end of the current conversation.

Dame Coco is the driving force of the party. She's an exceedingly mature university student who has made up her mind to compensate for the lost years when she was working and raising children, by energetically pitching into every course option and extra-mural activity that might conceivably interest her. The result is a glorious mishmash of politics, art history, literary appreciation, genealogy, psychobabble and mysticism. She has very strong views that are not overly troubled by any requirement for factual accuracy, and I quickly realise that arguing with her is a completely pointless activity.

The itinerary of her tour has been guided by her interests and principles. There have been plenty of the standard tourist stops but she has boycotted all royal palaces because of her disapproval for Prince Charles's treatment of Diana.

'I know what it's like to be on the receiving end of adultery.'

Scotland has been 'done' in three days and consisted of Edinburgh, Loch Ness and Loch Lomond. I long to ask at which of these locations the tam-o'-shanters were acquired, but I'm concerned that I might be unable to conceal my amusement, and I don't want to hurt their feelings. The three have just driven through the Lake District in today's rain, unable to see even the smallest of hills, or to distinguish between road, field and lake, but they pronounce the scenery lovely nevertheless, and they have a tea-towel to prove it. Next up is a day trip to Wales, followed by Cornwall and a search for family roots.

The hostel is full tonight and there are five other men in my bunk room. There's the usual huffing, groaning and farting as we all settle down to sleep. One person seems be going on longer than the rest.

'He's having a good scratch,' I think to myself

The scratching becomes more rhythmical and is punctuated by

small, almost inaudible gasps.

'It's not scratching.'

'Christ! Surely not. Does he think the rest of us are asleep?'

'Perhaps I'm wrong. He may have very bad eczema, I ought to give him the benefit of the doubt.'

'No, I'm not wrong. That isn't scratching.'

The last time I can recall being in a multi-occupancy room when this happened was at the age of fourteen, in a tin hut at a CCF summer camp. But then everyone was at it – if you weren't noisily playing with yourself within thirty seconds of the light going out, people thought there was something wrong with you. Forty years on, it's not really what I expect to encounter. I try to work out which bed the noise is coming from, and conclude that it's probably the chubby fellow with glasses over by the door.

Chapter 7

Next morning the rain has passed, but it's cool and cloudy with a blustery wind. I leave my bike in the hostel cycle shed and step out with my rucksack and boots, a walker once more. There's the small matter of the Kent Estuary to cross before I can make for the Cumbria Coastal Path and from there to the Cumbria Way. I could choose to walk to the nearest road crossing at Sampool Bridge but that would add fifteen miles to my journey and see me backtracking down the other side of the estuary in a southerly direction. The alternative is a five minute rail journey across the estuary viaduct to the station at Grange-over-Sands. This is the option I choose, telling myself that it isn't cheating. I'm not going any further north or east, just a westerly hop, no different to getting the ferry across the Camel estuary in Cornwall. There is a difference though, getting on a train doesn't feel quite right, even if the journey is mainly over water.

The train is thirty minutes late and a rumour passes along the platform that the line is under water somewhere near Manchester – the result of yesterday's heavy rain. I fall into conversation with small mousy woman who is off to serve on a market stall at an Edwardian festival in Grange. In her long dark skirts and lace trimmed blouse she would look very much the part were it not for the blue polyester anorak. She tells me that it's just for the journey. For the rest of the day she'll have to put up with the cold, because she hasn't got any other sort of jacket that would go. She also tells me, in confidence you understand, that she hasn't yet put on her petticoats, but she's not sure they'll offer much in the way of thermal protection. We commiserate with each other about the discomfort of having to spend the day out of doors in such unseasonable weather.

I definitely have the better deal, and I'm soon warmed up as I make my way up the hill from Grange and across the golf course towards Cartmel. This is a very attractive little village, dominated by a lovely priory that dates from the twelfth century and was saved from destruction during the dissolution of the monasteries because the people of the village had nowhere else to worship. It's said that the monks chose to build here because they were told in a vision they should construct their monastery on a site between two streams – one running in a northerly direction and the other southerly. Good job the vision wasn't presented to someone like me. I manage to pass through without noticing either of them.

But I do notice the market square – perfectly proportioned and bordered by thoroughly harmonious buildings with plenty of bright flowers. I notice too that the village shop sells sticky toffee pudding by mail order. Their advert invites purchasers to send one for Valentine's Day, Easter, Mothers' Day or new home celebrations. It seems there's no event, except perhaps a funeral, that can't be enhanced by the gift of a sticky toffee pudding. The product must be popular – there can't be many village shops that employ twenty-five people making puddings, and are able to boast a list of outlets that includes Harvey Nicks and Fortnum and Mason.

The village's second great distinction is possession of the smallest National Hunt racecourse in Britain. It must also be one of the most attractive in the country, surrounded by woods and rugged hills although, judging by the single narrow lane that leads to it, race-day traffic must be an absolute bugger. My route takes me along this lane and I stop to ask directions of an elderly man in a deerstalker hat who is taking car parking money. He directs me towards a white gate on the other side of the racecourse. At least, he tells me, it was white last time he saw it but his eyesight has deteriorated so that all he can do is point in the approximate direction of it. I confirm that I can see the gate, and it is still white. And I thank him and head on my way musing on the misfortune of living in such a pretty place and not being able to see much of it.

From the gate it's very easy going up to Howbarrow and I start to feel that I'm approaching Lakeland proper. I take my last look over the sands of Morecambe Bay and strike off northwards along a path that winds its way between outcrops of rock with idiotic sheep scuttling out of the way in typically panicked fashion. I'm conscious that at lunchtime today the rest of the country will be gearing itself up for the crunch match between England and Denmark in the World Cup. I've seen enough flags of St George over the past three days to strangle a thousand dragons, and I tell myself that I would like to see at least some of the match. The only likely pub stop is at Hatherthwaite, slightly off the route but, if I step out, I figure I can be there by one thirty – just in time for the second half.

By Bigland Tarn I'm on target. It's one o'clock and I judge no more than half an hour's walking to the village. I put on a spurt and I'm striding into Haverthwaite spot on half past one. But there's no pub to be seen. Shit! No people either – they're all inside watching the match. I consider knocking on a door and asking if I can join them, but that would take a deal more cheek than I possess. In the garden of the second to last house I finally locate someone – a woman who has come out to do some gardening as the only way of getting away from her football obsessed family. And what happens? No sooner does she get down to a little peaceful weeding than a wild-eyed walker comes stumping around the bend asking where he can find a pub to watch the rest of the match. She puts me out of my misery. The only pub is the best part of a mile to the east of the village – the direction I don't want to go. Haring over there may allow me to catch the last twenty minutes, assuming they have a television, but it will make for an unwelcome addition to what is already going to be a long day's walk. And I've already made an unnecessary detour off the path just to get here. I retrace my steps back to the path cursing.

Just a minute! There's a pub marked on the map at Greenodd. If I really go like the clappers, I could catch the last ten minutes. And off I go again, striding out with increased vigour, eating up the ground alongside the River Leven. But it's soon clear that unless there's extra time to be played I'm not going to make it. Never mind. At least I can have a drink at Greenodd and watch the highlights.

Another disappointment. There are two pubs in Greenodd and they are both closed. Indeed they look so closed that I actually wonder whether they are still in business. The place is a ghost town. The only signs of life are three young lads orming, scrapping and swearing at each other in a bus shelter. In a spirit of defeat I seek out the score second-hand from them.

It's ridiculous. I'm not big on football or patriotic hysteria. Why am I letting the World Cup hype get to me in this way? Not enough to occupy my mind I guess. I need to keep better control of myself. If I'm not careful I could start getting excited about the Queen's Golden Jubilee tour.

The Cumbria Coastal Path heads off in southerly direction from Greenodd and it's still a few miles before I can pick up the Cumbria Way proper at the southern end of Lake Coniston. Andrew McCloy's book of walking routes from Land's End to John O'Groats suggests a footpath along the banks of the river Crake. Well, there is a footpath, but it's shockingly overgrown. After a mile of fighting my way through waist-high vegetation, cursing the entire McCloy clan, I return to the lane on the eastern side of the river. It's almost free of traffic and makes for very pleasant walking. I plod on past the pleasant villages of Spark Bridge and Lowick Bridge – once thriving little cotton spinning centres – until at last I see the waters of Lake Coniston glinting through the trees.

I've been to the Lake District a number of times, but never to Coniston, which is strange because it holds a very special place in my childhood memory. Like many thousands of my generation and earlier, I grew up with the books of Arthur Ransome, a number of which were set on and around this lake. I read them all several times over, even on occasions starting again at the beginning of a book as soon as the last page was turned. No other writer quite did it for me like Ransome and, even now almost fifty years on, I'm able to identify landmarks that featured in my favourite stories. There is Wild Cat Island, it's called Peel Island on my map. And there's the promontory on the other side of the lake where the Swallows planned their first adventure. Somewhere off to my left shrouded in mist is Kanchenjunga, aka The Old Man of Coniston.

Ransome, a native of Leeds, attended a preparatory school in the Lake District and visited the area regularly on holiday. But it was not until later life, after a number of years abroad as the Manchester Guardian's foreign correspondent, that he came to live here and to write the books for which he is famous. Much of what went into them was drawn from his own childhood holiday experiences.

It's hard to put my finger on what was so special about books that featured a bunch of privileged pre-war kids who spent their hols sailing jolly dinghies on northern lakes while communicating in the most frightfully buttoned-up nautical language. They were certainly a million miles away from my own childhood experiences, but I guess at root the characters and the situations were believable. Ransome's adventures were not like Blyton's, my other childhood staple. They didn't involve children defeating evil, deformed or foreign adult baddies in mysterious castles on deserted islands. Essentially the Ransome adventures were concocted, just like ours, by the children themselves out of ordinary situations, and those who appeared to be adult baddies generally turned out to be just ordinary people going about their business. The great magic of Ransome was his ability to create adventure out of the mundane.

I was anything but a nautical child. In fact my boating experience was confined to the occasional pedalo and those smelly little self-drive motor craft that were to be found chugging around shallow, dirty concrete edged lakes at seaside resorts. They always had a car-type steering wheel and a little metal arrow on the prow that turned with the movement of the wheel to indicate the direction of travel. Invariably the arrow pointed in a completely different direction to that on which the boat was set, but this didn't matter too much because, even with the accelerator pedal pushed to the floor, performance was distinctly more sea slug than swordfish.

My first encounter with these vessels was at the age of five when my elder brother took me on one at a boating lake in Bridlington. I'm not sure which aspect of the technology caused him the greater difficulty: whether it was the unreliability of the little metal arrow or lack of understanding that at some point he would need to remove his foot from the accelerator pedal, but he proved completely incapable of returning the boat to the landing stage when our number was called. Time and again we approached the ruddy-faced boat owner, leaning out with a boat hook and shouting urgent instructions, only to veer way at the last moment leaving him thrashing at empty air. I know my brother wasn't doing it deliberately. He became increasingly anxious with each pass, to the point that he had to take one hand off the wheel to clutch the front of his trousers, as he tried desperately to respond to the pond-side exhortations. Towards the end he even had to contend with advice from a five-year-old who was convinced he could make a better job of driving. The rest of my family, meanwhile, developed a sudden and much more pressing interest in what was happening on the crazy golf course. The saga only ended when the boat ran out of petrol and the owner came out in waders to pull us back to the bank.

By the age of eight, fired up by the Ransome books, I fantasised about owning a boat and pestered my mother until she succumbed. Well, it wasn't quite the sleek clinker-built vessel I coveted, but the best I was likely to achieve in the circumstances – a cheap blue plastic lilo by mail order from the Headquarters and General Supplies advert in the Saturday *Daily Mirror*. The expenditure was justified on the basis that, when not doing service as an ocean going racer, the object could double as a guest bed if anyone came to stay.

At least I could sit on it and float along; in that respect alone it had the attributes I was seeking. I christened it *Swallow* and took it for an inaugural voyage on the children's outdoor swimming pool next to the seafront at Southsea. My sister and I paddled out into the middle, sitting astride it, with me calling out 'Belay'. 'Ready About' and other nautical sounding instructions. We were swiftly engulfed by a swarm of other kids who appeared oblivious to our *Swallows and Amazons* re-enactment. This was probably the first plastic airbed ever launched into that shabby 1950s pool, and everyone wanted to climb onto it. Our efforts at repelling boarders were pathetically inadequate and within five minutes the thing was hopelessly punctured – large rips along both sides. Despite my best efforts with Sellotape and Elastoplast it never again took to the seas and I spent a long time living down the charge of 'not looking after it.' In my mother's catalogue of possible wrongdoing, 'not looking after things' fell somewhere between heinous and despicable – the effect of years of scrimping, I suspect. Unlike other naughtiness it was not a crime for which you could serve your sentence and be forgiven. Incidents of 'not looking after things' could be resurrected as evidence in quite unrelated cases, months or even years after the event.

Arriving at Coniston feels as if it should be the end of the day's walk, but it isn't. The lake is second only in length to Windermere, and the village of Coniston, my destination for the night, is right at the top. What's more, the path is hard going, winding its way along a pretty lumpy shoreline. It takes me nearly two and a half hours to work my way from the bottom end of the lake to the top, and it's almost half past seven when I finally drag myself up the hostel driveway, desperate to clean up and get something to eat.

This youth hostel is heaving – walkers, climbers, and hordes of foreign students – but it's not the most welcoming of overnight stops. The washroom floor shows every sign of having been recently visited by a troupe of exuberant seals – surely mere humans cannot splash so much water around. And there's a distinct smell of vomit along the top corridor. Downstairs, the lounge has about as much character as an accident and emergency waiting room. There are slippery, plastic upholstered chairs arranged geometrically, and only leaflet holders to decorate the walls. Inmates move around the room in a desultory fashion, lighting on this leaflet or that and then perching for a few minutes and engaging in snatches of pointless conversation. The exception is a group of young teachers who have come here on a mountain leadership course. They have dragged their chairs into a revolutionary circle and are earnestly hanging onto the pearls of wisdom being dispensed by their instructor – a smug, frog-faced man about my age. He's treating them, and anyone else within earshot, to a scathing assessment of trainees he has worked with previously:

'People who are new to the hills do the oddest things. I have to spend a lot of my time educating them, changing their point of view. And it's not just the younger ones. There was this old bloke last week, nearly seventy. He'd learned that things get wet in rucksacks, and so he put all his things in carrier bags. When he opened his rucksack he had six Tesco bags. They're on a different planet some of them. The older ones especially. It's because they matured in the 1950s rather than the 60s.'

I ask you! What's wrong with keeping things dry in carrier bags? My rucksack's full of them. I don't understand how it brands me as a hiking inadequate. OK, you can buy a fancy waterproof rucksack cover or a polythene liner, but carrier bags come free. Might as well put them to some continued practical purpose. It's a lot better than letting them blow around the countryside and get stuck up trees for years on end – tattered and waving in the wind like witches' knickers.

And another thing, why so much stick for people who matured in the fifties? What was it about the decade that he feels served them so badly? Was it Suez? Did the final humiliation of Britain's world power aspirations leave them with identity crises that turned outwardly well-adjusted individuals into covert carrier bag people? In addition to a tendency to carry their belongings in Tesco freebies, might we also expect them to prefer cardboard boxes to sleeping bags and a drop of meths to the campfire cocoa? And was it only the brazen pop-fuelled confidence of the 1960s that rescued the next generation from a similar fate? What a plonker! I've taken a strong dislike to him.

To escape his boring drone and because my stomach is shouting even more loudly than my knees, I escape the hostel for what in normal circumstances would be a gentle stroll down to the pub in the village. Now that I've really stiffened up it feels like something that, had anyone else inflicted it upon me, would have warranted action under the International Convention on Human Rights.

The pub is full and I'm lucky to grab the last seat at a tiny table by the bar. Those who pile in afterwards have to stand. They're a strange assortment of sturdy-booted walkers and whippety-thin cycling types alongside glum caravanners and overweight weekend trippers. There's Donald Campbell memorabilia all around the walls – photos, news clippings and so on – all testament to the ill-fated 1960s Coniston attempt on the world water speed record. It's a subject that has been given added currency recently by the operation to salvage the wreck of Bluebird from the bed of the lake, recover Campbell's remains and attempt to work out the cause of the accident. Campbell and Bluebird are clearly important selling points for Coniston. One of the local beers is called Bluebird bitter. I drink two pints, hoping that it isn't named for its tendency to explode and go straight to the bottom.

There are eight men in my hostel room. Two are already asleep when I get back at half past ten. One by one the rest return and all get undressed in the dark. There is the inevitable snorer, but thankfully no wankers – at least not in the literal sense – but I do believe the frog-faced man is in here somewhere.

In the morning we all get up in complete silence. Not a word. Not even the hint of a word. It's as if everyone wants to preserve a sem-blance of the privacy that is so patently lacking. The bloke from the top bunk has his big hairy bum a foot from my face when I first open my eyes.

The silence continues over breakfast. I'm on a table with three others – all from my room. My attempts to whistle up a bit of conver-sation are run into the sand. One man who has so far responded with 'eh?' to all my other utterances at least manages to tell me what the weather forecast is – rain clearing by lunchtime and returning later in the day – but beyond that there is nothing to be said.

120

I'm sitting on a bench in the hostel porch donning my boots and waterproofs, and next to me a group of Japanese students is preparing for a day on the hills. High heeled boots and ordinary raincoats: it's somewhat inadequate weather gear, and they are conscious of it. One girl points to the flimsy footwear of her companion:

'I think your shoes are not the best to climbing a mountain.'

It puts me in mind of my own time as a young, single teacher of English to overseas students. Group weekend walking trips were, I discovered, an excellent way to chat up au-pairs. On a five hour trek, even somebody as socially inept as I was could manage a reasonable amount of small talk. The downside was that the most desirable individuals always seemed to arrive dressed for the catwalk rather than the cattle track. There followed the inevitable recriminations as mohair jumpers were snagged on barbed wire fences, designer boots were ruined crossing muddy ditches and city smart rainwear was exposed as a triumph of style over practicality. I was always left chatting to the plain but sturdy outdoor types with the corduroy trousers that made a rhythmical 'riffruff' sound from their thighs rubbing together as they walked, while the pretty ones I had my eye on sulked and dragged their feet at the rear of the party.

The rain stops shortly after I leave Coniston and I have a very pleasant day's walking, albeit along the rather meandering course that this stage of the Cumbria Way follows. There are more direct routes to where I am going but they would involve a fair amount of road walking, so I'm happy to go with the long distance path planners. For quite lengthy periods I hardly see a soul and then suddenly there are dozens. Inevitably the increase points to the presence of a car park. Tarn Howes is a particularly popular spot. This Lakeland jewel of a thousand place mats boasts an ice-cream van flogging overpriced cornets to shivering people who carry them back to their cars, from which they are best able to consider the view: blankly, evenly through the windscreen, mesmerically licking, engine running, blower on.

I'm pleased to find that, even after yesterday's marathon, my legs feel quite strong and my feet are intact. The boots that caused me so much trouble at the start of the walk have been left to fester in Falmouth, the St Ives impulse purchase has been put down to experience, and I'm wearing the ones I purchased specifically for the trip. I've discovered, a little late in the proceedings, that your feet swell considerably when you are covering long distances every day, and footwear that may feel loose to start off with soon becomes quite snug. Anything that is tight at the outset is a disaster.

The going is very muddy in places and I keep meeting people trying to tread gingerly around the bad bits or turning back defeated. But I gaily splash through, confident in the knowledge that nothing is going to get through my waterproof Brasher boots. I think I'm starting to fall in love with them.

And at last I've found the answer to a question I posed myself back in Cornwall. On some popular cliff top locations there was a commemorative bench every few yards, and I wondered what else one might dedicate to a departed loved-one. Well, here in the Lake District they've cracked it. Gates. Yes, honestly, gates. If you want to celebrate the life of a deceased countryside lover, you can pay for a gate in one of their favourite locations, complete with a little plaque and the usual dedications. Once I've got over the incongruity of it, I decide it's a pretty good idea. Gates serve an essential purpose. They are doubtless expensive to maintain and replace, and they're less obtrusive than benches. I resolve to have a gate when I die – one of those that's really hard to open and springs back on your ankles before you're halfway through.

After two nights in youth hostels I'm ready for a bit of comfort and I've resolved that my destination for the day will be the Old Dungeon Ghyll Hotel at the head of the Langdale Valley. It's not as far as I would like to walk, only about eleven miles in total, but there's not much alternative. Beyond the hotel there's no accommodation until you get into Borrowdale, about three hours hard walking further on. Anyway, I like the idea of staying at this famous old hotel. The building has occupied its beautiful location for around three hundred years. Previously it was a farm and an inn, but even as a hotel it retained some farming activity right up to 1949. The Climbers' Bar is a converted cattle shed, and still has the cattle stalls intact.

In the days when horse-drawn charabancs brought visitors up the narrow lane from Little Langdale, they would stop at the top of Blea Tarn Pass and sound the horn as a signal for hotel staff to start preparing food – the number of horn blasts indicting how many passengers the hotel should expect. Fortunately I don't have to resort to these methods, my mobile phone has done the trick for me.

And I'm pleased by the knowledge that there's a bed booked and ready for me. It has started to rain heavily over the last half hour of my journey and the terrain up here is pretty exposed.

The hotel is warm and comfortable with bags of character. It has been a Mecca for climbing clubs since the 1930s and all the big names in British climbing have stayed here. It's nice to think that my room might well have been occupied by the likes of Sir John Hunt or Chris Bonnington. There aren't any famous climbers staying tonight, at least I don't think so, but there is a group that is running the Coast to Coast Way for charity – four strapping blokes who don't look like runners at all and their support team, the mother of one, two wives and a girlfriend.

Overnight I'm wakened several times by the sound of torrential rain and howling winds, and in the morning it's still blowing a gale with ominous skies, although the rain has eased somewhat. My route today should take me across Stakes Pass, the second highest part of the Cumbria Way, and on to Keswick. As I take my shower I've already convinced myself that a trip over the tops isn't really a starter in this weather. But there isn't much in the way of alternatives. I either stick with the present path or put up with a substantially longer journey to Keswick involving some retracing of steps and a fair bit of road walking. Amazingly, as I'm getting dressed, the sun comes out briefly. I'm the last down to breakfast – the coast to coast runners were on their way by eight. The waitress brings me enough spare bacon to make a sandwich for lunch, and a weather forecast that promises gale force winds on the fells but only light rain, and that clearing later. I decide to stick with Plan A.

The upper end of the Langdale Valley is strikingly beautiful, and curiously familiar. I realise that the scene I have in front of me was once a feature of my school geography book – illustrating the classic effects of glacial action. I stop to take a photograph and manage to leave my precious map behind on the path.

I'm becoming quite concerned about this increased tendency towards absent mindedness. I'm forever putting things down and failing to remember what I did with them. I've run over two pairs of glasses in the last six months – left them on top of the car while attending to some loading task and then driven away, returning later to crush them under the wheels. It very nearly happened on a third occasion, but this time the sun was out and the reflection on the road caught my eye just in time.

And what about the time I spend searching for things I've mis-placed? I reckon twenty minutes a day would be a fairly conservative estimate. That's 120 hours a year, the equivalent of three weeks full time work. Over an adult life of, say, sixty years, I'm going to spend around three and a half years of full time employment just looking for things. Blimey!

But perhaps I ought to be comforted by Harvard professor and world memory expert Daniel Schacter. He claims that some of the most frustrating memory lapses are not so much products of a flawed system, more indicators of the strengths of memory. Absent minded memory errors arise from our ability to perform routine activities on autopilot – a facility that allows us simultaneously to give our atten-tion to other matters without having the memory cluttered by unnec-essary information. My failure to recollect that I put my map down when I stopped to take a photograph isn't so much a case of forgetting, more that I never committed that detail to memory in the first place. It can be immensely frustrating but, says Schacter, the benefits of a memory system that filters out unnecessary detail may far outweigh the disadvantages.

That's all very well, but the map was considerably more important than the photograph. And my compass was in the folder too. These paths require some navigation. Without them I could lose my way entirely.

I turn back cursing and full of anxiety, my head filled with visions of myself lost on the fells, being rooted out by a mountain rescue team who hold up to ridicule my lack of appropriate route-finding gear.

I've hardly gone any distance when a statuesque girl who has been overhauling me rapidly waves my map folder at me.

'I thought it had to belong to someone who had passed by just recently.'

She shrugs at my pathetic murmurings of gratitude and powers on her way. She is stunningly fit, six foot two with long, long legs that carry her over the ground at a quite remarkable speed. I'm not one to hang about, and I can't recall anyone overtaking me previously, but within a few minutes of her passing me she's a good quarter of a mile ahead, and clambering off towards one of the less accessible peaks.

Wow! I feel like a grey-flannelled wimp on a pootle in the park.

There's a stiffish climb to the top of Stakes Pass but nothing too demanding. It's very windy at the top but there's no difficulty in finding the path. A trio of middle-aged Americans following the same route as me come huffing along behind as I stop for a rest. We engage in the usual conversation – where we come from, what we do for a living, how long we are spending walking the Cumbria Way. I've had this conversation so many times already, that I'm beginning to think it might be worth preparing a typed résumé I can hand out to people – the easier to move rapidly to more interesting topics of conversation.

Borrowdale is even more beautiful than Langdale. It's so lovely it makes you want to cry. I slither down the stony path, my eyes fixed on the view. A bit more attention to where my feet are going might be advisable. I slip, and land heavily on my side – hip and elbow making painful contact with hard rock. As I pick myself up. I feel a worrying wetness seeping through my clothes. Blood? No, just water. I've managed to burst my water bottle in the fall. Apparently it can cope with John Prescott sitting on it, but perhaps not playing hopscotch on it.

This is first day since the West Country when I've needed my hiking stick. Everybody seems to have one, and I certainly find mine handy on the steep descents: reduces the impact on the knees, and provides an extra point of stability. Some people have two, which strikes me as a bit posey, maybe because they tend to be the same people who carry GPS systems and wear red knee-length socks. Most ridiculous are those who use a pair of sticks along completely flat surfaces – even on tarmacked roads, propelling themselves along like cross-country skiers.

The afternoon passes amongst austere crags, waterfalls, beautiful woods, lush valleys and a peaceful lake. Derwentwater is both prettier and easier walking than Coniston. I'm feeling light-headed and at one with the universe as I drift the last mile into Keswick.

The youth hostel is full, but I'm not overly perturbed. Keswick has plenty of B&Bs and I easily light upon a double en suite above a slightly tatty café for eighteen quid. With breakfast, that's only just over three pounds more than the hostel and it comes without snorers or wet washrooms. True, the place has a rather bizarre decor – livid red flow-ered walls and an astonishing metallic gold shower curtain – but there's a telly (volume control stuck on high), a kettle with a six inch flex that plugs in down by the bathroom door and two packets of custard creams. Sir John Hunt probably didn't stay here, but I'm sure he would have gone for it like a shot if it had been located on the foothills of Everest.

I like Keswick – pleasant town gardens, nice-looking theatre and a lovely lakeside outlook. I have smoked trout with a reasonable selection of vegetables for a remarkable £4.90 in the Oddfellows Arms. It's not the most stunning meal I've ever eaten but what can you expect for that? In the corner a slab-faced woman from Hartlepool is explaining the sweet menu to her wild-eyed mother-in-law.

'You can have sticky toffee pudding.'

'Stick it up me what?'

And later 'Where are we going tomorrow Brenda, Keswick?'

'No Mum, this is Keswick. We're going to Kendal.'

'There's a Boots there, isn't there?'

'There's a Boots here Mum.'

'Yes, but not like that one. That's a big un.'

My cheap B&B serves me a gargantuan breakfast – the biggest I've had to date – two eggs, two rashers of bacon, sausage, mushroom, beans, hash browns, tomatoes. And for once I have to say it's not bad. There's even decent fresh coffee. Of course, this fried stuff is useless fuel for a heavy day's walking but it keeps the hunger pangs at bay during the strenuous pull out of Keswick towards Skiddaw.

Three sheep dog owners are putting their dogs through their paces on the hills. I'll readily admit that the only attention I ever previously paid to this sort of activity was to leap for the off switch whenever the opening titles for *One Man and His Dog* started to roll. But I'm well impressed. The dog and sheep are a third of a mile away across the valley. One whistle for left, a different sound for right. The dog responds immediately. And so it goes on – look back, stop, creep forward. The control is quite amazing. The sheep look thoroughly pissed off as first one dog and then another is sent across to use them for practice.

Skiddaw House Youth Hostel has to be one of the most remote in the country. There's not another building to be seen in any direction – just bog, hills and sky. When I put my head around the hostel door to ask if I can fill my water bottle the warden jumps about a foot into the air. After she has recovered her composure, she tells me the water is off the mountain and not guaranteed for drinking, but I fill up anyway even though she offers to let me boil some. She says she volunteered for a stint here because she loves solitude, but all the same seems pleased for the chance to talk. It's nice to find a youth hostel that is true to the original spirit of the movement. No car drivers here. Everybody including the warden arrives on foot – a five mile walk from Keswick. The only motorised access is a weekly visit by a quad bike delivering supplies.

For the next couple of hours I don't see a soul. The path is a quagmire in places and there's a tough climb alongside Grainsgill Beck up to Carrock Moor, but the view from High Pike at 660 metres is wonderful. This is the highest point on the Cumbria Way and I can see across to the Solway Firth and the hills of southern Scotland. Then, quite suddenly, the Lake District is at an end, and it's a different kind of hill I bounce down to Caldbeck – rounded contours, springy turf. There are disused mines by the dozen – lead and copper.

My destination for the night is the Oddfellows Arms (is this becoming a habit?). The rooms in a converted mill at the back of the pub are excellent and the food's pretty good too. I'm eating my eastern lamb casserole when a film crew comes in. – eleven of them, all flush-faced and full of it, ready for a few drinks and something to eat after a hard day in the field. It's always been a mystery to me why they need so many people to make a film. There are no actors in this group, just the crew. The director is instantly recognisable with his close-cropped grey hair and anorak that resembles Joseph's coat of many colours. The rest of the ensemble appears to be in orbit around him. Foremost among his planets is the assistant director – green wellies and arms full of different coloured ring binders. She immediately launches into an inventory with a skinny cameraman – checking off what they've put in the can today, what's gone to the labs, what they are going to be doing tomorrow. The sound team lurk quietly on the fringes, staring into their beer glasses, checking their levels. Then there are the beefy guys in fleeces and sagging jeans – an inch or so of topside rump protruding between the two. Best boys? gaffers? People included on the crew just to make the credits list longer and more impressive? And so it goes, down the pecking order until we get to Rob. It is an indication of Rob's status that, while the rest are downing pints and tucking into hearty meals, he is sent out to guard the Range Rover because there's a camera in it. God knows, in this sleepy little village, what opportunist thief is going to look inside a Range Rover and decide that what he really needs is a couple of stone of professional movie gear – unless of course it's that furtive guy in the corner who's just heard the director announce its presence to everyone in earshot.

I can tell that I've been on my own too long now. I've started trying to date the bathroom suites I find in my B&Bs. No, it's not as bad as you think – just an attempt to work out how old they are from their colour. It's the absence of any serious mental stimulation, I'm sure. Today's suite is avocado – that means 1983 unless I'm mistaken. Yesterday's was pink – circa 1972 I think. I'm hoping for a 1979 burgundy before the trip is out, and if I'm really lucky, a 1985 brown. Such a shame that future generations of bathroom spotters will be denied this thrill if the current preference for boring old white isn't soon overthrown.

At breakfast two cyclists who arrived latish last night are tucking in at the next table. They're in their late sixties, bald and wiry, and as brown as nuts. They remind me of two lithe sand lizards. And they're also doing the Land's End to John O'Groats trip but in the opposite direction to me. They tell me they are following a route recommended by the ACC or the CCA or the CAC or some other three letter abbreviation that stands for a cycling association with which they assume I have, at the very least, a paid up life membership. I've never heard of it, but I simulate familiarity with a smile and a knowing 'Oh Yes.' They've taken a meandering route down through Scotland, including some of the Western Isles, and they're knocked out by the friendliness they've encountered along the way. For some reason I can't quite ascertain, they are also tremendously impressed by the Highland Co-ops which have provided for their every need. I obligingly promise to look in on some Co-ops as I travel north.

Before leaving Caldbeck I take a walk around the pretty little church of St Kentigern. This chap, also known as St Mungo, was born around 518 AD and has been credited with founding the community that became Glasgow. His mother was a princess of Northumbria who fell pregnant at a tender age following the unwelcome attentions of a prince from Strathclyde. Her father showed only limited parental sympathy for her plight, ordering her to be thrown over a cliff and, when that failed to kill her, to be cast adrift in an open boat. But, against the odds, both she and the child survived. This early brush with death must have convinced Kentigern of his durability because, at the age of twenty-two, he agreed to become the Bishop of Strathclyde after the previous incumbent was murdered. He managed to hold down the job for thirteen years and was pretty devout – reputedly reciting the Book of Psalms every day while standing up to his neck in Scottish rivers. Such antics were clearly popular with his flock and a community grew up around him which became known as Clasgu (dear family).

But after all that, how did Kentigern wind up in the Lake District? Well, in 553 he fell foul of a new king of Strathclyde who was poorly disposed towards Christians and he was forced to take his ministry elsewhere – first to Wales and then to the Lake District. He finally returned to Glasgow in 581.

So that's the origin of St Kentigern's church in Caldbeck. Around the back there's a well which is believed to mark the site of his original sixth century chapel.

But the church has other claims to fame. It's also the burial place of John Peel and the Maid of Buttermere. John Peel was a local farmer whose life would have passed into obscurity had it not been for the song written by his friend and hunting companion John Woodcock Graves. The two were sitting boozing and recounting hunting stories one night in the mid 1820s when Graves was inspired to write the song to the tune of a lullaby being sung to one of his children in the next room. He wrote down the words there and then, and when he had finished said, ' By Jove, Peel! You'll be sung when both of us are run to earth.'

But the song was far from being an instant hit. Indeed, it would have remained unknown had it not been reworked and included in a book of Cumberland songs and ballads produced some twelve years after Peel's death. This prompted a man called William Metcalfe to change the tune from the rather dirge-like original to the version that everyone knows. So there you have it – different tune, different words, such is immortality.

The huntsman's grave isn't hard to find; it's been recently restored in brilliant white and stands out like a sore thumb from the rest. I'm staggered to discover that this ordinary person-sized plot contains not just the man himself and his wife Mary, but eleven of their thirteen children: they must be packed in like sardines down there. When the last trump sounds and the graves give up their dead it'll be like watching the successful conclusion of one of those Guiness Book of Records phone box cramming attempts.

A group of middle-aged women have come looking for the grave at the same time as me and, when they find it, they gather round and strike up a fluting rendering of 'D'ye Ken John Peel with his coat so grey.' I guess this is a pretty common occurrence, but the grave hasn't always been treated with such respect. In 1977 a group of anti-hunting protestors set about it with hammers, cracking the headstone, and dug a hole into which they threw a fox's head. I have never been a supporter of blood sports, but I can't think of a more prattish way to reduce sympathy in your cause.

My final homage before leaving this little churchyard is to Mary Robinson, the Maid of Buttermere, whose story has been fictionalised in Melvyn Bragg's book of the same name. She was a celebrated beauty whose parents kept the Inn at Buttermere during the 1790s. Her famed looks attracted the admiration of tourists of the time, including our old friends Wordsworth and Coleridge, and her reputation spread far and wide. In 1802 a dashing gentleman calling himself Colonel Hope, MP for Linlithgow, stayed at the Inn and was immediately smitten with Mary, as she with him. Only after they were married, an event that occurred in double quick time, did it emerge that the groom was a fraudster and bigamist, by the name of John Hatfield, who had been impersonating Colonel Hope in an effort to seduce another young woman, and get his hands on her loot. The resulting scandal had all the ingredients of a latter-day tabloid frenzy. Hatfield went on the run but was eventually detained in Swansea and brought to Carlisle Assizes where he was tried and sentenced to hang – the job being delegated to an inexperienced hangman who had to be shown how best to position the noose by the condemned man.

Despite the nefarious objective of Hatfield's foray into the Lake District, he remained constant in his declarations of love for Mary. Ironically, had she not been so well known, the marriage might well have escaped the notice of the newspapers, and his deception remained concealed.

After Hatfield's death, Mary married a local man and together they kept the Inn at Buttermere for many years. They moved back to

Caldbeck in later life and that is how she wound up in this quiet little churchyard. What drama in such a peaceful place. I think I had better move on before I uncover anything else.

The path strikes off through the woodland of Parsons's Park. It's very muddy in places and the going is slow. Ominously, the map shows a place up ahead called Bog Bridge, but by the time I get there the ground is as hard as a rock.

I pass through a field that has been laid out for a gymkhana. It's incongruously full of sheep which skitter away at my presence. Some of them make as if to run at the fences and, for a moment, I'm confronted by a bizarre vision of them saddled and bridled, each bearing a plump little rider with freckles and a hard hat. I'm puzzled by sheep. You'd think after all the millennia of domesticity they'd be used to having human beings around. Why they have to scatter in abject panic whenever anybody walks through or past their field is beyond me. And always they crap themselves as they run. They must spend their entire lives running away and crapping themselves. Sheep! I hate the things, they're so unutterably stupid. I can't stop myself shouting at them and berating them for their silliness.

By the time I get to Dalston the beauties of the Lake District are dwindling to a memory. I follow a bland cycle track between railway and river, past a Nestlé factory that is making an urgent attempt to establish its environmental credentials. Notices by the path tell the user about its campaign to plant 35,000 willow saplings which will take up excess water, improve the quality of the surroundings and encourage songbirds. The cynic in me wonders what havoc they have wreaked in the past that they need to be so publicly embarking on this.

As I arrive in Carlisle the riverside path suddenly stops and deposits me in a terraced street with cobbles. At the end of it there is one of those wonderful old-fashioned hardware shops that used to be everywhere – the sort that dispensed Aladdin Pink Paraffin from a hand operated pump with a permanent paraffin sheen, via diverse metal jugs and funnels, to the can you had brought with you. Ah! I can smell the stuff now. And did any of those cans ever have a lid that fitted properly? Ours never did. The return journey home was always accompanied by the steady dribble of Aladdin Pink down your leg and into your sock.

131

Chapter 8

A quick train trip to Arnside via Lancaster and I'm reunited with my bike. Boots and rucksack once more crammed onto the back rack, I leave Carlisle via the A7 in the direction of Longtown, sailing past a petulant line of slow moving vehicles that fizzles and spits behind a horse-drawn caravan driven by a 'couldn't give a monkeys' girl with dreadlocks and a nose ring.

At Longtown I cut back in a westerly direction along a minor road and, after a little while, the Scottish border pops out at me from behind a tree. Just a short distance further on is the village of Gretna Green. Incredibly, this place lays claim to being the second most visited tourist location in Scotland (Edinburgh Castle is the first), but it's just a totally anonymous, not even attractive, one-trick village with its ridiculous raison d'être plumb in the middle of it.

It's all down to a piece of legislative disparity in 1754. The Marriage Act introduced that year in England sought to do away with the irregular marriage trade. It required that all marriages be recognised by the church and that weddings of people under the age of twenty-one could only occur with parental consent. In Scotland, however, the law remained unchanged. Anybody over the age of sixteen could marry, parental consent or not, and they could do so simply by declaring their intention in front of two witnesses. And so Gretna Green took advantage of its location. As the first village beyond the most southerly section of the Scottish border, and sitting as it did on the main route north, it was uniquely positioned to take advantage of the brisk trade that developed from those who had been unsuccessful in gaining parental blessing and had convinced themselves they were unable to wait around until such time as it wasn't required. A number of enterprising individuals established themselves in the business of conducting on-demand weddings from various houses and inns around the village, and one of these locations was the village smithy located at the coaching road junction. In time it emerged as the most noted of all the irregular wedding venues, and those who conducted the short, sharp ceremonies came to be known as anvil priests. They were, by all accounts, a pretty unsavoury bunch and had nothing in the way of qualification for their duties other than a general readiness to drop everything and conduct ceremonies at any time of the day or night – for there was often an angry father or brother with a gun up his vest in hot pursuit – and sufficient command of English to ask a couple of simple questions in front of witnesses hauled from their beds in neighbouring houses. These irregular weddings continued for almost two hundred years until they were outlawed in 1940.

However, the inhabitants of Gretna Green were not going to let a change in the law get in the way of their main industry. They still knock out weddings at around two thousand a year, although these days they're conducted according to the same rules as the rest of the UK. On this weekday lunchtime there's one in full flow and another party fidgeting by the door awaiting their turn. I just can't understand why anyone would want to subject themselves to this – jostling with coach-trip pensioners in the gift shop, being ushered into the Wedding Suite by living impersonations of Action Man in kilts, then back to the pensioner melee before posing for photos beneath a hideously twee little arch fashioned from horseshoes or in front of the sculpture of a naked couple embracing. Yucko!

Still, there are plenty who seem to like it, so who am I to scoff. One of the past customers was our old chum John Peel from the Caldbeck churchyard. At the age of twenty he fell in love with the eighteen-year-old daughter of a neighbouring farmer and, when her parents vetoed the marriage, he spirited her out of her bedroom window at midnight and rode off with her to Gretna Green. Despite the unpropitious start, it was a marriage that lasted for fifty-seven years.

I notice from my map that the village of Lockerbie is quite close, and I actually think about visiting it. My only reason, of course, is that a sabotaged airliner came down there, I wouldn't give it a second thought otherwise. I know the place from a thousand televised images and the motivation to go there is simply to look at where it happened. It's nothing more than an excursion into other people's misery and, when I think of it like that, I'm ashamed of myself for even considering it. I quickly decide that I won't go there, after all.

I was recently reading an article by a resident of Dunblane who pointed out that, six years after the event, minibus-loads of people still turn up at the site of the massacre to weep and hold each other up. She described them as 'strangers in a town they think they know'. For these visitors Dunblane is solely defined by the dreadful events of 1996, whereas for all its residents it has to remain a living, breathing community with a past and a future, and not just a symbol of wickedness fixed in the nation's consciousness by thirty minutes of lunacy.

So Lockerbie is off my itinerary. But here's an interesting question – how long does it take before you cease to be a ghoul and become simply a tourist visiting a site of historic significance? Dunblane is out but Drogheda and Glencoe are fine. But then what about the twin towers? Only a year or so after the event, the site is a major place of pilgrimage. And if you can't visit in person, there are websites that purport to offer tribute to the dead by letting you take a virtual tour through the buildings as they were before September 11 and even leave your name in the visitors' book. Now if that's not ghoulish, I don't know what is.

I take the B724 along the Solway Firth through Gretna (not the same as Gretna Green) and Eastriggs. These townships had the most curious of origins during the First World War. They were secretly built to house thirty thousand workers bought in from all over the world to staff a huge new munitions-producing facility. This was the government's response in 1915 to a severe armaments crisis that was threatening Britain's ability to prosecute the war. So secret was the project that the towns were known only by a code name. Fifteen thousand construction workers were involved in building them, and the drunkenness and disorder they brought with them became so great that the government took over direct ownership and management of all the pubs from Annan to Carlisle. But the new townships were not merely slung up in haste as you might expect. They were designed with thought and care by leading architects of the time, and included shops, schools, churches, pubs and dancehalls. It makes you wonder how long the government expected the war to last. The munitions factory complex was one of the biggest in the world, stretching over a distance of almost nine miles. When it was fully up and running it produced more 'devils porridge' – the explosive paste from which cordite was produced – than all the existing plants put together. More than a thousand tons of cordite a week was packed into shells and cartridges at the complex.

A few miles further on I pass through the village of Ruthwell, home of the world's first savings bank. The building from which it was run is a small whitewashed cottage in a road of nondescript modern bungalows. I'm afraid that I can't summon up much enthusiasm for savings banks, old or new, so I don't bother to stop, but I wonder, as I pedal on, why it is that we feel compelled to celebrate the first of everything, no matter how dull? I'm sure that somewhere in Britain there must be a plaque commemorating the first bus shelter, the first traffic island, the first commemorative plaque even.

I do stop at Brow Well. My guidebook tells me that Robbie Burns took the waters here shortly before his death in 1796. Well, rather him than me. If the supposedly health-giving contents were anything like the murky, greenish-tinged liquid that lurks in there today then I suggest that the ill-judged drink could have been what killed him.

Dumfries has made an industry out of Robbie Burns. There's the Robbie Burns Tea Rooms, the Robbie Burns Museum, the Robbie Burns Mausoleum and much else besides. That's all pretty good going since he only lived here for the last five years of his life. He took a job as an excise man after a distinct lack of success as a farmer, and busied himself seeking out evidence of tax evasion on goods like brandy, beer and whiskey. It was during this period too that he wrote Auld Lang Syne, which is rather ironic given the alcohol-fuelled celebrations to which this verse has been an accompaniment ever since. When Burns died at the age of 37 he was buried in a simple grave in St Michael's churchyard, but in 1815 he was dug up again and moved to an elaborate and hideous mausoleum on the other side of the churchyard, and he has occupied this less than des res ever since.

I light upon Dumfries as my stopping point for the night and start to seek out some suitable accommodation. There are three comfortable looking guest houses across the river from the town centre – nice outlook, pleasantly green surroundings. One of these will do. I knock on the door of the right-hand house. There's no reply. I try again. Still no response. After the third knock I give up. On the doorstep of the middle house a French couple are trying to arrange a room for the night. They seem to be having a little difficulty. I'll give that one a miss. The third hostelry is the Haven Guesthouse. A heavily made-up lady in her seventies comes to the door and gives me a look I can only describe as less than welcoming. In response to my question about a room for the night she says:

'I don't have a single. I only have a twin.'

'OK. How much would you want for that?'

'More than a single person would pay.'

I'm open mouthed. She doesn't want me at any price. That 'dog shit on my shoe' look she gave me when she opened the door wasn't just my imagination. I'm seized by a desire to present her with my credentials as an upright citizen, to show her my library card and my over-fifties discount coach card. But the look on this lady's face suggests that even a personal recommendation from His Holiness the Pope wouldn't cut a whole lot of ice. I struggle for some suitable words to mark my displeasure but nothing comes. 'Oh' is all I can manage, and I stump off down the path muttering.

My search continues to go downhill. I cycle fruitlessly around neighbouring roads without spotting a single guesthouse sign. Eventually I light upon another enclave of B&Bs to the north of the town centre, but they all have 'no vacancy' boards up, and when I do find one that indicates available rooms, there is once again no response to my knock. I'm beginning to get rather paranoid – cold and hungry too. Finally I find a place that's prepared to take me. The Waverley Hotel next to the station has clearly seen better days but it looks clean enough. In the lounge area there is a man slumped in a relaxer chair watching television and drinking beer. As I walk to the reception counter he shuffles to his feet and wanders across to serve me, and I realise with mild surprise that he is the management's representative. He shows me to a room decorated in vivid lilac woodchip and available at a jolly reasonable price. I enquire about a garage or shed where I can secure my bike. There isn't one, but he offers to let me bring it into the residents' lounge, where we lean it incongruously against an armchair next to the telly and he fixes a large label to the crossbar indicating its ownership.

Dumfries doesn't appear to be the easiest place in the world to find a meal at a quarter to nine in the evening. Perhaps I have chosen the wrong part of the town to look, but the few pubs that serve food have already finished, and the rest are austere drinking dens. Is it something to do with the Scots' national psyche that so many of their public houses have the appeal of public lavatories? I push the idea of a pub to one side and seek out a restaurant.

Here's a Chinese. Hmm don't really fancy Chinese tonight.

Ah! That looks like another restaurant sign just down the road.

Oh! Chinese again. There's one opposite too, and another a little further on. Either the residents of Dumfries are extremely partial to Chinese food or there is some sinister town-twinning arrangement going on. Somewhere in Shantung Province there's a little town stacked out with haggis and neeps shops. I decide that Chinese food is what I want after all, and choose the restaurant with no other customers, where the manager and waitress are standing in the window anxiously scanning the street. It's not that I have a desire to eat in splendid isolation, just that I don't want to hurt their feelings by going in somewhere else. Actually the food isn't bad, and the service is lightening fast. It's almost as if they have been keeping my dinner warm for me out at the back. I like to think too that my presence is the deciding factor that brings in four more customers while I'm eating.

After my meal I amble along by the river, where a man in waders is mid-stream, fly-fishing. It doesn't seem like the place for it somehow – in the centre of a town with traffic pouring past just fifty yards away. But he looks at peace in the semi-darkness and enjoying it as much as if he were on a remote Highland stream. As I walk on past the Haven Guest House, I'm pleased to see that the vacancy sign is still up.

I'm starting to wonder whether my hotel is a DSS location. There is an air of long-termism about the other residents I have encountered. A very young single mother with a permanently crying baby is occupying the next room, and on the wall of my room is a notice indicating that anybody discovered using drugs on the premises will be evicted. It's obvious too, from the sounds issuing up through the floor, that at least one inmate has a hi-fi system in his room.

Sleep doesn't come easily. The baby next door is working itself into a ferment and its mother is becoming increasingly rattled. I lie in my lilac room, its hue mercifully muted by the streetlights' glow, hoping that I'm not going to become witness to a child beating episode. I'm sure the music isn't helping. Not only is it inflicting itself uncomfortably on my ears, and no doubt on the baby's too, but I can feel its percussion in the pit of my stomach. At gone midnight this is wholly unacceptable. Under normal circumstances I'd be down there complaining, but I'm feeling a bit of an outsider here and not sure of my ground. Just when I think that I will have to do something, the music stops, the baby stops and we all go to sleep. Well I do anyway.

I get up at seven in the morning to watch England's exit from the World Cup at the hands of Brazil. Wish afterwards that I had chosen an extra ninety minutes in bed. But not all the residents of Dumfries share my disappointment. There are several youths in the shopping centre cheering and gleefully shouting out the result.

It's a grey overcast day and looks a lot like rain. I had intended to view some of the Burns memorabilia before leaving the town, but now I'm more intent on putting in some quick miles before the weather deteriorates further. I follow quiet undulating lanes that take a meandering course in roughly the same direction as the main A76, but apart from crossing it twice, I'm able to keep it well out of sight and sound. The rain starts about eleven and quickly develops into a steady unremitting downpour. By the time I get to the Duke of Buccleaugh's ancestral pile at Drumlarig I'm very damp indeed. Do I want to inspect the pad of the biggest landowner in Scotland? Well, it might offer me a spot of warmth and a chance to dry out. Just as I'm parking up my bike, four coachloads of school kids pull into the car park. I get back into the saddle and cycle slowly away down the long, straight tree-lined drive.

The nature of the terrain changes radically at Mennock, from where I take a narrow winding road up into the Lowther Hills. Before long I'm into a thick blanket of low cloud. Rocks turn into sheep and sheep into rocks as I heave and groan my way slowly through the mist. The rain still pours down the back of my neck where it mingles with a freshly generated surfeit of sweat. Only the miserable weather and the sheer bleakness of the landscape, or what I can see of it, prevents me from stopping for a rest. But just when I'm thinking that I will have to take a break, the road levels out and a few ghostly buildings swim into view. This has to be Wanlockhead. I'm not going any further today.

I can't think that Wanlockhead would be the prettiest of villages even on a nice day. Today in the steady rain and enveloping cloud it has an appearance so grey, so desolate that one is tempted to assume that its inhabitants must have been forcibly transported here as punishment for dreadful crimes. At 1531 feet it's the highest village in Scotland and its existence is explained by the presence of minerals.

Typically the Romans kicked off the action, mining lead and gold here, and extraction continued throughout the middle ages. With the industrial revolution and its attendant urbanisation came a rocketing demand for lead, so that by the mid-nineteenth century there were nearly 300 mine-related employees living in the village. It was a grim life – harsh climate, poisonous dust, underground accidents and unpredictable effects of explosive used to blast the rock. By way of supreme insult, the miners even had to pay for their own gunpowder and candles.

All that activity has gone now; the last mine closed in 1929. But there is still amateur gold panning in the area. In 1992, the village played host to the World Gold Panning Championships. Today's population numbers 158 and a third of the houses are holiday homes. There's little sense of planning or layout – cottages are scattered at random around the hillside as if thrown there, the discarded playthings of some giant's offspring. They really are toy-like – tiny two-roomed affairs with scarcely room to swing a haggis. Apart from the houses, there is a small mining museum, a village shop, the second oldest subscription library in Scotland, a youth hostel and a pub that looks well and truly closed. As in fact it is: loss of custom during the foot and mouth epidemic dealt a death blow to it and rumours of an impending re-opening have so far proved unfounded.

The youth hostel is a dismal off-white building that used to be the doctor's house. It's not open for business yet, but the door is unlocked and would-be residents are invited to come inside and make themselves a cup of tea. Three ladies from Cannock arrive as I am removing my saturated gear, and they are followed a little later by five cycling Lands End to John O'Groatsers on day eleven of their trip. They have cycled eighty miles today and are so cold, wet and exhausted that they have to climb into bed and eat a packet of chocolate biscuits each before they can begin to hold a reasonable conversation.

With no pub in the village and no food for sale in the hostel, it looks as if the only prospect of sustenance is a visit to the shop. But then the hostel manager reveals that there's a pub in Leadhills three miles down the road, and that the landlord is prepared to operate a pick-up service from the hostel – a sort of pizza delivery in reverse. We all seize upon his offer with enthusiasm.

Leadhills is slightly larger and a little more presentable than

Wanlockhead but everything is relative, and it's immediately clear that the publican's pick-up service is not a matter of pure altruism. Without our patronage, customers would be very thin on the ground (there are just two others). But the bar is pleasant enough – decent beer and good food. There's a fire blazing in the hearth and, on this the longest day of the year, we huddle around it warming our hands and bottoms.

Apparently Bonnie Prince Charlie passed through this village on Christmas Eve 1745, a Hanoverian army hard on his heels, while retreating north after his incursion into England. From the photo above the mantelpiece I can see that Not So Bonnie Prince Charlie has been here too, slightly more recently. It's a very young and gawky Prince Charles who enjoys pride of place, pressing the flesh outside the very bar in which I'm sitting.

Saturday dawns grey and cold but thankfully not raining. A trip to the village shop is a necessity if I'm going to have any breakfast at all. The shop owner is from Stoke-on-Trent – moved here some 18 months ago.

'Are you pleased you moved?'

'Yes we love it. We can get our boots on and be up onto the hills in five minutes without driving anywhere.'

I consider it would be discourteous of me to point out that for just about every other human activity apart from walking, they do have to drive somewhere. But then, looking around the shop, I start to wonder whether my assessment might be inaccurate. This is clearly an establishment that aims to provide most of what I might ever want in life. If I'm after an original watercolour, pet food, photocopying, ice cream, or even a clock made of matchsticks there's no difficulty. But all I want is breakfast for one – no wastage and nothing to pack up and carry away with me. It's not the shop's fault – they can manage breakfast for four, six, or even ten – but I'm damned if I want to buy a packet of cereal, a pint of milk, a loaf and some jam, only to use a fraction of it. After much poking about the shelves, I settle for a tin of rice pudding, an apple and a banana.

The first part of the day is a comfortable downhill run followed by a pleasant cycleway alongside a B road to Douglas. Well, pleasant apart from the weather, which switches in an instant from gentle sunshine to torrential rain. It's the sort of bubbling-puddles downpour that would have any sane individual looking immediately for cover. But there's none, not even a bush. Nothing for it but to press on. For the rest of the day I'm treated to a game of climatic tag. One minute it's pissing with rain, the next the sun is shining. I'm sweating in my waterproofs, but as soon as I take them off I'm being doused again.

After Lanark I take what is euphemistically called the Clydesdale Tourist Route – a busy main road, lined with seemingly identical garden centres. Several miles of this tedium follows and I'm delighted when I see a cycleway promising seven miles to Hamilton. I head off along it, but within three hundred yards find myself deposited back on the main road again. At Cambuslang the road is blocked off completely for a street fete. I wheel my bike self-consciously between bands, stalls and drum majorettes. Finally I reach the towpath of the River Clyde and enjoy an easy pleasant ride into the city.

The youth hostel in Glasgow is in a grand Victorian terrace close to Kelvingrove Park. The area is somewhat gone to seed but the building is still magnificent with a particularly attractive staircase which I am able to examine thoroughly during the lengthy journey to my room on the fifth floor. I'm sitting on a vacant bunk mopping my brow when in comes a lad with a rucksack the size of a wheelie bin. He is carrying a guitar in one hand, and under his other arm is a snowboard, partially wrapped in corrugated cardboard and newspaper. He pitches down on the remaining vacant bunk and launches into the opening bars of 'The House of the Rising Sun'. In between this and snatches of other geriatric play-in-a-day favourites, he tells me he's from Tasmania and has been travelling Europe for eighteen months. I ask if the guitar has been with him all that time. He shakes his head:

'Bought it last week in Edinburgh.'

I don't like to ask about the snowboard. Drawing attention to a snowboard in midsummer Glasgow feels somehow unseemly, like asking somebody how they came by a nervous tic or a particularly nasty squint.

After tartan and shortbread, the third great export from this country has to be the ubiquitous Scottish drunk. And if Glasgow is the cradle of this Diaspora then Sauchiehall Street on a Saturday night has to be its sacred precinct. A typical devotee stands in the middle of the road, rocking gently on the balls of his feet, arms aloft and outstretched, his short-sleeved shirt undone almost to the waist allowing his cheeky little beer belly to take the evening air and join in the fun. His attention is centred on two potato-faced girls with impossibly blond hair, teetering along on pavement-stabbing heels, and in skirts that have been cleverly designed to consume no more of the world's resources than are necessary to protect them against allegations of public indecency.

'Hey yew, Lassie. Come here and tock tae me.'

They ignore his invitation. He ups the decibels.

'Ah haven'e got the pox. Ye'll be awright wi' me.'

Surely no-one could resist a chat-up line like this. But amazingly they can. They nudge each other and hurry on. He takes a step forward, stumbles, almost goes down but grabs onto a bollard in the nick of time. He resumes his position and refocuses with difficulty on the next likely prospect.

'Look at the arse on that yin.'

Glasgow is to be the end of this stage of the trip, but I've arrived here a day earlier than expected and the cheap railway ticket I booked in advance is only valid for travel on the named date. Returning earlier means paying the full single price – an unsupportable idea. I decide that I'll spend my additional day exploring the town and cycling out to Milngavie, the starting point of the West Highland Way, so that the final walking stage won't have to begin with a tedious trek through Glasgow suburbs.

First though, I have to arrange an extra night in the youth hostel. The receptionist, with barely a glance in my direction, tells me that there are no beds free for Sunday night. Glasgow's heaving this weekend. I'll have to find something else or take a chance on cancellations. What's the next step after the youth hostel – the doss house? I gather that once upon a time in Glasgow the least expensive sleeping arrangement was known as 'a penny hang'. Those who couldn't afford a bed for the night would pay a penny to dangle their arms over a clothes line and sleep in a semi-standing position. In the morning, the line was simply unhitched, pitching the sleepers to the floor. Sounds pretty dubious to me but, with this uncomfortable image at the front of my mind, I make three visits to the hostel reception in the hope of cancellations before the receptionist, keen to get rid of me, offers the phone number of a private backpackers' hostel two miles away.

Accommodation sorted, I seek out the cycleway that will take me the twelve mile off-road journey to Milngavie. It starts off through the parks – pleasant, if a little muddy. But as I get to the town fringes it starts to resemble an assault course. The mud becomes much thicker and there are numerous obstacles I have to lift the bike over. I'm minded of those pieces of early film footage where First World War troops struggle to push their heavy cycles through the Flanders quagmire. At the point my wheel rims disappear completely in the thick smelly ooze, I turn around and toil back to the road.

Milngavie is a nice little place. There's a stone pillar announcing the start of the West Highland Way outside Bottoms Up. I take a photo of it, buy a sandwich from Marks and Spencers and head off back into town feeling curiously content that I can be back here in a month or so for the final three hundred mile walk with no big cities between me and John O'Groats.

A sudden onset of rain drives me into the Glasgow Art Gallery with its renowned collection that includes work by Rubens, Van Gogh, Whistler and Cezanne among a panoply of European and British art. I'm enchanted by it all – not least because entry is completely free – but I rather let myself down by laughing out loud in front of one of the home-grown works. *The Last of the Clan* painted by Thomas Faed in 1865 depicts the sad aftermath of the Highland Clearances – a group on the quayside bidding farewell to an emigrant as the rope is cast off. It's seen from the perspective of the person on the boat, looking back at the mournful faces of all those he will never see again – a sorry collection of old people, women and a few children. On a knackered old horse the ancient head of the clan sits, slumped like sack of spuds in his cloak and tam-o'-shanter. His long white side whiskers and terminally miserable expression are exactly mirrored on the face of the horse. It's not meant to be funny, of course, but it creases me up.

Out in the park there's a complete contrast – a South American style carnival procession, rhythmical drums and whirlygigging scantily-clad dancers – all somewhat out of place on a damp Glasgow Sunday afternoon. One of the revellers, a wild-eyed whippet of a man, tries to galvanize the small crowd of onlookers with the aid of rhythmical blasts from the referee's whistle clamped between his teeth. His expression suggests that he might nut anyone who fails to show sufficient enthusiasm.

My replacement hostel is decorated in a particularly garish pink and mauve – almost enough to deter me from going in. But in fact it's more comfortable than the previous one – pleasant rooms, decent facilities, breakfast included in the charge. When I enter my room the curtains are drawn and somebody is asleep in one of the bunks. He rears up, a chubby shaven-headed youth, peers at me blearily and mutters something about not feeling very well. Then he rolls out of bed in one fluid movement and lurches through the door. Later I see him downstairs, gulping some bright blue alcoholic concoction from the bottle. Several of the other inmates tell me he has won the lottery; like really won it, six numbers. Of course he won't get his hands on the money for a few days yet, so he's staying put in the hostel and blowing his available funds on booze.

My other roommate is a quiet American who quit his job a month ago in order to undertake a cycling trip from Orkney to Cornwall. He tells me it's the route of a pilgrimage made by an obscure Arthurian knight, and I'm prepared to take his word for it. Halfway through his available time he has only made it as far as Glasgow and, in the four weeks before his return flight date, he's hoping his bike will take him to Newcastle, York, The Lake District, Cardiff and the West Country. From the superior vantage point of Land's End to Glasgow veteran I suggest he will need to up his daily mileage somewhat. One of the items slowing him down could be the weighty volume of Cervantes' *Don Quixote* which he is reading for inspiration along the way. He considers that he has much in common with the eponymous hero and has christened his bicycle Rosanante. And, while he has yet to encounter any windmills that look like giants, he has been in plenty of pubs that have the appearance of castles – at least after a drink or two. I point to the conspicuous absence of Sancho Panza and he tells me that he too was worried that he lacked an appropriate trusty companion until he noticed that the maker's name on his cycle lock was 'Squire'.

There's just one drawback to this hostel. I discover it when I'm in bed and trying to sleep. Talent night! It's coming from a pub somewhere over the back. An electronic organ and drum-kit provide the backing as all-comers troop up to mutilate a succession of predictable standards – 'My Way', 'Delilah', 'Mack the Knife', 'Take Me Home Country Road' – all bawled out at a volume considerably greater than the sound system can handle without distortion. Each performer is given the same passionate introduction by a compere who has all the verbal eloquence of the man who calls the scores in televised darts matches and, as the last ragged discord of each number rattles around the surrounding streets, the poor sods chained to the walls of the pub are invited to put their hands together for Jimmy the Fish, Sharon Gorbals or Willie John McCophany. I lie in my metal bunk, that has inexplicably become a lot less comfortable, and wonder whether there is an afterlife.

When I pick up my bag to leave at a quarter to ten next morning, the lottery winner is unconscious in his bunk, lying on his front, face scrunched into the pillow, his bullet head hard against the metal frame of the bed and one naked leg hanging over the side. I hope he'll still be able to remember where he put his ticket when he comes round.

Chapter 9

To someone who regards Birmingham as almost within the Arctic Circle, Glasgow feels about as far north as you can get. But, on the route I intend to follow, there are still almost three hundred miles before I can drink in the crystal air of John O'Groats. And it's walking all the way – no more namby-pamby cycling to eat up the miles.

As I wait for the train to Milngavie (confusingly pronounced Mullguy) it's obvious that I'm not the only one heading for the start of the West Highland Way this morning. Prominent are a brown and wiry couple in their sixties wearing identical baggy grey polyester walking shorts and large blue rucksacks. They contrast quaintly with the pale but nattily dressed Glasgow commuters thronging the platform. Trains have been delayed by a power failure near Bellgrove and the projected disruption to the day's walking schedule is causing the female member of the duo severe distress. She repeatedly scurries out from the dingy glass and concrete waiting area to scan the line in both directions and enquire from anyone whose nose isn't buried in a newspaper whether they know when the Milngavie train is due. To be fair, her anxiety isn't helped by the frequent platform announcements relayed from some control centre in the bowels of the earth. The combination of inadequate platform speakers, volume set a shade above totally inaudible, and an announcer with an accent as thick as yesterday's porridge, who has been successfully trained to remove any trace of modulation from her delivery, produces a net result bordering on complete incomprehensibility. It's noticeable that regular commuters pay the announcements no attention whatsoever, preferring to take as their only reliable source of information the destination indicators on the fronts of approaching trains.

At Milngavie I provision my journey with a paving-slab-sized bap from Greggs, and supplement it with some yoghurt-coated nuts from the health-food shop next door. These come in a packet that bears the warning: 'Processed in an environment where nuts may be present.'

I've indulged in a bit of advance guidebook research for this section, and everything I've read has emphasised that the West Highland Way is a tough challenge, so it's a surprise to find that the early bits are something of a walk in the park. Literally. The path meanders through a country park before heading into a more open landscape and following the course of a disused railway. It's very easy going and I quickly realise that the guide's recommended first day of just twelve miles to Drymen is going to fall well short of my hard-won capabilities. Unfortunately though, I've booked ahead for the first four days of the walk, taking my cue from the second guidebook warning about severe shortages of accommodation along the Way. So, unless I want to unpick the arrangements and start again from scratch, I'm rather locked into the itinerary. I decide to go with the flow and amble gently along enjoying the day. A sign by the path tells me that Loch Lomond is flowing in the other direction six feet below my feet on its piped route to quench the thirsts of the Glasgow population. That's nice to know; I just hope there will be some water left in the loch when I get there.

There is no need for map skills on this path. Every turn and deviation is clearly and prominently waymarked. And there's more: on gates, stiles and fences there are adverts for a service called Travel-lite that for £25 will transport luggage between your various evening destinations, leaving you with nothing more to carry than waterproofs and a snack. Maybe not even that, for there are other signs that point to the presence of nearby rest and refreshment. One tatty piece of A4 decorated with red felt tip in a very childish hand offers, 'Pancakes for the Walkers – 200 yards.' It all smacks of pampering to me. In the official West Highland Way leaflet there's even an advert for a mobile massage service which will attend your hotel, B&B or campsite. Walkers are invited to hop into the mobile clinic, cunningly disguised as a van, and have those aches and pains eased away. I find myself musing on the possible entrepreneurial opportunities that have so far been left untapped – clean underwear by parachute perhaps, or coin operated blister plaster dispensers along the path.

I stop to eat my sandwich by a sluggish stream and am joined within a few minutes by Mr and Mrs Baggy Shorts from the Milngavie train. He stretches out on the ground without a word and starts to read his book while she scurries into what is clearly a familiar lunch preparation routine – unpack and light stove, fetch water from stream for tea, exchange pleasantries with man eating sandwich by stream, share out rations equitably and neatly, accidentally kick stove over just as water is coming to the boil, fetch more water from stream etc. I figure that it would be unkind to tell them about an item from last night's local news revealing that bacterial pollution of the Milngavie reservoir, probably fed by this very stream, was behind a recent outbreak of gastro-enteritis. Should be all right if they boil it.

Despite every effort at taking it easy, I'm in Drymen by a quarter past two. I'm almost embarrassed to be knocking on the door of my B&B at this time, but the landlady doesn't seem to mind. She makes me a cup of tea and apologises for the state of the carpets. I confess that I can't see anything wrong with them but she points out that the attractive brownish sheen is not a feature of the weave, rather residual mud from recent torrential rain that brought a flash flood in through the back door and out through the front.

A walk around Drymen reveals not much of interest, so six o'clock finds me in the bar of the Clachan – best pub in the village according to my B&B landlady. Two flush faced individuals around my age – checked shirts, polyester trousers and matching paunches – are exchanging notes about their ex-wives:

'The current wife and I are estranged and my American girlfriend's on the Isle of Wight, but my first wife came up for my fifty-fifth and organised a party for me.'

'That was nice of her. We're loveable souls really aren't we?'

'The second wife still keeps in touch though. I'm quite fond of her. That piece of music I wrote about Labrador was for her. She thinks it's about the dog.'

The Clachan proudly proclaims itself the oldest inn in Scotland. Founded in 1734, it was originally run by the youngest sister of Rob Roy who went by the name of Mistress Gow. I suspect that when she was in charge it didn't have the log effect gas-fire, the artificial beams and all the downlighters. Nor, I would hazard, did they serve butter-flied Cajun chicken, and breaded haddock with chips. My poached salmon is passable but it's swimming in butter, and the addition of honey to the sauce strikes me as something of an error.

There's the obligatory gloomy Victorian highland print over the fireplace – brooding, cloud-enveloped mountains reflected in deep skulking lochans. All dark greens and greys enlivened only by a smudge of dull orange as a terminally weakened sun sets for the last time ever, somewhere behind the dour peaks.

Morning reveals the extent to which Drymen's tourism is dependent on the West Highland Way. Out of the doors of B&Bs all along the road in which I'm staying, booted and waterproofed figures emerge to face the steady drizzle. Here are two very attractive girls from Berlin, in Scotland for twelve days to walk the Way and see some of the sights. Next, a couple from Switzerland in matching gear and very little to say apart from Hello. Here is a group of five – four colour-fully cagouled women and a man with bare legs and shorts tight enough to be hailed as a break-through in male contraception. We make our way in a ragged procession up the hill and through an extensive Forestry Commission plantation in which dreary rows of conifers are enlivened by the occasional discarded fridge or cooker.

Just as I emerge from the trees, the rain magically clears and draws back the curtains on Loch Lomond and its surrounding hills. As payment for the view I'm required to make the stiff climb up to the top of Conic Hill and then the equally steep descent down the other side to Balmaha on the shores of the Loch. The guide book tells me that this village has the last shop for many a mile and, fearful that I may be unable to get hold of the wherewithal for a meal later in the day, I purchase some bread rolls, a packet of that thin processed ham that looks and tastes like wet toilet paper, two golden deleterious apples and a tin of spaghetti bolognese. All have mysteriously acquired the status of collectors' items since leaving the Glasgow wholesalers, but I manage to close a deal on them with the aid of a hastily arranged mortgage.

I celebrate this minor triumph with a trip to the pub. It's called The Highland Way or something like that. I'm the only customer and there's a smell of bleach from the morning clean up. Even though it's gone midday, mine is the first draught beer to be drawn from the pump, and two or three pulls of what has lain in the pipes overnight have to be thrown away before my meagre half pint is in a position to stare at me rudely and defiantly from its glass. To show who's boss I down it quickly and head out to the path.

Loch Lomond is the largest inland stretch of water in Britain and, for the next day or so I shall be following its eastern shore. The Way leaves Balmaha in picturesque fashion – out around a headland with views across the lake to the chain of islands that mark the fault-line between the Scottish Highlands and the Lowlands. But it's an irritating path nevertheless. For the next five miles it traces a tortuous route through the remnants of oak woodland that once skirted the entire loch shore. Down to the waterline it goes, then sharply back on itself to climb over high spurs and rocky promontories. It's pretty enough but slow going, and all rather unnecessary when there is a quiet and gentle, almost traffic-free, road just a little way back from the shore.

So I'm not as hugely enamoured of 'yon bonnie banks' as I had hoped to be, but that doesn't stop me humming the wretched tune over and over as I walk along, until I have to shout at myself out loud to stop it. Do you know why we get tunes stuck in our heads in this way? Well, according to one eminent academic who has nothing better to do with his time and his university's money than research the issue, ninety-five percent of us suffer from the problem and it arises from what he calls a 'cognitive itch': some repeated phrase or incongruity in the tune that niggles away at the brain causing us to have a 'cognitive scratch' – repeating it over and over to ourselves. I don't buy this explanation. For me the impetus is always something about the lyrics rather than the tune – something that strikes a chord with people and events around me. I'll have a conversation with someone called Angela Wrigley and within seconds I'll be off whistling 'Eleanor Rigby'. But it's not always as innocuous as that: on occasion I've found myself humming such inappropriate numbers as 'Hit the Road Jack' at an industrial tribunal and even 'Stayin Alive' at a funeral.

The precise origins of the Loch Lomond song are not known, but a commonly held explanation arises from the aftermath of the 1745 Jacobite Rebellion when a large number of the captured Scots were imprisoned in Carlisle Castle. The English treated these captives inconsistently, hanging some while setting others free. The words to the song were written, so the story goes, by one of the condemned men, to be carried back to his sweetheart by one of those being freed. The song taps into an old belief that when a person dies away from their homeland, their spirit returns to its earthly haunts via the low road of death. So while the free man would plod his weary way back to

Scotland along the high road, his colleague would make it a deal sooner along the low road.

I'm early arriving at Rowardennan, too early for the youth hostel, so I call in for a drink at the Rob Roy Bar of the Rowardennan Hotel. The polished floor looks rather smart and I offer to remove my boots at the door – a proposal that attracts laughter from the barman and some discourteous remarks about mud being preferable to sock odour from a couple of female customers. So, slightly indignant, I tramp across to the bar in my boots leaving, I'm pleased to notice, muddy marks as I go.

The two female aromaphobics, thirty-something Londoners, turn out to be West Highland Wayfarers but not altogether enjoying the trip. They've never walked any distance before and, despite making use of the Travel-lite baggage transportation service, are finding these early stages hard going. But I warm to them quickly because they are able to laugh at themselves as well as others and they're determined not to take the journey too seriously. They ask me when I expect to get to Fort William and what I'll do afterwards. I find myself readily admitting to my true destination – now I'm past Glasgow it actually feels achievable – although I'm immediately embarrassed by the wave of incredulity that comes back at me, and I hurriedly explain about doing the journey in stages and half of it by bike. The barman tells me there are a couple of Australians also heading for John O'Groats a day or two ahead of me. 'Walked all the way in seven weeks,' he says pointedly.

The Rowardennan Youth Hostel is a fine, red-gabled house on the very shores of the Loch. It's understandably popular and I have to queue at reception behind three eight-foot German lads, a balding Belgian and a diminutive Australian in torn combat trousers and an outsized tartan cap worn backwards. We are booked in one by one and given detailed directions to the same six-bed dormitory. By the time my turn comes I'm ready to set the directions to music or find my way to the room blindfold. Undeterred, the hostel manager goes through them yet again for me.

The kitchen is wild. A group of Spaniards have commandeered a large part of it and are noisily throwing together tortilla and mixed salad. In and around them are people boiling up vats of rice, juggling pasta, sloshing soups and sauces in all directions. I'm deeply ashamed of my pathetic tin of spaghetti bolognese and am lurking in the corner shielding it from view when the two pretty German girls I met on the way out of Drymen appear on the scene and open tubs of pot-noodle. I can hold my head up again – at least I haven't quite been reduced to that.

Mr and Mrs Baggy Shorts are here too. She is darting around the kitchen knocking up a meal with the remains of a chicken carcass, vegetables and rice. He is sitting in the lounge reading his book. She reminds me of somebody famous I can't quite place – small brown face, button nose, permanent look of wide-eyed astonishment. Then there are the baggy shorts, thin brown legs and jerky movements. Of course! Pinocchio. But I'm unkind – she's a friendly soul and chats away to me about experiences on the trail since we met yesterday lunchtime. We're nattering like old chums when her husband calls out from the lounge – 'I thought you were going to get the mushroom soup' – and she scurries off to salvage a pan from the debris of other people's dinners.

And, what a surprise, here comes somebody I know – the daughter of an old friend. I smile and greet her warmly. 'Hi Becky. Fancy meeting you here.'

It's not her. I realise as soon as the words are out of my mouth. For goodness sake, she's not even English! How on earth could I make a mistake like that? Better book my place in the geriatric ward without further ado.

But she smiles, responds, brushes my embarrassment aside, and I realise that as a conversation starter the mistaken identity ploy would probably be a winner. If only I'd thought of using it thirty years ago. An hour and a half later I'm grateful for the error. It's allowed me to make the acquaintance of two delightful and entertaining Belgian medical students and we've shared opinions on everything under the sun.

Browsing through the glossy colour leaflets advertising local attractions, I find one entitled 'Hire a Celt'. For a daily fee you can get a strapping fellow who will escort you around the principal attractions of his homeland. You won't understand a word he is saying, of course, and you may need to turn a blind eye to his tendency to smear himself with woad and run naked into battle. In the event that any Romans decide to advance upon him, he is liable to retreat to his hill fort where he will suspend the head of his enemy above the front door. But he can take up to seven in his Renault Espace, and he claims that his local knowledge is second to none.

It's raining quite hard in the morning and there are knots of gloomy hostellers jostling in the lobby, trying to harness the well-known power of collective griping to effect changes in the weather. I refuse to join this pagan practice and, pausing only to adjust the toggles on my hood, I stride off into the dripping landscape.

I think I've got the wrong shape of head. I've never been able to find a waterproof jacket with a hood I can see out of. If I leave the toggles loose, the sides bear in on me so that, like a blinkered horse, my vision is restricted to five degrees either side of straight ahead. Turning to look sideways will only present me with a close examination of the inside seams of the garment. But if I pull the toggles tight, as one is meant to do in bad weather, the peak comes down so low over my eyes that my only view of the outside world is that of my boots and the final six inches of my waterproof trousers.

Not that this matters too much today. The visibility is so poor that there is little to be seen beyond the well-defined track edges. So I spend the morning counting my footsteps and marvelling that with so much water on the ground my feet are remaining remarkably dry. The rest of me isn't, but I've learned on this trip that feet are what really matter.

The noise of falling water has increased, and I realise with a start that it's more than just the sound of rain landing on my hood. I'm smack next to a torrential brown waterfall. This has to be Inversnaid, there's no other stream of this size on the map. It's twelve-thirty, I'm hungry and cold, but just over the bridge I should find the Inversnaid Hotel, the only place offering shelter and refreshment along the course of today's walk. My spirits soar.

Five minutes removing boots and sodden outer garments with numb fingers and I'm able to pad into the lounge bar, to find that quite a few of the people I've met on the trail so far are already ensconced there. Over by the window is the tight-shorted man with his four female companions. Next to them the silent Swiss lookie-likies, and down at the end the two girls from London. And of course Mr and Mrs Baggy Shorts are here too. Mrs BS conspiratorially admits to me that they have been drinking coffee and eating other people's sandwiches, but her husband still ignores me and says nothing. Why would they want to eat other people's sandwiches? I don't get them at all. They seem intent on spending as little as possible. She told me yesterday that on the first night of the walk they bought a special-offer supermarket cooked chicken and ate it in their room. There was still enough left, she proudly announced, for sandwiches and a meal the next day. Blimey! I've been doing this trip on the cheap, but their skilled penny-pinching exposes my rank amateurism. They don't look hard up: they're well clothed and equipped. Perhaps they are just conforming to a Scottish stereotype.

They leave shortly after my arrival, decked out in matching green hooded ponchos that envelop not only their upper bodies but their rucksacks too, and come down almost to knee level. They are still wearing their shorts despite the foul weather and their skinny bare legs are the only discernibly human features emanating from the huge green poncho humps. They look for all world like the back ends of two gaily coloured pantomime horses as they clip clop down the path.

As I don my own damp waterproofs once again, the German girls arrive and, just behind them, four ladies from a South Devon walking club. They all wear that look of relief that was doubtless on my face when I stumbled through the door half an hour previously.

The rain stops as I trudge away from the hotel and, warmed up by a pint of decent beer and a tuna sandwich, I manage to fool myself that it is about to clear up. It isn't. Fifteen minutes later it's coming down harder than ever.

About a mile along the path a little wooden sign directs me towards Rob Roy's Cave – reputed to be one of the famous man's hideouts during his period as an outlaw between 1715 and 1725. I decide to take a look, but it's a precipitous scramble across tumbled boulders, slippery from the rain. I become quite anxious about losing my footing and winding up in the loch, so remove my pack in order to make the going a little easier. But I still have to edge my way along a downward sloping ledge with the water tantalisingly beckoning ten feet below me. So convincing is the image of falling in, that I'm looking along the shoreline for a suitable place where I might clamber out. There doesn't appear to be anywhere. I'm still pondering the prospect of having to swim back to Inversnaid when I reach the cave. I know I'm there because somebody has obligingly written 'Cave' in two-foot-high white painted letters on the rock face. Without the slogan I might have been in some doubt, because the cave is nothing more than a sorry little cleft in the tumbled rocks. It would have to be a pretty desperate outlaw who chose to make this his hideaway. And a small one too. If Rob Roy really used this place then I estimate that he was not much more than three feet tall. I retrieve my bag and continue along the tortuous path.

A herd of about fifteen feral goats tiptoe among the rocks above me, leaving a prodigious stench in their wake. Apparently, there are quite a number of these creatures in the Lomond area. Once domesticated, they are a relic of the eighteenth and nineteenth century Highland Clearances – returning to the wild when their owners were driven off the land. They're not out of place in these surroundings, unlike the colony of red-necked wallabies – founded by escapees from captivity – that runs wild on one of the islands and occasionally shows up on the loch shores too.

The rain continues to fall, steady and unremitting, and it's with some relief that I arrive around half past three at a simple stone shelter called the Doune Bothy not far from the top of the loch. I've saved a sandwich made from this morning's breakfast bread, and the prospect of a bite to eat in the dry is most welcome. I push open the heavy wooden door and immediately wish I hadn't bothered. It's dank and cold with smoke-scarred walls and a debris-littered floor – reminds me of the bomb site buildings I explored as a child. I half expect to find human turds in the corner. Charred newspaper and sticks in the fireplace point to a recent unsuccessful attempt to warm the place up. Along the sleeping platform which runs the length of one wall sits a line of damp dejected German lads with expressions reminiscent of captured troops after a particularly bloody campaign. Mr and Mrs Baggy Shorts are here once again. They've made a cup of tea on their portable stove and are drinking it somewhat apart from the others. The silent Swiss man has stripped down to his underpants, and is wringing out his soaking T shirt onto the floor. Nobody says a word. It's about as cheerful as a pantomime on death-row.

The last hour and a half passes in a weary wet trudge. I overtake the girls from London who are stumbling along grimly, hair plastered to their faces. They are starting to hallucinate about steaming glasses of hot toddy. Half an hour beyond the head of the lake and I'm beginning to think I may have strayed off the main path in the murk and

155

gone past my destination but, just when I'm starting to panic, the wigwams at Beinglas Farm Campsite come into view. Well, they're not really wigwams at all – just small wooden sheds about eight-foot square, with sloping side walls and two tiny windows. Each sleeps three, top-to-toe on a wooden platform that runs round three sides of the interior. Pretty basic stuff, but alternatives are scarce and, on a day like today, they're as welcoming as a suite at the Ritz.

On waterlogged ground towards the river, a few poor bedraggled sods are manfully setting about the erection of lightweight tents. Apart from a toilet block and small shop which doubles as the farm office, the only other shelter is a prefabricated metal lean-to of the sort commonly used for storing tractors and sacks of fertiliser. It is open to the elements at both ends and the wind is whistling through. It serves as a location for laundry, meals and what passes for communal activity. A couple of enterprising Belgian lads have hit on the notion of erecting their tent in here and only carrying it out into the rain when they are ready to put the pegs into the ground. Those who have already put up their tents in the downpour eye them with hostility and huddle mutely on wooden benches and plastic picnic chairs.

Even the most imaginative of estate agents would have difficulty describing my wigwam as anything other than titchy, but it's dry and even has a rudimentary heater. So far I'm the only one occupying it. I sort out some dry clothes and scurry to the shower block. When I return from the most wonderful hot shower any human being has ever experienced, my wigwam-mates have arrived. None other than Mr and Mrs Baggy Shorts. With three of us trying to hang up wet clothing and organise supplies, our home for the night is suddenly less spacious than an aircraft toilet. I exit backwards and head for the communal shelter with my damp gear.

Hovering beside the £1 in the slot tumble drier, a Scandinavian couple are looking for someone to share a load. I agree to put my stuff in with theirs. It's a mistake. My synthetic trousers, tee shirt, pants and socks are thrown into the drum with their fleeces and woollies. After three pounds worth of tumbling (all contributed by me) my stuff comes out wetter than it went in.

People are begging old newspaper at the back door of the farm and stuffing their boots with it in an attempt to have them wearable by morning. One girl with no alternative footwear gleefully seizes upon a plastic carrier bag that I had been using to transport my damp things. She looks so crestfallen when I claim ownership that I relent and let her have it. She uses it, along with one she has acquired elsewhere to fashion a pair of carrier bag bootees tied around the ankles, and does a happy little shuffling dance in them to show her gratitude.

Ah the simple things!

I seek comfort in food, but it's £1 in the slot again just to light the gas on the communal cooker. Seems a bit excessive when the pasta I'm intending to cook on it only cost eighty pence. Mrs Baggy Shorts comes to my aid with an offer of her petrol stove. It's fine if a little smoky. And is it just my imagination, or does my pasta carry the subtle fragrance of premium unleaded?

Now that we're roommates, Mr Baggy Shorts finally engages in conversation. Over petrol pasta I discover that the couple were originally from Scotland but emigrated to South Africa twenty-five years ago. Now retired, they have sold their house in order to fund a life-long wish to travel. They've been on the road constantly for the past two years, have travelled throughout Europe, North and South America and Australasia. And they intend to keep going for as long as health and their funds will let them. The collapse of the rand – two to the pound when they emigrated, sixteen to the pound now – has made this a tricky business. They have to eke out their money very carefully, staying in hostels and bunk houses, and living on pasta and soup. 'We can afford to travel but we can't afford to eat in restaurants.' Now I understand the freebie sandwiches in the pub and the supermarket chicken in the bedroom. I'm full of admiration for them. Fancy flogging your house and going on the road like this in your sixties; I think I'd curl up and die from the worry of it all.

Apart from my wigwam-mates, there's only one individual of similar vintage to me. He's a haunted soul with long wispy grey hair tied back in a pony tail, a beard that Ben Gunn would have been proud of and 1980s John Selwyn Gummer glasses. He lights upon me in the shop and embarks upon a diatribe that I take to be about the weather, although in truth I cannot follow a word of it. The problem is a stammer like a machine gun which, combined with a strong accent and a tendency to miss the endings off words, renders him quite incomprehensible. I try my best, nodding and murmuring my agreement at what I think are appropriate points, but it's bloody hard going.

Now I'm certainly not one to make fun of a person's speech difficulties, but for somebody who has a serious problem getting words out, he seems compelled to talk. He does it pretty well non-stop. He tells me things about himself that I can't comprehend, asks me questions I don't understand, and when I do think I'm on the right track and giving him the response he is looking for, he has that hugely irritating habit of finishing my sentences for me. Or perhaps I should say *starting* to finish my sentences for me. His interjections take three times longer than what I was intending to say and are generally incorrect.

It gets to the point where I'm embarrassed about constantly asking him to repeat his questions and statements. I've noticed that every time I do so, the stammer gets worse. I will just have to ask a question myself to show that I'm playing my full part in the exchange. I cast around wildly for something relevant. His legs! He's wearing shorts and there are midge bites all down both legs.

'Where on earth did you get all those bites?'

Yes I know it's not a particularly brilliant conversational ploy, but I've heard all about the legendary ferocity of the Scottish midge and I've managed to avoid them so far. It seems a perfectly sensible question to ask. These things matter when you're walking in the Highlands.

The rain eases off around eight thirty and I decide to take a walk across the bridge to Inverarnan where there's a pub. I leave my roommates tucked up in their sleeping bags, reading.

The Drovers' Inn is the business. A genuine stopping point on the old cattle droving road from the Highlands, it has managed to escape any hint of the twentieth century dollying-up that afflicts so many pubs of character. There are bare wooden floors without a hint of polish, and a wonderful array of stuffed animals including a distinctly moth-eaten bear. The walls carry the grime of centuries and the rickety furniture has the authentic appearance of stuff that has simply wound up here over the years rather than having been selected for its period qualities. The veneer is peeling off my table so badly that I'm hard pressed to find a level surface to stand my pint, and I love the hat stand that has long since lost its claim to any function other than covering a patch of wall. Its hooks are broken, its mirror cracked; a pair of deer antlers have been dangled across the top of it, as if to give some reason for it being there.

The male bar staff are all in kilts – not the peelie-wally souvenir shop and shortbread tin ones – sturdy plain dark grey tweed with thick woolly ankle socks and big boots. The female bar staff are in trousers and tattoos.

A group of comfortable, smartly-dressed, middle-aged women at the next table greet me like an old friend. 'Hello, we saw you at lunch time.' I struggle to recollect them. Only after the rusty cogs have turned through 360 degrees does it dawn on me that these are the self-same bedraggled creatures from Torquay who tumbled into the pub at Inversnaid just as I was leaving.

A cheer goes up at the far end of the bar as a well built man resplendent in highland dress enters. He preens himself and acknowledges the acclamation. Then he jumps like a man who has just learned there's a hornet in his underpants and starts to rummage inside his sporran which has started to play 'Scotland the Brave'. When he finally finds his mobile in amongst whatever else it is that Scotsmen keep in their sporrans, he isn't able to hear the caller because of the racket his friends are making. It's his stag night in a manner of speaking, except that the bride is here as well. Not surprising since they are already married. They've come all the way from America for a second wedding ceremony in an open boat on the Loch. Just hope the weather is better tomorrow than it was today.

My God! What's going on now? There's somebody else greeting me.

'Here's the guy who passed us at Conic Hill. And you were in the pub today weren't you?'

He's a genial chap from Aberdeen, and once again I have no recollection of meeting him. Nor can I recall any of the four people he has with him. Am I losing it completely? Does my memory for people deal only in good looking women and weirdoes? Then I realise – it's because he's wearing trousers. He's Mr Tight Shorts – I haven't really looked at his face before. And these ladies are Bright Cagouls numbers One to Four. I think it's most unfair the way people keep doing this – turning up in unexpected places wearing different clothes. I'm constantly being embarrassed by it. Individuals I know well as suit wearers appear in jeans and tee-shirts at car boot sales and, though I know I know them, I'm incapable of recalling the who, the how or the where of our acquaintanceship. It's my firm hope that, before too long, behavioural scientists will reveal this weakness to be a medically recognisable syndrome, not just the result of forgetfulness or stupidity, and they'll give it a respectable title with its own acronym, such as CODFISH (Clothing Dependent Facial Identification Syndrome). And they'll pinpoint the causes – over-frequent nappy changing in infancy perhaps. Then people like me will be given the special help we deserve and spared the embarrassment and ridicule that has dogged us to date.

This is a wonderfully atmospheric pub and I'm thoroughly enjoying being here. Still, I can't help but think of my little roommates back in the wigwam reading their books. What's the point of all the travelling if you're unable to sample the local atmosphere, and you have to eat petrol pasta in a tractor shed?

In the morning Mr BS is awake first. He leans over and shakes his wife's shoulder.

'Wake Up!'

She dutifully gets up and heads off to the communal tractor shed to make the tea while he lies in bed reading his book. I'm appalled, but she doesn't seem to mind at all. And I get the impression that he would be horrified too if the nature of his behaviour was drawn to his attention. From talking to him, he doesn't appear to be a boorish unthinking chauvinist. I guess it's just the way things have been throughout their marriage. Neither has thought to question whether the domestic role she has always fulfilled is still appropriate in their new circumstances. She pops her head back into the wigwam to tell him that breakfast is ready and he heaves himself out of bed groaning slightly.

At breakfast a very believable Glaswegian girl walking the path from north to south tells me that the place I'm planning to stop tonight is crap. 'Tired and run-down' she says. This bothers me as I had chosen it for its advertised extras – a swimming pool and a sauna. A cut above your basic bunkhouse, I thought. She also tells me about two Australians bound for John O'Groats whom she met the day before yesterday. I guess they're the same pair I heard about in the Rowardennan pub.

Most of my clothes are still damp but I put them on anyway, figuring that once I'm on the move there will be as much dampness from sweat as from yesterday's rain. But the underpants have to come off again; they feel like used nappies. Not that I have much recent experience of that sort of sensation, you understand.

I dawdle over my preparation and I'm the last of the northbound walkers to leave the campsite but, through the morning, I gradually overhaul most of the others. This offers an opportunity for a pleasant chat with each successive group before I press ahead again. I realise that I'm one of a small minority who are carrying all their gear with them. Those using the Travel-lite service are full of praise for it's convenience and efficiency.

I come upon Machine Gun Malcolm, the man with the stammer, sitting at the side of the path, boot and sock off, his hands and foot a mass of crimson.

God! What's happened here? I'm trying to recollect my long-lost first aid training – now tourniquets, are they in or out these days? 'What have you done Malcolm?'

It's only antiseptic, some bright red continental variety. He was tending a blister and knocked the bottle over. I leave him to mop it up, feeling slightly cheated that my skills have not been called upon.

There are more wigwams at Strathfillan. These have perhaps a little more claim to authenticity in that the occupants are all dressed as Red Indians. They are sitting around playing cards and drinking fire-water. It's another stag do, and the guy dressed up as Chief Sitting Bull is the impending bridegroom. I guess it beats being handcuffed naked to a lamppost.

A little further on I catch up with an American lad who is creeping along at a snail's pace. All his gear looks fresh out of the shop – bright new rucksack, top of the range walking trousers, pristine sweatshirt, expensive looking bandanna, and unstained trainers. Trainers? Not really the best footwear for this path. I ask him if he's OK and he shakes his head.

'Got a problem with my foot.'

He describes it to me and I'm instantly reminded of childhood outings when my father's fallen arches used to wreak their havoc. I lived in fear that I would be struck down in the same way and regularly examined the undersides of my feet for any indication of weakness. Come to think of it, I was beset with concern about acquiring the whole range of my father's many physical afflictions and, throughout my teenage years, anxiously monitored my body for manifestations of stomach ulcers, hernia, slipped disc and premature baldness. None of them have made an appearance which leads me to the inescapable conclusion that, contrary to popular belief, worrying is a highly effective means of preventing illness and incapacity.

Anyway, I pass on my fallen arches diagnosis to the unfortunate American, and suggest that rest might be the only solution to his problem. He seems unconvinced; he's desperate to complete this walk and hopes that he will be able to find something to alleviate the problem at the outdoor shop in Tyndrum. God knows what he has in mind. I have nothing to offer but sympathy and some of that, doubtless infuriating, gentle head shaking beloved of self-appointed experts. I leave him hobbling painfully along.

The path skirts the site of a battle in 1306 which Robert the Bruce lost to the MacDougall Clan. Its main significance is that it immediately preceded a turning point in Mr Bruce's luck. Up to this point he had been a singularly unsuccessful leader, but shortly afterwards he had his encounter with the spider and things started to look up. I keep my eyes peeled for an arachnid that might have similar effect on my own fortunes, but there aren't any to be seen.

By the side of a pretty little lochan there's an impressively inscribed stone block that tells me this is the Loch of the Legend of the Lost Sword. I'm intrigued and want to know more. Who lost the sword? What is the legend? The guide book is no help, my map is no help. The information bureau at Tyndrum is no help. Even that global repository of useless information, The Internet, is no help. I wouldn't care if the inscription hadn't been there, but now I really want to know.

Tyndrum is reckoned to be the smallest settlement in the UK to have two stations and two railway lines: one on the route to Fort William, the other on the line to Oban. In the nineteenth century the village flourished briefly as a centre for gold and lead mining, but now its primary purpose appears to be as a staging post for people passing through. There's a Little Chef, a tourist office, a service station, some B&Bs and a quite upmarket hotel. The location, halfway along the West Highland Way, is marked by a substantial outdoor shop, and a general store with a sign that proclaims in large letters 'last shop for 28 miles'.

The Pine Trees Leisure Park where I had been planning to stop looks OK despite what the Glaswegian girl said about it. Sure, the camping area has a slightly neglected air, and the swimming pool, one of the main reasons I booked, is little bigger than a fish tank. I peer into the bunk house windows – the two bedded rooms look quite comfortable. But is there something I'm missing? I check out the café before making up my mind whether to stay. It's excellent, and very reasonable. But it's still only 3pm and I feel as if there's a whole lot more walking left in my legs. Then again, it's another eight miles to the next conceivable stopping point – Bridge of Orchy. What to do? I'm in a ferment of indecision.

After dithering for 20 minutes over a cup of tea and a scone, I decide to honour my booking. Yes, the bunk house really is comfortable, and I appear to be the only one in it. Then I leave my pack behind and stride out in the direction of Bridge of Orchy. From the map it appears that I can walk another four miles, then cut across to the main road and hitch back. If I start from where I finished today, I'll have a shorter walk tomorrow.

I walk the four miles, and it's delightful. Without my pack I can literally bounce along the path. The afternoon sun is warm and pleasant – what a change from yesterday. I pass a couple stretched out next to the path sunbathing with their shirts off. There are two men in the stream panning for gold. None of your Charlie Chaplin style prospectors these. They're wearing wet suits and face masks, and are scouring the bottom of the stream with a petrol-driven suction pump. The expensive four-wheel-drive vehicles parked nearby suggest a successful enterprise, but they profess to be doing it only for enjoyment.

I get to the place where I had intended to rejoin the road and I'm still feeling full of energy. Damn! I could have walked all the way to Bridge of Orchy after all. No chance of that with my bag back in Tyndrum. But it's so nice, I think I'll make the return journey to Tyndrum on foot – after all I am a bit too long in the tooth for hitching. Halfway back I meet Machine Gun Malcolm who tells me he's carrying on to the Bridge of Orchy.

Later in the pub at Tyndrum I encounter the girls from London. They tell me that they have cancelled their booking for the Kingshouse Hotel, my intended destination for tomorrow night, because the ladies from Torquay told them that somebody else had told them it wasn't very nice. Here we go again. Am I to trust this information or will it be as unreliable as today's was? I really don't know what to think.

Despite the comfort and solitude of the bunkhouse, I lie awake for hours planning the whole of the rest of the trip in my head, working out mileages, possible stopping points, when I might reasonably expect to arrive at John O'Groats. Come morning I'm knackered, but a huge bowl of muesli and a mug of decent fresh coffee in the campsite café restores me to the point where I'm just about prepared to contemplate a day's walking.

The proprietor of Tyndrum Taxis tears himself away from his Sunday paper to take me to the point where I turned around yesterday. As we bowl along the main road I can see, across the valley, the little figures of my previous day's companions setting out along the path. I feel irrationally guilty about stealing a march on them, as if the extra miles I did yesterday somehow don't count. No sooner has the taxi dropped me off than I discover that I've left my map and compass behind at the campsite. I'm initially quite anxious, after all I'm approaching the wildest part of the whole walk. But for God's sake the path is so well marked even a toddler could follow it. Just hope the standards of way-marking so far are maintained. I don't fancy getting lost on Rannoch Moor.

At Bridge of Orchy railway station there's a wonderful little bunk house and café on the platform. It's called the Bridge of Orchy Sleeper and has put to use the former waiting and refreshment rooms. I'm only sorry not to have arrived hungry or at the end of the day. It seems such a shame to pass it by unpatronised.

The isolated Inveroran hotel is the last possible stopping point before Rannoch. I quite fancy a pint, but it's only half past eleven – too early really for a break. I notice that the hotel gives the lie to the claims of the Clachan back in Drymen. The date on the stone façade is some 20 years earlier than that claimed by the Drymen pub. But there's none of that 'oldest pub in Scotland' malarkey.

Rannoch Moor lives up to its wet and wild reputation, but the path follows a sturdy eighteenth century parliamentary road that winds away into the distance. No chance of getting lost here. There's a solitary figure about half a mile ahead of me and I'm obviously gaining on him. It's Machine Gun Malcolm, I'm sure it is. Oh Blimey! I'm not in the mood for another of his juddering conversations. I stop by a stone bridge to eat my sandwich, the better to give him a little extra lead. But in no time I'm catching up again. There's nothing for it, I'll have to overtake.

It's not him at all. Just a genial old Scotsman with a walking stick, hobbling somewhat, and wondering whether he's bitten off more than he can chew. We work out how much further it is to Kingshouse, and he reckons he'll make it as long as he takes it steadily.

After the empty quietness of Rannoch Moor I come over the final ridge to be greeted by the main road once again – way down below and a good mile distant, but the noise of motorbikes darting along like small angry wasps is clearly audible. There is the Kingshouse Hotel sitting on its own at the head of Glencoe. And there is the most gloriously photogenic of all Scottish mountains – the perfectly conical Buchaille Etive Mhor.

The Kingshouse Hotel is great. Comfortable, quite reasonable and full of character. I'm so glad I took no notice of rumours to the contrary. The two German girls arrive and are less happy. They've also been talking to the ladies from Torquay and have changed their plans to stay here in favour of a B&B in Kinlochleven which offers to pick up walkers from the hotel car park and return them there the following morning. Most of the others who were in Tyndrum last night have opted for a shorter walk today. Apart from the German girls, the only familiar faces to have made it this far are those of two Belgian lads, an older Belgian man and, of course, Machine Gun Malcolm. These four are ensconced in the informal camping area on the other side of the stream.

The Hotel has its origins in the seventeenth century but acquired its present name in 1745 when, after the Bonnie Prince Charlie uprising had been quashed at the Battle of Cullodon, it was put into service as accommodation for the troops of George III. Understandably, it was not the sort of hostelry that locals felt comfortable popping into for a pint and a packet of crisps. But by the end of the century it was back in use as a normal inn, and I'm not in the least surprised to learn that those ubiquitous tourists Coleridge and the Wordsworths stayed here in 1803. What the two men thought of the place is not recorded but Dorothy Wordsworth was singularly unimpressed. She wrote:

Never did I see such a miserable wretched place. Long rooms with ranges of beds, no other furniture except benches, or perhaps one or two crazy chairs. The floors far dirtier than an ordinary house could be if it were never washed...With length of time the fire was kindled and, after another hour of waiting, supper came. A shoulder of mutton so hard that it was impossible to chew the little flesh that might have been scraped off the bones.

Well, things have looked up a bit since then. There's a glowing fire in the comfortable lounge and my venison casserole is excellent. The combination of a glorious hot bath, a good meal, friendly bar staff and decent beer is giving me a warm feeling about the place. I'm not even overly put off by the prominent signed photo of Jimmy Savile relaxing on what is clearly the next settee along from the one I'm occupying. As the light fades, the mountains are bathed in soft pink and deer come down from the hills to nibble the grass outside the front door. There's just one small irritation – the cheery Kiwi barman tells me yet again about these wretched Australians who passed through a couple of days ago bound for John O'Groats. 'Fit as fiddles and raising money for the NSPCC as they go,' he tells me.

The guidebook suggests that the next day's stage should be a short one – just nine miles to Kinlochleven. It points out that this is the toughest section of the walk, including a climb up the Devil's Staircase. Beyond Kinlochleven there is no accommodation of any description until Fort William a further fourteen miles away. I ponder the prospect of twenty-three miles of tough walking. It's a little daunting, but I've found the previous short stages frustrating and I've no accommodation booked tonight. I decide I will crack on to Kinlochleven and if I'm there in good shape by lunchtime I'll go the rest of the way to Fort William.

It's warm and sunny as I leave the hotel and I quickly overtake other walkers on the track that leads along the valley to the start of the Devil's Staircase. Just before I get there I catch up with Machine Gun Malcolm who has attached himself to a girl from Holland. As we start to climb I realise that she's dropped well back while he remains alongside me.

Despite its name and reputation, the Devil's Staircase is not particularly difficult. Just a stiff zig-zag track up to a height of around seventeen hundred feet. The name was given, not for the difficulty of climbing it but of building it, and was bestowed by the eighteenth century soldiers who had the task, along with that of constructing the

166

rest of the military road of which it forms a part.

To be brutally honest the greatest hindrance to easy travel comes in the form of Malcolm. When he's alongside me he selects the best line of the path so that I'm pushed into the loose rocky stuff at the edges. And when he's behind me, he takes such close order that he keeps treading on my hiking stick, bringing me up with a sudden jerk. He maintains an incessant commentary on the journey which is infinitely more wearisome than any discomfort inflicted by the climb. I don't wish to be unsociable, but I've come to cherish my own company on the hoof. And particularly today – it's gloriously warm, the visibility is perfect, the views stunning. I just want to soak up the emptiness and wonderful silence of it all. But what do I get? Malcolm chattering constantly in my ear like a bloody jackhammer, and it's such hard work understanding him that I'm barely able to concentrate on my surroundings at all.

As we make the long descent to Kinlochleven, Malcolm announces that he is thinking of joining me on the second leg to Fort William, having earlier been flatly dismissive of my intention to complete the whole trip in one day. I'd been consoling myself with the thought that at least I would only have to endure his chatter until lunchtime, and I fail to greet his new plans with the enthusiasm he anticipates.

We're at Kinlochleven by half past twelve, and stop for a pint at MacDonald's Hotel, sitting on the benches outside and looking down the picturesque loch. The place is empty but for two middle-aged ladies engaged in elaborate planning for an afternoon drive. I eat the crisps from my packed lunch and Malcolm has some toast and marmalade he saved from breakfast. Then the hefty climb out of Kinlochleven which shuts him up for a bit. But once we're on the excellent eighteenth century military road that runs along the ridge he's off again. Fortunately I'm beginning to understand him a little better so it's not such a physical strain as this morning and, in a masochistic sort of way, I'm starting to warm to him. He's a committed traveller and I hear about a large number of his trips in considerable detail. It seems that wherever he goes he manages to lose a camera. He's left them on top of cars, in airport departure lounges, on lavatory cisterns and under cross-channel ferry couchettes. It's as if there's some strange pre-evolutionary animal behaviour at work that compels him to mark his presence with photographic equipment rather than more conventional substances. He tells me the make, model and market value of each instrument, and he prides himself on perfect recall of exactly where each loss occurred. Why, with this knowledge, he wasn't able to retrieve some of his missing possessions is not explained.

By three o'clock I'm getting pretty hungry. I have this excellent packed lunch from the Kingshouse Hotel, but I haven't wanted to gobble it in front of Malcolm because I'm aware that all he had was the bread and marmalade he ate back at the pub. But that's not my fault for God's sake! He had opportunity enough to get something else in Kinlochleven. Nevertheless, I share my baguette with him to ease my conscience.

Shortly afterwards we catch up with Marc, a fifty-year-old trombone player from the Antwerp Philharmonic who is walking the trail in five-and-a-half days and plans to do some of the Great Glen. I've seen him on two or three occasions since Tyndrum but this is the first time we've had the opportunity to talk. Marc admits that he's stretching not only his legs along the trail but his face too. When there's no-one else around he does mouth exercises as he walks, the better to keep in trim the muscles on which his livelihood depends. He's very good value and particularly welcome because he provides an interlude from Malcolm's running commentary.

With about four miles to go, Malcolm starts to blame me for the fact that his feet hurt. I tetchily remind him that I didn't ask him to accompany me all the way to Fort William and that this morning he had been intent on stopping at Kinlochleven. He falls into a moody silence. We make the long slow descent of Glen Nevis, punishing our knees at every step, and Marc peels off at the campsite around six-thirty. Malcolm and I continue into Fort William, and just after seven we take each other's photos by the finish post of the West Highland Way. There are several others who have just finished the walk and we are pressed into service as photographers to record their achievement. They ask us if we've walked from Kinlochleven today and become disgruntled and suspicious when we tell them we've come all the way from Kingshouse. Malcolm checks into the first B&B we come to but I've decided to suss out the backpackers' hostel. It looks a bit run down and I'm put off by the sight of dirty boots lining the windowsills, so I book into a small B&B just down the road.

I was looking forward to Fort William, but my joy at reaching it is short-lived. What I want is a nice pub meal with a couple of pints. Not a lot to ask. I go into four. The first isn't serving food, the second is packed, the third and fourth have cramped and fetid first floor restaurants where customers lower their voices or chew in guilty silence as if eating is on a par with sex – something not to be performed in public. And the choice of food is the same uninspiring crap in each – fish and chips, scampi and chips, pie and chips and the ubiquitous Cajun chicken or haggis and neeps. I don't really want any of these things. In the end I admit defeat and settle for an eat-in fish and chip shop where the staff are wearing tabards so bespattered with grease they could keep the propeller shaft of the QE2 happily turning for a month. My 'haddock and chips supper' (pappy fish and waggly chips with one lettuce leaf, a sliver of tomato and a slice of lemon) is utterly dreadful and leaves me more in need of a pint than ever. But that too is a disappointment. I investigate seemingly interesting cellar bar, but find myself in a dank vault that smells strongly of bleach and appears to be patronised by creatures who have not seen daylight for many a month. The beer is not too good either, but the barmaid is pleasant.

As if twenty-three miles wasn't far enough for one day, I determine that I'm in need of a little stroll to settle the garbage I have inflicted on my stomach. As I shuffle along the main street, I catch sight of Malcolm emerging from a bar and instinctively dodge into a doorway. I'm ashamed of myself for being so antisocial, but in all truth the action happened without any conscious decision on my part.

Towards the bottom end of the street there's a green tiled tourist trap called McTavish's Kitchens where you can book in for a meal and a Scottish show performed by singing shortbread tins in an upstairs room. One of them is romping through 'Roaming in the Gloaming' as I walk past, and the 'Bonny Banks of Loch Lomond' as I walk back. He's straight out of *The White Heather Club* – neatly-crimped white hair, scrubbed pink cheeks, a broomstick down his back and such an exaggerated roll to his Rs that he's in danger of getting his tongue tangled up with his tonsils.

Gloomily tucked up in bed back at the B&B, I hear the couple from the next room helping each other up the stairs in paroxysms of drunken laughter, followed a few moments later by the noise of vigorous grunting sex – headboard banging against the thin partition wall.

Mercifully it lasts for slightly less than the time it took them to get upstairs, but as I lie there, unable not to listen, I feel a long way from home.

Chapter 10

The Great Glen Way is a brand-new long-distance footpath that runs seventy-three miles from Fort William to Inverness. Well, it isn't entirely new – for a large proportion of the route it follows the same tracks as the Great Glen Cycleway that has been in existence for a number of years. For me, it's the most convenient means of getting over to the eastern side of the country for the final trek up to John O'Groats. The start is not particularly distinguished. It meanders around the back of an industrial development, through a housing estate, along a road and into another rather gloomy housing estate. My map tells me this second place is called Caol. Without my glasses I mistake the C for a G and think that it's aptly described. What a dreadful snob I am! It's nowhere near as miserable as some of the places I've passed through, and doesn't deserve to be dismissed in this manner. My attitude must have something to do with the sudden switch from the glorious views of the last few days.

Once the path links up with the Caledonian Canal and the Fort William environs are left behind, things start to look up. Neptune's staircase, a flight of eight locks that lift the level of the canal by sixty-four feet, provides a fine photo-opportunity. But my thoughts are focussed on rather more basic needs. The locked toilets at the upper-most lock (for boat users only) put me into a seriously uncomfortable and mardy frame of mind. And I'm still more disgruntled to find that I've picked up a couple of midge bites. Almost everything has to come out of my pack before I can reach the insect repellent which has worked its way to the very bottom. At least bad temper speeds my progress and I quite quickly cover the six or seven miles to Gairlochy.

Next there's a bit of quiet road walking to Clunes and then a thoroughly boring, straight and seemingly interminable Forestry Commission track through the regimented rows of spruce that colonize the banks of Loch Lochy. What a silly name that is. Imagine if there were to be a stretch of water in England called Lake Lakey; people would fall about.

The track stays close to the loch shore, but there are long stretches with no view at all, unless you count rows of bloody Christmas trees as a view. There's nowhere, and I mean nowhere, to sit down and take a break – not a log, not a stone, not a bridge, not a clearing of any sort. Even where the track runs directly adjacent to the loch, and I can see bits of shoreline where it would be possible to grab a spot of recuperation, there's always an impenetrable tangle of brambles or a precipitous drop to stop me taking advantage of it. Every now and again a massive timber transporter rumbles along, squeezing me into the track-side scrub and leaving me choking in clouds of grey dust. My mood sours even further and I start to curse the Forestry Commission for the way they manage their land.

But perhaps I shouldn't be directing my ire at the Forestry Commission. It's Forest Enterprise that actually manages the land. And what is Forest Enterprise? It's an agency of the Forestry Commission, of course, with its own armies of bureaucrats and its head offices in different towns from those of its parent body.

Still, I have to admit that they've bucked up their ideas since the time when, as a teenager, I thought I might make a career with them. I was casting around for a stimulating and active outdoor job that didn't involve killing people or handing out parking tickets, and thought that life as a forester might fit the bill. I hasten to point out that this was in the days before the Monty Python lumberjack sketch. The requirements were two years practical experience as a forest worker followed by two years in forestry school halfway up a mountain in North Wales. I never made it to the second phase, so disillusioned was I by the first. It wasn't just the stultifying nature of the work – a month planting out six-inch Christmas trees, followed by a month cutting down gorse around two-foot Christmas trees, followed by a month clearing drainage ditches alongside six-foot Christmas trees – it was more that those on my forest who had made it to the ranks of qualified forester all seemed to be unhappy or ill. The head forester, whose name escapes me, had the look of a man who should have been in a sanatorium. He would creep, grey-faced and wheezing, from his forestry house into the morning mist, and drive the couple of hundred yards to his office where he would remain throughout the day –

windows shut, electric fire on (all three bars) winter and summer. His deputy, an overweight ruddy-cheeked man called Tackney, suffered from high blood pressure and angina. His two delights in life were eating and trying to catch his men sitting down on the job. This at least provided him with slightly more exercise than his boss. His usual trick was to park his Land Rover some distance from where we were working and creep through the trees in the hope of emerging in triumph with a booming shout of :

'What the bloody hell's on then?'

We became wise to his methods and whenever we sat down, which was frequently, we made sure that one of our number was on his feet like a meerkat sentry, nervously looking out for Tackney.

Did you know that there are two billion trees in Scotland? A football pitch full of them for every resident. I got that from a Forest Enterprise leaflet. It also told me that Scotland has the oldest living organism in Europe – a three-thousand-year-old yew tree at Fortingall – and that the tallest hedge in the world is a Scottish beech hedge. To be fair to the Organisation, they have become much better in recent years at fostering diversity of tree cover and re-establishing ancient woodland, but there are still too many of these characterless production forests. Still, with only sixteen percent of the country covered by trees, there's probably plenty of scope for getting it right.

The appearance of Laggan at the head of the Loch is very welcome. I've covered another twenty-three miles today and am more than ready for a rest. There's an attractive floating pub and restaurant moored on the canal close to Laggan lock. It's the first place offering any form of refreshment that I've passed all day. Even though I'm but a mile from my destination for the night, I have to drop in for a beer. One half of the proprietorial partnership – a cheery English woman – tells me it's a brand new venture, only in business since June but looking good so far.

The combination of alcohol and a ten-minute sit down at this stage in the day might have been a mistake. I find I've seized up completely and the final mile from pub to youth hostel is a torment. When I get there I'm completely knackered, and go through my chores like an automaton: make up bed, take shower, wash tee-shirt, socks and pants, prepare pasta, eat it. The stuff is so vile that for a moment I suspect that, in my zombie-like condition, I might have mixed up my chores – mistakenly washed the pasta and am now attempting to eat my socks and pants. But it's pasta all right. I force it down and feel a bit better afterwards.

There's an absence of stimulating conversation in this hostel. Most of my fellow residents sit in stony silence, and I'm feeling too tired to make the effort. The only people saying anything are two gormless English girls engaged in a wittering exchange about when one of them knocked a jar of jam off a supermarket shelf several years ago. Their conversation is liberally punctuated with those irritating rising inflections that turn every statement into a question.

'Like I decided I didn't want it? so I put it back on the shelf? And it fell off, right? And there was this jam all over the place? And I just walked on like it was nothing to do with me, right?'

'Yeah, cool'.

I think I hate the word 'cool' even more than the rising inflection. Cool is so, well, uncool. Back in the sixties, the people I knew who used it were the terminally naff – pretentious prats who thought themselves to be where it was at, but who were generally a thousand miles adrift. The same people used equally crummy expressions like 'groovy' and 'right on'. They called girls 'chicks' and boys 'cats'. I just can't understand how, from such pathetic beginnings, 'cool' has made it through to general currency among the youth of today.

My mood is brighter in the morning and, perhaps in consequence, I find the path from Laggan along the banks of Loch Oich a deal more pleasant and picturesque than yesterday's forest track. This one follows the course of a disused railway – a particularly ill-fated enterprise, only in operation for about 25 years. It's remarkable how many railways were constructed that never really had a hope of commercial success. I guess they were the late nineteenth century equivalent of the dotcom boom, only with rather more in the way of ironmongery.

Walking through this country you can't help but be aware of the amount of land that is still in the hands of large estates. Nothing is more likely to draw me to the barricades than the peremptory signs I see everywhere nailed to trees: 'Ochy Nochy Estates. Strictly Private. Permits for breathing anywhere within two miles of this notice are only obtainable from Mr Hector McServant, 2 Grovel Cottages. By order of the Duke of Clarts.' I read recently that the over-privileged owners of obscene quantities of land are all up in arms about a new law to be passed by the Scottish Parliament which will give us members of the public access to an astonishing fifteen million acres from which we have been previously excluded. Not before time I say. And not before time also for tenant farmers who, under the same Act, will be given the right to buy land they and their forbears may have farmed for generations.

After a quiet morning, I arrive at Fort Augustus and I'm suddenly pitched into tourist land. My five minute walk through the village is recorded for posterity on at least two dozen holiday snaps and videos. The car park is full of coaches and there's a queue for the next Loch Ness cruise. All a bit of a shock, but it's an attractive little place nevertheless, and at least the competition between eating establishments makes for a cheap and appetising lunch.

There are more Forest Enterprise tracks between Fort Augustus and Invermoriston. Curtains of dark green conifer shut out the view as I climb 800 feet up the steep loch sides, then down almost to the shore, then back up again. Along one completely undistinguished stretch of track there's a small cairn surmounted by a yellow plastic tub containing faded plastic flowers. No outlook, no inscription, no cliff edge, no explanation of why it might have been placed here. This irritates me.

I've decided that the Great Glen Way is a bit of a con. In large part it's the old cycleway with just a few walkers-only bits thrown in. It disregards the fact that what is good for cyclists is not necessarily so for walkers. Many of these forestry tracks are not only immensely boring with few walker's stopping places, they're iron hard and give my poor joints a real hammering. I had to take pain killers last night just to get to sleep. And the ascents are a nuisance too. Cyclists have to toil up them as I do, but at least they can swoop down the descents, while I jolt my way to the bottom cursing my knees at every step.

Invermoriston has a well stocked food shop that isn't shown on the facilities key of my special Harvey's Map of the Way. I've lugged food for my evening meal all the way from Fort Augustus when I could have stocked up much closer to my final destination. Such things assume high importance at the end of a long day. And it has been a long day – it feels longer than suggested by the map. I pore over the distance chart, adding up the mileages shown for each stage, and discover that the total falls five miles short of that given for the path as a whole.

Hmm! Resolve to write to Harvey's Maps about this.

Loch Ness Youth Hostel has been given a very personal makeover. Its manager, a forceful and enthusiastic lady, has furnished the place with all manner of bric-a-brac and painted the walls in bright primary colours – the drying room is yellow and blue, the washrooms red and green. Dried flowers are everywhere, and there are pictures even in the bedrooms. I love it: such a refreshing change from the usual stark hostel interiors. I notice too that the manager eschews the common hostel trick of assigning people to one bunkroom until it is full, and only then moving on to the next. This practice obviously cuts down on cleaning but it makes for an uncomfortable stay in hostels that are way below capacity. At Loch Ness people appear to have been spread between the available rooms so that, although there are a lot of people in tonight, there are only two of us in my six bedded room.

My roommate is Hugo, a lad from La Corruña, whom I chanced to meet earlier on the last mile of today's walk. He was taking photos of Christmas trees and ambling in the haphazard fashion of somebody who is only where he is because he can't think of anywhere else to be. He is travelling alone through the UK and I suspect that he's starting to feel rather homesick. He is very keen to talk to me and tell me about his life and travels.

Three Land's End to John O'Groats cyclists have also arrived just ahead of me. They're instantly recognisable by their end-of-day ritual clothes-washing followed by the consumption of huge mounds of tinned spaghetti. I talk to them over dinner but their conversation is exclusively about cycling and I'm quickly bored by it. The youngest and fittest of them is nineteen and looks about twelve. He is planning to do the Paris-Brest-Paris road race next year, twelve hundred kilometres in a maximum of ninety hours. Now where have I heard about that before? A second member of the trio thinks that when he gets to John O'Groats he might turn around and cycle back to Land's End.

I drift away from what they're saying to ruminate on whether walking or cycling offers the easier proposition for a long distance trip. I think I would rather ride sixty miles than walk twenty, but is that because I'm walking at the moment? Cycling is so much more efficient as a means of transmitting bodily effort into forward motion and you're spared the weight of the pack and the impact on your joints. On a decent machine I reckon Land's End to John O'Groats along minor roads in three weeks would be fairly comfortable, even for someone like me. These guys are doing it in two, but they're pushing it, seventy five miles a day

I excuse myself from the cyclists, they don't notice me leaving, and chat for half an hour with Hugo who is sitting on his own at the other end of the lounge. He's delighted to have somebody to talk to, but his friendly cultivation of me ends abruptly when he hears Spanish being spoken by some newcomers who have just entered the dining area. He's off like a shot and I see no more of him until he comes crashing back into the room around one-thirty in the morning, groaning slightly as he gets into bed. In the morning he packs his bag in the manner of one who has just heard the four minute warning and tells me that he's off to Inverness with 'the Spanish boys.' He appears much happier with life, and I figure it would be unfair of me to remind him that he told me yesterday he had already visited Inverness and would be heading south from here.

After breakfasting on tinned rice pudding, just the thing for a miserable day, I head out into the steady drizzle. The path takes another of its zig-zag courses up the steep sides of the loch to a height of 1,000 feet. I curse the rain, the path, the person who planned this route and, above all, the unseen RAF fighters that periodically come screaming along the Glen. This has been getting on my wick since I left Fort William. The military obviously like to use the steep-sided glens for low flying practice, and I'm told they're particularly active at the moment. It's pretty startling in fine weather, but the imminent screaming presence of a low flying jet obscured by curtains of cloud and rain has a terrifying Nazgul-like quality to it – very unsettling.

As I arrive at Drumnadrochit around half past one, the rain appears to be stopping. I take a pint and a sandwich at Smiddy's Bar just outside the village. This enterprising establishment has coaxed me into patronising it with small notices promising comforting drinks and appetising food, posted on fences and stiles along some of the more dreary and inaccessible parts of the path. The messages have invaded my brain-stomach communication channel to the extent that, by the time I get there, I'm desperate for what they have to offer. And it's excellent – nourishing, friendly and cheap. The owner advises me on my route after Drumnadrochit. I've already worked out that I will need to leave the path before Inverness and head off northwards. He suggests a back road and the village of Kiltarlity as the only likely accommodation point within striking distance.

I pop into the Drumnadrochit Tourist Information Centre to suss out accommodation options in Kiltarlity. Waste of time. These places are always staffed by pretty girls with BTEC National Diplomas in Travel and Tourism. They have nice smiles but the service they offer seldom exceeds a cursory consultation of whatever brochure is to hand and, if you're lucky, a phone call or two. So it is today. The girl tries to be helpful and offers to find me accommodation in Inverness. I'm sure it's a fine city, but I'm not actually going that way. Of Kiltarlity she knows nothing, despite the fact that it is only ten miles away. I venture the radical notion of consulting the accommodation booklet and, after a little thumbing through it together, we locate a couple of B&Bs in Kiltarlity. I give them a call. The first lady is very sorry but she is completely full. She offers me additional phone numbers but they turn out to be in other, more far flung, villages. The second lady has a room available, it's reasonably priced and the house is located in the village. Fine! Then she asks me where I'm coming from. I tell her I'm walking from Drumnadrochit so won't be there until about half-past six. There's a pause and I realise that her attitude towards me has changed.

'I'm sorry I don't have facilities for walkers. I had one once and it wasn't a success for me.'

I don't know what to say. Who was this walker, Godzilla? Did he go to bed with his boots on, or light a campfire in his room? I tell her 'I'm a very clean walker.' But it makes no difference to her attitude. 'I'm sorry,' she says.

Ho hum! Well, if there are two B&Bs in Kiltarlity there have to be more. It looks like a fairly substantial village, and the girl in the tourist office said that the brochure only had a selection of what's available. So I set out.

I've walked six or seven miles when I come to a sign indicating a B&B half a mile down a lane to the right. There is no phone number and anyway I'm out of range. If they're full I'll have walked an extra mile to no avail, but on the other hand I have no guarantee that there will be accommodation when I get to Kiltarlity. I dither at the junction then resolve to invest the extra distance to suss the place out. It's a bit more than half a mile but I don't mind because it looks so pleasant and welcoming – not just a B&B but a stables too. I stride through the yard, up to the door and give the bell a confident push. I hear it ring but no one comes. I try again, still no answer. This is silly – there's a car carelessly parked right outside the front door, and the door itself is open. I could just walk inside. I put my head into the hallway and call out 'Hello'. Still no answer. Perhaps they're at the back. I walk right around the house, peering in the windows as I go. No sign of anybody. I go down to the stables, thinking they might be there. No – completely empty. I can see three or four horses in an adjacent field – maybe the proprietor is there. I trek off in that direction. No joy. I circumnavigate house again, ring the doorbell three more times, peer into every available outhouse and finally give up, wondering vaguely as I head off down the drive whether I'm going to be picked up by the Northern Constabulary somewhere along the road and charged with the opportunist murder of a much loved local stable owner.

Having gone out of my way I'm a deal less inclined to walk all the way to Kiltarlity. I tell myself, if there's one B&B at hand, there must be more than one. But the logic of London buses doesn't extend to accommodation in the Highlands. There are no more, and so around seven o'clock I find myself stumbling into Kiltarlity via an extensive detour.

It's immediately apparent that this is not prime B&B territory. Most of the houses are two bedroom terraces or three bedroom semis. I approach a pinch-faced young couple with a push chair and ask if they know of anywhere. They look astonished, not by the specific question, but by the fact that anybody should have stopped them to ask about anything. They've clearly never turned their minds to the question of accommodation in the village but, after a lot of head scratching they agree that there might be a place up by the post office. An older couple with a dog prove more knowledgeable. Yes there are two places – they describe to me the two establishments I have already phoned, but helpfully suggest that there are lots of guesthouses in Beauly. I'm grateful to them but it's not what I want to hear. Beauly is another four miles away and its knocking on for half-past-seven. I consider a taxi but it doesn't feel right. Oh what the hell! I resign myself to another four mile plod.

But what's this? Half a mile down the road, a hotel comes into view – a bloody big one too. Nobody said anything about that. It's going to be a bit more expensive than a B&B but who cares? I need a bed. With renewed vigour I march up to the reception desk. 'Awfully sorry,' says the girl, 'We're full.'

I trudge back out to the road again.

I remember that, in my notebook, I have a couple of phone numbers for accommodation in Beauly. I pick one, the Caledonian Hotel, and phone to book a room. If I've another four miles to walk, at least I'll have the comfort of heading for a place that's expecting me. The last couple of miles are hard going – I figure I've walked 26 miles today. There's a brief shower and then, as I'm approaching the town, a rainbow that appears to end at exactly the spot I'm heading for.

Well, there's certainly no shortage of accommodation in Beauly. The place is littered with hotels and B&Bs. But hold on! The one I'm booked into looks like the tattiest of the lot. It may be a 300-year-old inn, but it has a scruffy bar with chipped yellow paint, cramped dining room and worn stair carpet. Still, I'm so tired I wouldn't really care if there was a pile of shit on the stairs. The pleasant girl behind the bar leaves it unattended in order to show me to my room through a maze of corridors. It's OK. It has a bath. Wonderful!

'Would you like anything to eat?' she asks.

'What time do you finish serving? I'd like to have a bath first, if I've time.'

'Just come down whenever you're ready .'

This is more like it.

After a brilliant hot bath I drag myself back downstairs, and find that the beer is good and the food quite excellent. I take another couple of pints following my meal and sit talking with the landlady, a short slightly untidy lady, but warm, knowledgeable and interesting. And I'm starting to realise that my initial impression of this place was way adrift. It may look a little tatty, but there's a genuine laid-back friend-liness and concern to deliver on the important things, that lots of outwardly smarter hostelries would be very hard pressed to match.

My reassessment of the hotel is further bolstered the following morning. Breakfast is served by Ian the landlord, who sits and chats with us while we eat. He serves me the best kippers I have ever tasted in my life and excellent home-made jam with the toast. He is full of local knowledge and relaxed humour. My fellow guests, a couple from Yorkshire, tell me they come back every year and there are plenty of others who go out of their way to stop here. A family from Germany regularly fly into Inverness and arrive by taxi. I can understand why.

As I make ready to leave, Ian advises me on quiet lanes to follow through to the Muir of Ord and even offers me a lift up to the ridge from where my route will commence. I thank him but say reluctantly that it would be cheating.

I can't believe my legs are well again. Yesterday I would have thought that I might never walk again, but today I'm striding out as good as ever. It's a grand fresh morning and the sun is shining. I bounce along quiet lanes with fine views across the Beauly Firth. Almost the only car to pass me is driven by an elderly lady who stops to offer me a lift. I decline once more. The route is a meandering one but much more pleasant than the direct busy road I can see in the distance. After Muir of Ord I do have to brave the traffic but at least two of the six miles to Dingwall are along pavement and cycleway.

Since I finished with the long distance trails I've been getting increasingly irritated about some of the items in my pack I no longer need. The large scale maps, guide book, compass and gaiters probably total no more than a couple of pounds, but I convince myself that they are an insidious drain on my energies and I must get rid of them. Perhaps I can find a few other things to dispense with too. At Dingwall I cadge a large cardboard box from the Victoria Wine Store and make up a parcel on the post office floor. There's no other surface that's large enough, but I'm hopelessly in the way and other customers have to keep stepping over me. The counter assistant breathes a barely audible sigh of relief when I'm finally finished. I walk out six pounds lighter and, telling myself it makes all the difference to my speed and comfort, I positively race away from the town along an unclassified road in the direction of Evanton. I feel like an Antarctic explorer shedding surplus equipment in the final dash for home.

I reckon Evanton must have moved closer to Dingwall at some time without the map makers spotting it. Or it could be that I've fallen into a hypnotic trance counting redundant drilling rigs along the Cromarty Firth. For whatever reason, I'm there much sooner than I expected to be. But I'm not going any further. A school caretaker, interrupted while loading trestle tables into an estate car, isn't sure but he thinks they might do B&B at the tea room next to the pub. They do – it's cheap and excellent – £17.50 with lovely clean rooms newly furnished. The pub's good too. The only drawback is the bus-stop

181

outside my window where the youth of the parish congregate throughout the evening. There are skateboards and banter, lots of effing and blinding, and numerous petty skirmishes. One voice out-talks, out-swears, and out-argues everybody else. I note that his accent isn't Scottish but Scouse. But then I've heard that there are more English north of Inverness than there are Scots. I wonder why this should be?

My companions at breakfast are two market researchers from Dundee. The first is a stork-like woman who appears to have modelled herself on Maggie Smith, or Maggie Smith on her. She does that sudden insincere Miss Jean Brodie sort of smile that drops from her lips almost as soon as it arrives, and as she speaks she flashes swift sideways darting glances to ascertain your reaction to what she is saying. And there's dangling jewellery, lots of it, that tinkles gently as she talks. The second is an ideal foil, shorter, rounder – navy blue sweatshirt, stay-pressed trousers, matter-of-fact manner. They're on a rare foray into the northeast, knocking doors and asking people about their job aspirations on behalf of Scottish Enterprise. This is the same organisation that is currently laying off several thousand people in the Highlands – a fact that has not escaped some of their respondents on the doorsteps. They tell me that yesterday they were sent to Golspie with twenty addresses to call on. One was a holiday cottage, and fifteen were old age pensioners ineligible for the survey. But they don't mind: 'Just as long as we get paid.'

The walk to Allness isn't great. It's a B road, but fast and busy with no verge. I have to put on my fluorescent bib and keep my wits about me – ramming myself painfully into roadside bushes as lorries miss me by inches.

One of the things you notice when you're challenging commercial vehicles to run you down is the large proportion of enterprises that have made up their corporate identities by combining the names of their founders – Colfred Transport, Grajan Tours, Jimpaul Contract Cleaners. They're so unimaginative, they irritate me to death. If the Government is interested in quick and easy ways of reducing the amount of traffic on our roads, and God knows it should be, I reckon that banning any commercial vehicle carrying a sign made up of two people's names should come pretty near the top of the list. And while they're at it, they can include any vehicle that has coloured lights hanging up inside the cab, and all juggernauts owned by Norbert Dentressangle, whoever he is.

Allness is making a bid for the Scotland In Bloom Competition. They've won it three times before and, if sheer quantity is anything to go by, they'll win it again. There are flowers everywhere: on roundabouts, hanging from lamp-posts, in tubs and boxes occupying every available space. Even the dustbin lids are planted with multi-coloured petunias. No they're not, that was a joke. But seriously it's just a bit over the top, although I do have to wonder how dreary the place might be without these blooms. And I notice that not all residents have yet been persuaded to join the community effort. One prominent rebel along the main road into town has obviously gone to great lengths to stock his front garden with a comprehensive collection of the best in British weeds, unsullied by even the smallest flower or shrub.

The town centre is busy this Saturday morning and the only visible café looks horribly crowded. I decide against a refreshment stop and continue along an unclassified road in the direction of Tain, which takes me some twelve miles in almost traffic-free conditions. It's a pretty if slightly boring lane through quiet farm land and the occasional conifer plantation.

Tain has the air of a town that has occupied its patch for a long time, and intends to remain for a lot longer. It sits solid and respectable on the southern side of the Dornoch Firth. I arrive at three-thirty in the afternoon having not eaten since breakfast. I'm desperate for a cup of tea and something to fill the void between head and legs. Here's a café and bakery, name of Harry Maw or something. The menu doesn't look too exciting, but a sandwich will do for starters.

'Sorry we've finished doing sandwiches. We've only got cakes.'

I take a look at the pathetic eight or nine cakes that have been rejected by the rest of the day's customers and are now sheepishly gathered on a tin tray at one end of the counter. Most are those dreadful iced cubic things in nasty yellow that I know from experience contain overly-sweet sponge. They are accompanied by a few similarly shaped coconut-covered objects. Even the sight of them makes my teeth ache.

'I think I'll pass on these. I'll just go for the tea.'

It comes in a mug, has too much milk and hasn't been allowed to brew for long enough. As I sit there gagging on it, the assistants start to wash the floor. A man at the next table, the only other customer, leans over and tells me there's a better café down the road where I can get something to eat. 'They're always like this in here, he says.'

I have to wonder what he's doing here when he could be in the other place. Any café where they start to wash the floor and clear the shelves at half-past three would soon have me voting with my feet. And in fact it does. I drink a quarter of my tea, retch, wipe my mouth on a serviette and make for the road out of Tain.

It's the A9 unfortunately – there is no other option for getting to the other side of Dornoch Firth. But it's not as bad as I expected. There's a reasonable tarmac margin and a verge I can leap onto if I'm about to be mown down. A mile or so from Tain I pass the Glen Morangie distillery – it offers a visitor centre and free tours – but I'm not interested. I've consumed plenty of its product in the past, but the romantic in me likes to think of distilleries tucked away up picturesque glens. Finding one smack next to a busy trunk road shatters that cosy image and leaves it of no more interest than a paint factory.

The bridge over the Dornoch Firth offers me my first sight of a road sign marked with the distance to John O'Groats – just seventy-five miles. My route will be somewhat longer than that, but still it feels as if I'm almost there. The wind is blowing in quite strongly from the sea – glad I'm not walking over here in a gale – and I'm made particularly aware of my vulnerability when an MPV zips past me at seventy miles an hour with the boot hatch wide-open and a stack of luggage ready to fly out into the road. A seventy mile an hour suitcase in the chops would be a less than auspicious end to the walk.

Once over the bridge, I climb a fence and make my way to a narrow lane that takes me the three miles to Dornoch. A man in a yellow fleece stops his car and offers me a lift into town. Again I politely refuse.

Dornoch is Tain's sister on the northern side of the Firth. It exudes a similar air of permanence, politeness and privacy. But it hasn't always been that way. The town was the location of the last witch burning in Scotland in 1722. The old lady in question was accused of turning her daughter into a pony and then riding the creature around the town. I really don't understand what was wrong with this – I wish I could turn some of my family into ponies – but the worthies of Dornoch decided it was an abomination and sentenced the poor old biddy to be burnt alive in a barrel of boiling tar.

Nowadays, Dornoch is known mainly for its golf course, and this could represent my undoing. There are stacks of B&Bs, but I'm shocked to find that they all have 'no vacancy' signs up. It's Saturday evening and golfers have converged on the place for the weekend. Bring back the witches, I say. I circumnavigate the town twice to no avail. There are dense black clouds building just to the south, a torrential downpour is minutes away and I start to become concerned that, if I eventually do find a place with vacancies, I will be so wet and bedraggled that they will refuse to take me. I meet the man in the yellow fleece again and he helpfully suggests that I start knocking on the doors of private houses. He thinks there's an old lady somewhere down the road who occasionally takes in visitors.

I'm not quite ready for that; the 'my little pony' story is still slightly worrying. I'll just take a further look around first. As I walk past the cathedral for the third time I spot a B&B sign that has obviously been erected at the bottom of a back garden in an adjacent street so that it can just about be seen from the main road. It takes me a bit of exploring to locate the front entrance – a sprawling bungalow in a small road opposite the fire station. The door is opened by an apple-shaped lady in her seventies. She has the welcoming but slightly intimidating air of a retired teacher or health worker.

'Come in, Come in. Don't be shy.'

She gestures impatiently at me with a rolled up newspaper and ushers me through to a cluttered room lined with books. Entry formalities completed, she rustles up tea and biscuits and talks to me about retirement in Sutherland. Fourteen years since moving up here from Bristol, and life is so much more full and active than it would have been down south.

'I've seen far more ballet and theatre than I ever did in Bristol. In fact, I went to see a play last night at Brora. Written by a Sutherlander. Lots of swearing mind you – mainly bloody and fuck. There was a ninety-one-year-old with us and I don't think she wanted to hear that.'

Tea and custard cream threatens to come down my nose but, with an extreme effort of will, I manage to compose myself and dab my eyes with a tissue. Funny how obscenities from the mouths of angel faced children and respectable old ladies are so much more startling than from the rest of us. We move on to a three biscuit exchange of views on the f-word in art and literature with particular reference to the northeast of Scotland.

Dornoch Cathedral is the town's second major attraction. A fine building, but not as venerable as it looks, having been reconstructed in the mid-nineteenth century on the orders of the Duchess of Sutherland. This might seem to indicate philanthropy, but the frequency with which the family name appears on monumental masonry around the building suggests that it might have had more to do with preserving in death the status her relatives had enjoyed during their time on earth. Still, it does have a very good stained-glass window.

The weekend popularity of Dornoch extends to its eating places. The first I go into is absolutely crammed, not a seat to be had, but the second is half empty. When the meal comes I can understand why – toad in the hole, with real toad I think.

I have a table by the window, and in the square outside a pipe band is warming up. I've never understood why bagpipes are classed as musical instruments while chain saws and car alarms are not. Anything more than five minutes should be sufficient to warrant action for nuisance, but these are allowed to continue for the best part of an hour – staying on the move, up and down the square, to avoid presenting an easy target. A crowd of what I take to be protesters has assembled outside the cathedral and greets with relieved applause the silence that descends every time they stop to wipe the spit from their chanters. Halfway through the performance a pony disguised as an old witch comes around the restaurant with a collection box labelled 'pipe band'. It whinnies politely when I ask if I can have something from the box for putting up with the racket.

Someone else has been in my bathroom. The landlady said it was exclusively for my use but the toilet seat is up, I know someone else has been in there. My wife says I'm the only man in Western Europe who puts the seat down. In her eyes it's probably my sole attractive trait. Not that I'm prissy or anything; I wee on the floor like other men. I just can't stand to walk away from a raised seat. Even in the men's changing room at the gym where they're almost welded to the perpendicular I have to put them down. Freud would probably have an explanation for it, but I reckon it's down to simple childhood conditioning – growing up in a family where females outnumbered males. And the way I see it, even if you have the same number of males and females in a household, there are bound to be more occasions when people need to sit down than when they wish to stand.

The mystery seat lifter preys on my mind. I listen out for him as I lie in bed, ready to leap out and catch him in the act. But in time I drift off, lulled by distorted but clearly audible tones of the late evening entertainer at the Dornoch Castle Hotel who is hammering out geographically misplaced standards like 'Dirty Old Town' and 'The Leaving of Liverpool' to the accompaniment of an electronic organ.

In the morning the seat is up again.

Chapter 11

My route out of town takes me alongside the famous golf course – 'an ever varying course of rare subtlety' according to the blurb. Golf started its life back in the fifteenth century a bit further down this eastern coast of Scotland, when locals discovered what fun it was to hit a pebble with a stick across the dunes and to see who could get their pebble from one point to another in the smallest number of strokes. The game became so popular that it distracted young men from their military training and in 1457 was banned by King James II. Unfortunately, it was reinstated fifty years later and has never looked back. It has been played at Dornoch since 1616. History doesn't record whether the town worthies went off for a round of golf after they burned the witch.

People often ask me if I fancy taking up golf and I'm in dread of the day when the word 'yes' comes out of my mouth. It nearly happened last year, but I managed with a great effort of will to fight it; to convince myself that life still had some meaning and purpose. My family is right behind me in my struggle, but my GP doesn't seem to understand the danger. I've already lost so many good friends to it – personal tragedies, individuals who should have had years of useful activity in them – and I know the time cannot be far off when I too succumb, stumbling into my dotage in a pink Pringle sweater with wildly mismatched checked trousers.

Golf course owners always contrive to make walkers feel like trespassers. Footpath signs are subtle, and the paths themselves indistinct compared to the main traffic routes. As I negotiate the Dornoch course I take the wrong track and find myself fighting through brambles and gorse. The skirmish is made all the more painful by my ability to see the path I should be on. It has taken a diagonal route across the links and now wanders gently along the shore. But I can't get to it –

there's a barrier of lethal gorse, a wire fence and a fairway between me and where I want to be. With shredded limbs, I finally extract myself from the bushes and locate another track leading in roughly the right direction. And after that it's easy going along the shore to Embo, yet another disused railway line and then a quiet lane around Loch Fleet.

Once again there's no option but to rejoin the main road, and it could be the start of a lengthy acquaintance. If I want to stick to the east coast, the more direct route to John O'Groats, I will have to walk along it for about thirty-five miles. There really is no choice – no footpaths no minor roads between Brora and Lybster. Andrew McCloy's Land's End to John O'Groats book, which I have had with me from the start, suggests an alternative, a minor road from Lothbeg which cuts across the empty moors and peat bogs of central Sutherland to hit the north coast thirty-five miles west of John O'Groats. It looks a more attractive route, but it means an extra day's walking and at this stage in the game I'm less than willing to contemplate it.

Just before I reach the main road I meet two end-to-end walkers heading south – the first I've met the whole trip. They're about my age, on their fourth day out of John O'Groats and absolutely full of it. They plug me for information about accommodation on the West Highland Way and I, in turn, want to know about their route from John O'Groats. They tell me they've taken the main road and, whilst it wasn't very pleasant, they never felt it was dangerous. Well, that's my dilemma sorted. I don't think I'll be following Andrew McCloy's route after all.

The A9 traffic it isn't too bad, but then it's Sunday. I tell myself it will probably be different tomorrow. It starts to rain heavily and I paddle along, sweating in my waterproofs.

The landscape around Golspie is dominated by an enormous statue of the first Duke of Sutherland which stands on the top of Ben Bhraggie overlooking the town. The hundred-foot-high monument would be a preposterous piece of arrogance whoever the subject, but this is none other than the guy who instigated some of the most vicious nineteenth century Highland Clearances. Around fifteen thousand Sutherland crofters were evicted in the name of land improvements – a euphemism for greatly increased landlord income from sheep farming. And who were the landlords? Why the Sutherland family of course. They owned one and a half million acres of the stuff. Some of the uprooted crofters were forced to the coastal areas, to scratch a precarious living from fishing or kelp gathering. Others wound up in the slums of Glasgow and Edinburgh, foot soldiers of the industrial revolution. And for many the only solution was emigration: to Canada, the USA, Australia and New Zealand. Nova Scotia alone received twenty-two thousand cleared highlanders between 1815 and 1838.

When the Duke died in 1833 his widow decided to erect this monstrous memorial to his memory and, as the supreme insult, his remaining tenants were invited to contribute to the cost – an invitation that came with the threat of further trouble if they failed to comply. The statue bears a plaque which acknowledges the contributions of the Duke's 'grateful tenants.' Makes you want to puke, doesn't it?

Over the years there has been no shortage of people ready to blow the thing up, and since 1995 a vigorous campaign has been mounted to have it dismantled and handed over to the family, so that they can re-erect it in the grounds of their own little castle if they wish. A counter view says leave it be. Not out of any affection for the bugger, but because only by it remaining will people remember the shocking injustices performed in his name. Good point, I guess. After all it is the presence of the statue that has led me to spend the last three paragraphs slagging off the geezer.

A less ostentatious monument to a dominating presence is the Golspie Business Park. The sign outside its neat surrounding wall says it has been built with the help of EU funding – nearly a million pounds worth, in fact. It has a smart new roundabout, well laid out tarmac roadways, and neatly spaced business plots. But there's not a single enterprise in it. Not so much as a bike shed. Perhaps they'll be along soon, but for now it looks like an urban wallflower at a country dance.

In the picnic area next to the main Golspie car park there are two waterproof clad figures huddled over a portable stove. I greet them:

'Not much of a day for a picnic.'

'It's not really a picnic', says the small one from under her hood. Australian!

'Hey, are you the two Australians people keep telling me about?'

It is them, Steve and Donna, two very fit and engaging physiotherapists. I've caught them up because they had a couple of easy days earlier in the week. They're quite flattered to learn that celebrity has been left in their wake. I'm handed a damp sandwich and offered a cup of tea, if I can provide my own cup. Unfortunately I can't. They've come all the way from Land's End in one stint, around twenty miles a day, carrying their camping gear and raising money for NSPCC. The finish line is in their sights now and they're powering to the end. A couple more days should do it. We walk together along the shore towards Brora, exchanging life histories and reminiscences about the journey. I discover that their last adventure was a cycling trip across Australia from Perth to Sydney – more than three thousand miles and some pretty inhospitable terrain.

'After that, this trip must be a doddle.'

'No' says Steve. 'I'm finding it harder.'

It's an attractive walk along the beach past Dunrobin Castle – a Disneyland extravagance which is the seat of the Sutherland family. Grey rocks in the shallow water just offshore move and reveal themselves to be seals. There are puffins too. Up ahead, on the expanse of otherwise totally empty beach, we are surprised to see three human figures entering the water. They shriek and leap as the cold waves hit them, but bravely remain in the sea throughout the five minutes or so it takes us to approach and plod slowly past. Only when we are about 100 yards further on do we glance back to see them urgently scurrying back up the beach – naked. This is one skinny dip that went on a bit longer than initially intended. The trail of discarded clothing we find over the next 400 yards reveal that company was the last thing they expected.

Brora was to have been my destination for the day, but when we get there I feel ready to go further. My companions are making for a campsite some five miles distant, but inquiries in the local shop suggest that there are no B&Bs between here and Helmsdale – twelve miles further on. That would be too far for today. So I reluctantly set about finding accommodation in Brora. I plump for the Sutherland Hotel in the main street because it offers evening meals as well as rooms. It's an odd place; some of it has obviously been renovated, but it looks as though the job has yet to be finished. Who cares, my room's fine, recently decorated and fitted out to a high standard.

I go downstairs in search of a drink. There's a comfortable but empty dining room without a bar, although a sign indicates that a public bar can be accessed via a separate exterior door at the far end of the building. I walk around the hotel and into a very scruffy car park, but can see no evidence of a bar, just a dirty grey door that looks as if it leads to some sort of storeroom. There's a guy in an advanced state of drunkenness practising figures of eight in the road outside. He shouts and gestures at the door, urging me through it. Can this really be the pub entrance? Tentatively I venture inside and am greeted by the ugliest dog I've ever seen in my life – a pensioned-off hound of the Baskervilles with great rolls of muscle gone to fat and one hideous red eye. My instinctive 'Oh! you're an ugly bugger' could equally apply to some of the customers. And the room itself would surely feature in the grand finals of the Bar from Hell competition – brown tobacco stained ceiling, brown tobacco stained walls, unrelieved by anything remotely cheery. I can't say that I would want to take a shit in here, let alone relax over a pint. But with all eyes upon me I feel I can't walk out again.

The staff somehow don't seem to fit the general ambience. Behind the bar there's a neat little waitress, traditionally togged in black and white, and an English barman, casually smart. He serves me with good humour, but as he does so he's being berated by one of the customers, a paid up member of Alcoholics Ominous, who appears to have a grudge against the world in general and English people in particular.

'You fucking English twat with your Union Jack in the garden,' he says to the barman. 'That's racist man – ramming your fucking Union Jack down our throats.' (NB I've toned down his actual language here for the benefit of my more sensitive readers) The barman smiles, he's clearly heard all this before: 'It's your flag as well, I'm merely showing my patriotism.'

But the drunken man has moved on with that sudden switch of logic so beloved of the seriously inebriated. He now believes the barman is playing games with him.

'Are you trying to take me apart psychologically? You don't understand what I've got to put up with.'

The barman says something like 'Here we go again,' and that sends his antagonist into a total frenzy. He shouts and swears even more prolifically, composing whole sentences that consist of just pro-nouns and f-words. And he threatens all manner of terrible retribution on the barman and his progeny. Then suddenly he stops and turns his attention to me. He's intrigued by my notebook and wants to know what I'm writing about. I'm uneasy because I'm actually writing about him, but I have little inclination to tell him so. He cranes across and tries to read my writing and, for one of very few occasions in my life, I am deeply thankful for the total illegibility of my scrawl.

I figure it's probably time for me to go in search of some food, so I make the trek back around the hotel to the quiet respectability of the dining room. The same little waitress comes through to take my order, and the same amiable barman brings me my drink. He apologises for the conduct of his public bar patron. 'He gets like that, but he's perfectly harmless really.'

My chicken stir-fry is very tasty indeed, but I'm quickly into a familiar fowl-phobic routine. The meal arrived so quickly and, I tell myself, the chicken's not quite fibrous enough – too waggly. I cut open some of the pieces and examine them closely. They look perfectly all right. Probably just the water that producers inject into the birds these days to increase profit. Or is it? For God's sake! I'm forever doing this with chicken – the effect of too many media horror stories about unwitting supermarkets and catering establishments being supplied with dodgy meat. There's nothing to justify my fears but, by now I've got the idea firmly in my head and it won't go away.

When did I last have a bad experience with chicken? Never! I've been laid low by liver, I've puked up on prawns, but the humble hen has never harmed my health. However, that doesn't stop me treating it like a culinary landmine every time it appears on my plate. The sequence goes something like this: eat some; worry about it; poke it around; decide to leave it; figure that, as I've already eaten some, the damage is done; eat the rest; worry some more.

At breakfast I choose a double ration of cereal rather than the cooked – a better weapon against the runs, I tell myself. They still occupy my thoughts despite a complete absence of any concrete evidence, so to speak. I'm on the road before nine and make the twelve miles to Helmsdale by midday. Traffic is nowhere near as bad as I had expected and, contrary to the forecast, the weather is really nice. As for my own forecast of storms in the alimentary canal area, not a sign of course – a belated five stars for the chicken stir fry.

Within spitting distance of the campsite where yesterday's companions were intending to stay there are two quite prominent B&Bs. So much for drawing on local knowledge. You'd think that, in such a thinly populated area, locals would remember what's what within a five mile radius of their homes. But it's proof, I guess, that people only see what has direct relevance for them.

In a lay-by close to Lothbeg there's a stone that commemorates the killing of the last wolf in Sutherland – dispatched by a hunter in 1700. What I want to know is how could they be certain it was the last one? More likely in my view that it was the penultimate wolf in Sutherland. What would you do if you were the last of your kind for miles around? Would you sit about close to centres of human habitation waiting to be killed? No, I reckon you'd hole up somewhere you weren't likely to be caught. I'm convinced that the last wolf in Sutherland died of lonely old age in the empty hills, unmarked by any commemorative stone.

I'm starting to see increasing numbers of end-to-enders. No further walkers but quite a few cyclists and motorcyclists. One particularly speedy cyclist is being shepherded by a motorcycle, hazard lights flashing. I learn that he has recently recovered from cancer and is aiming to make the trip in four days to demonstrate his return to peak fitness. Makes my efforts look pretty pathetic.

Helmsdale has an attractive harbour, some pleasant looking restaurants and a church clock that is twenty-five minutes fast. I buy a Scotch egg and an apple and eat them on a bench by the river, mentally noting that the town would be a good place to stay if I'm ever in these parts again. Three overweight youngsters are whingeing and quarrelling on the next bench. To relieve my irritation, I ask them why they aren't in school. They stop momentarily to stare at me before resuming their noisy disunity.

The terrain changes suddenly after Helmsdale. The narrow coastal plain disappears and the road winds up steep hills. The only real opportunity to get away from the traffic occurs in places where some road straightening has taken place and the looping course of the old road remains. On one of these loops a plumbing contractor's van is parked – just having a bite of lunch I suppose. I glance into the cab as I pass and am shocked to see that the driver is having his own pipework attended to by a female companion. Now call me old-fashioned, but I really don't want to be a witness to people engaging in oral sex, wherever in the country I happen to be walking. And it seems the Government is behind me on this. I gather it is planning to introduce a new criminal offence that's aimed at reducing the incidence of unacceptable sexual behaviour in public, but it's mired in definitions and I'm not sure it would be much help on this occasion. For example, the Bill deems activity to be private if it takes place in 'a structure which in the circumstances would be expected to provide privacy.' Does that include vans? The Bill doesn't say, but while the definition of public places will be taken to include private gardens, private places will in future include the cubicles of public lavatories. And the activity will not be considered an offence if it occurs in an 'isolated' place. Does this lay-by constitute an isolated place? I don't know. Only time will tell.

An opportunity for a break with road walking occurs with a track leading to the ruined hamlet of Badbea where a community of crofters evicted in the Clearances tried for a while to scratch a coastal living, before finally giving up the struggle and emigrating to New Zealand. I make the detour to take a look, but the gravitational pull of John O'Groats is irresistible and I quickly return to the road.

A steep, mile-long, knee-crushing descent takes me to the pretty village of Berriedale at the mouth of a little river of the same name. And right at the bottom of the valley is a most welcome café. There are four people, English again, behind the counter and only two other customers in the place. One of the staff takes my order, a second prepares my bacon sandwich, a third makes my cup of tea and the fourth cleans the surfaces. It's an excellent little café – friendly, clean, tasty and cheap – and I suspect it hasn't been under its present ownership for all that long. But like so many admirable little enterprises I've passed on this trip, it appears to be on the margins of viability. I don't know about a nation of shopkeepers, we seem to be a nation of over-optimistic café owners.

A thick mist descends around four-thirty and I'm very glad to have my fluorescent bib. Visibility is down to about thirty yards and lorries come looming out of the murk. I'm extremely relieved when a pavement emerges from the mist and shortly afterwards the village of Dunbeath.

A quick circumnavigation of the shrouded village confirms that the Dunbeath Hotel offers the only overnight accommodation. It looks a bit pricier than I've been used to, but in these conditions, and after twenty-seven miles, I'm not prepared to walk any further. The presence of a coach outside has me worried for a minute – Oh God! I hope they're not full. But there's certainly no-one much around, just a sandy haired chap standing outside the front door. I nod to him as I walk past and he follows me into the reception area. Only when he moves behind the counter do I realise that he's not a fellow guest. He books me in, enters my details on the computer and shows me to my room. Later he cooks and serves my meals, pulls me pints at the bar, shows me how to work the telephone and makes up my bill. He and I are the only two people in the place – the coach, I discover, hasn't moved from its spot for at least five years. My host is English of course, and with the formality and reserve for which we are stereotypically famous. Studiously polite, sparing of speech, sober-tied, check sports-jacketed and with the slightly goofy teeth that are so much a mark of good English middle-class stock – in an Elstree Studios black and white film he'd be a Surrey banker rather than a Caithness hotelier.

The hotel has all the ingredients for a pleasant stay. My room is quite plush and the en-suite bathroom is larger than some of the bed-rooms I have occupied along the way. The food and the beer are good too, but I can't say I'm finding it entirely comfortable. Being the sole guest is the difficulty. If only the proprietor was a bit more forth-coming it would make all the difference. I try to engage him in conver-sation but, apart from the revelation that it's always quiet at this time of year, it's like seeking to extract espionage tips from MI5. I eat my meal in silence and down a couple of pints in the empty lounge bar. There is a public bar served by an external entrance and I'm aware that this too has just one customer. I can hear his mumbled conversation with my host who has positioned himself between the two bars. The proprietor is giving his public bar customer some pension advice.

'This policy would be fine if you were married. It has provision for your partner, but in your circumstances you would just be throwing extra money down the drain for something that you're not going to get any value from.'

The mumbled reply of the invisible customer suggests that he may have already committed himself to the policy in question, and they move on to consider what next he might do about it. I feel a surge of sympathy for my host. He's clearly not a man for idle chatter but has no problem when there's a practical purpose to the conversation. I just can't help wondering whether he's in a job that best suits his talents.

In the morning, the mist has cleared and it's a bright, breezy, sunny day. Dunbeath reveals itself to be an interesting little village, and I'd quite like to stick around a bit longer if it weren't for this obsession I now have with getting to the finish. There has been a settlement here for some six thousand years – Celts, Picts and Vikings have all at some time been represented on the residents' committee. In more recent years it was a fishing village and during the herring season up to three thousand additional people would move in temporarily. Now all that is gone – just an empty harbour with the odd recreational boat. Fishermen who come here these days are after salmon in the rivers. But this year even that pursuit has been curtailed. There has been so little rain in this northeast corner of the country that the river levels are too low to allow the salmon upstream.

There's a single place set in a dining room that could easily accommodate thirty. I'm starting to understand how Rudolph Hess must have felt as I ladle grapefruit segments from a bowl containing enough to provide the whole of Dunbeath with a healthy start to the day. My host comes out to ask whether I would like brown toast or white. 'Brown' I reply. Did I imagine it, or was there a slight tut as he walked back to the kitchen? A moment later he passes the front window on his way to the shop, and returns, brown loaf in hand.

I allow myself a brief walk down to the harbour before hitting the main road again. There's a bronze statue of a small boy with an enormous salmon over his shoulder, dedicated to the memory of Neil Gunn, the novelist, born just three doors away from the hotel where I'm staying. Somebody has put a pair of glasses on the salmon's face, and it peers over them like a quizzical old schoolmaster.

The six or seven miles to Lybster pass off quite quickly and I reward myself with a drink at the upmarket Portland Arms. A female cleaner comes into the Gents while I'm standing at the urinal. She apologises profusely and backs out in confusion. I call out, 'It's OK. Don't worry'. When I come out I'm surprised to find that she is still there – standing immediately behind the door, holding her mop and bucket, transfixed with embarrassment. We have to go through the profuse apology and the 'It's OK. Don't worry' routine all over again.

A little way after Lybster I'm able to turn inland off the main coastal road and down an arrow-straight single-track lane that leads twelve miles to Watten. There's scattered habitation at first – an odd mixture of rather run-down farms, abandoned crofts, and brand spanking new houses. After a couple of miles there are no more dwellings and the terrain gives way to empty moorland and peat bog coloured by occasional conifer plantations and the odd red deer in the distance. But it's not all boring wilderness. Obvious attempts have been made to brighten the view. There's a complete MFI teak-effect chipboard desk in the ditch, drawers spilt among the heather, and further on a half-submerged TV set looming, shipwreck style, from the waters of a small lochan. I'm three miles from the nearest house; who on earth drives out here to dump this stuff? But perhaps I'm missing something. Maybe it's an obscure Caithness custom to return consumer goods to the wild. The local paper would seem to bear out this theory. It has an item about a Thurso man arrested for the theft of a vacuum cleaner after he was spotted trying to hide the appliance up a tree.

This is a very very quiet road, maybe one vehicle every ten minutes, but it still gives me a closer shave with death than the couple of days I spent on the A9. A lunatic in a Mondeo comes past me like a bat out of hell, missing me by an inch or so and sounding his horn as he goes. The incident leads me to reflect on my status as a walker on the roads of this country. If I'm daft enough to walk alongside a main trunk road I'm prepared to pay homage to the motor vehicle. I'll hop onto the verge if I can so they don't have to pull out to get around me. I'll be touchingly grateful to the drivers who acknowledge me and try not to get angry with the majority who stare out through their windscreens with faces like bowls of cold porridge. I'll even suffer the stench and buffeting wake of juggernauts with no more than a couple of shouted obscenities. But on a lane like this I reckon I'm of equal status to the stinking, ravaging automobile. It's not as if I'm invisible: they should slow down, they should move out. If the opportunity were presented, I'd deploy that Mondeo gear stick in a manner that Corporal Jones would have approved.

Midway between Lybster and Watten I come to the Grey Cairns of Camster. These five-thousand-year-old Neolithic burial chambers have been restored so that they are presented in very much the way they would have appeared when originally constructed. A bit of internal concrete reinforcement here and there to prevent the whole lot dropping on people's heads when they crawl inside, but otherwise the genuine article. There are quite a few proper tourists shuffling back and forth along the wooden walkways. Three Japanese in light beige trousers are on their hands and knees at the entrance passage, intent on videoing the chamber interior. I mentally question whether the grainy images will be worth the dry cleaning bill.

Back when the cairns were constructed, the climate around here was much more favourable to farming and the soil wasn't bad either. It was able to support quite a large and thriving agricultural community. The desolate boggy wasteland that characterises the area today is a product of, not only the intervening climate change, but also over-exploitation of the land, carried out in part by the very people who were buried here. Odd thought that, isn't it?

Watten is a long time coming. It's almost five when I arrive, but I'm so keen to get to John O'Groats tomorrow that I consider going further, and I ask in the post office about the possibility of accommodation in the next four or five miles. An extremely helpful postmaster, English yet again, pores over his Ordnance Survey map and advises me, with greater authority than I've encountered, so far that I am unlikely to find anywhere within the next hour-and-a-half. He recommends the Brown Trout Hotel two doors away. I'm relieved on two counts – the prospect of walking several more miles is not attractive and the Brown Trout Hotel, which I had earlier earmarked as a possible destination, is not at all the pretentious establishment I had anticipated from its name. It's just an ordinary little pub on a corner. The rooms are neat and clean, and there's a smell of fresh paint. The girl who shows me to my room tells me they get quite a few Land's End to John O'Groats people stopping by.

I like the place, it's pleasantly understated. In fact, everything about it is fine until I get my evening meal. The menu says pink trout in an almond crisp with a white wine sauce and seasonal vegetables. Sounds great, but what comes resembles a scale model of Mont St Michel fashioned out of mashed potato, an oversized fish finger balanced on top and the whole thing standing in a white sea dotted with red and green pepper dinghies. Why, all of a sudden, do pubs and ordinary little restaurants feel they have to go in for this gastronomic Jenga? I'm all for food looking good, but when your meat is six inches above plate level it's got to come down before you can eat it. Whoever started it has a lot to answer for.

With just seventeen miles to go, I'm determined that the next day will mark the end of the journey. And the sooner I get there, the better I'll be able to manage the southward exodus. I'm on the road by eight-thirty and make good time on the traffic-free lanes. But the long straight lane to Gills, on the shores of Pentland Firth, just goes on and on. The last few miles is an undulating succession of dips and low rises and as I come towards the top of each one I prepare myself for a view of the northern coast. Each time I'm disappointed as another wave of countryside opens up. Finally I approach a slightly higher rise topped by a mobile phone mast. This, I tell myself, must be the last hill. The telephone mast is surely serving the main road and the small north coast communities that are marked on my map. But as I go over the rise I'm shocked to see land stretching away into the far distance. My God! I've made a serious miscalculation here. There must be some-thing desperately wrong with my map. Then, a few paces further on, I realise that the land I'm looking at is not part of the mainland at all. It's the Orkneys. A stretch of blue sea has opened up before me. It's great to see the end at last. And it really couldn't be a finer day for it. The sky is cloudless, the sun is warm, there's a gentle breeze, and I really can see for miles. Just a little way to go now.

My pace quickens without any conscious effort on my part, and I hammer the last four miles. The John O'Groats Youth Hostel in Canisbay is a real misnomer – I wonder how many hostellers have been dismayed to find that it's three miles from the place itself. I pound on through Huna, almost jogging now, and there it is – a huddle of buildings down by the shore – that has to be John O'Groats.

I flog down the last four hundred yards from the main road with a mounting sense of anti-climax. Car park, toilet block, gift shop, hotel – the place is a deal less interesting than umpteen tourist locations I've passed along the way. Am I seriously saying that I've travelled eleven hundred miles to arrive here? Well perhaps not. Land's End and John O'Groats were never the important element. What mattered was the bit in between. But in all truth this really is the arse-end of nowhere. Unlike Land's End it doesn't even appear to be the last bit of anything. Just to the east is a headland, Duncansby Head, that looks a lot more final, and everyone knows that the most northerly point of the UK is actually Dunnet Head several miles to the west. But for some reason John O'Groats has become fixed in the national consciousness as

Britain's most northeasterly point. Well, it's the location I've been aiming for so I'm really not going to argue about whether it's the best spot to finish. Here I am.

I take a look at the bus timetable – Oh Shit! There's one leaving for Wick in a few minutes and not another for several hours. If I don't catch this one I'll be too late for the train that links with the overnight express from Inverness – the idea of another night in B&B has suddenly become deeply unattractive. Huh! Turnstiles on the loo. Twenty pence and I've no coins of the right denomination. I could so easily have gone by the side of the road before I got here. A relief break snatched away like this means that what was merely desirable will suddenly become urgent. But I've no time to mess about getting change. I hurry over to the signpost, a twin of the one at Land's End, that serves as the main photo location. A bunch of people are standing around the pole, videoing each other. Nobody shows even the slightest smidgen of interest in me. Well, what did I expect, pipe bands and drum majorettes? A couple from Acle in Norfolk are having the mileage to their home town put up on the signboard. Christ! I can't even get my photo taken without lining up. Oh what the hell! I'll just get some postcards.

The giftshop is packed. Visitors are chattering over tartan this and tartan that, and forming an orderly queue at the checkout with their knick-knack purchases. I'm getting quite anxious now. For a couple of minutes I jiggle around behind two women who appear intent on buying up most of the stock, then leap to the front of the queue and throw 60p on the counter for four postcards.

I race back out to the bus, my Aussie companions from two days ago are lounging on the front seats. They tell me they got up at five this morning like children on Christmas Day and, when they arrived a couple of hours ago, did a celebratory dance around the pole. I confess that I have only just arrived and what dancing I've done has been borne of frustration. The bus driver enquires about photo opportunities and takes pity on me when I reveal that I haven't had time.

'Go and get one now. I'll wait for you.'

I run back to the signpost where numbers have declined. Just an elderly man videoing his wife who is standing as still and rigid as the post itself. He reluctantly agrees to take my photograph, then punishes me by taking an age to line me up. The smile of achievement is well and truly glued to my face by the time he presses the button. A final sprint back to the bus and I'm out of here. Not quite the triumphant arrival I had anticipated.

In Wick I take a celebratory pint with Donna and Steve before they depart for a night in a hotel, 'with real beds and real towels', and I go in search of the railway station. The painfully slow train journey to Inverness, stopping at every second telegraph pole, is like a rewind of my last few days walking, but it offers me ample opportunity to reflect on the trip as a whole.

So what have I discovered?

Well, the journey was nowhere near as daunting as it appeared before I started, and I'm convinced it's within the capabilities of any reasonably fit person of my vintage. I can't quite escape the feeling that I've cheated somewhat by breaking it into stages and covering half the distance by bike, but that strategy certainly helped to keep it enjoyable and achievable. I suspect that if I had set out to walk the whole thing in one stint, I might well have lost heart before the half way point. But now I'm quite fired up to think about other trips – a European cycle tour perhaps or some long UK walks.

I've been delighted by some of the countryside I passed through. For all the galloping urbanisation, congested roads, faceless retail parks and national lack of consideration for our surroundings, we still have a great deal to be proud of in this country. And the people I've met? I guess they've been the greatest pleasure – even the ones I was glad to be separated from. They've kept me interested, amused and appalled. Without them it would have been a dreary journey indeed.

I can't help feeling that the self-actualisation part of my quest didn't quite pan out as anticipated. Plenty of time alone with my thoughts but somehow consideration of those cosmic, life-changing issues eluded me. The opportunity to discover my position in the grand scheme of things was always elbowed out by questions of the moment. How far have I gone? How far still to go? Can I eat my Mars bar yet? Is this a good place to stop for a pee?

But I guess the big question, the really big question, as I rumble southwards is: am I any less of a miserable old git than before I started?

Hmmm, I think you'll have to be the judge of that.